THE REFERENCE SHELF

Vol. 19   No. 4

REPRESENTATIVE AMERICAN SPEECHES: 1945-1946

Selected by

A. CRAIG BAIRD

Department of Speech, State University of Iowa

THE H. W. WILSON COMPANY
NEW YORK   1946

Copyright 1946
By The H. W. Wilson Company
All Rights Reserved
Published October 1946
Printed in the United States of America

PREFATORY NOTE

REPRESENTATIVE AMERICAN SPEECHES: 1945-1946 is the ninth in an annual series. Each volume includes some thirty addresses of important public speakers on current issues. Together these nine publications include some two hundred speakers and more than two hundred and twenty-five selections.

The speeches are roughly grouped according to content, such as Victory and Retrospect, Management and Labor. An alternative classification, however, according to speech types, such as Congressional Debates, Judicial Speeches, Radio Commentaries, is given in the Introduction to this volume.

Each volume aims to reflect the typical speech-making done in the United States during a twelve-month period. The addresses represent varieties of subject matter and type, such as deliberative or congressional, persuasive or hortatory, educational, courtroom, pulpit or radio. A further aim of each edition is to include speeches as examples for study. The ideas, structure, language and other elements of each speech should be of interest and application to the students.

This year's collection, like the earlier ones, may be used as a reference for the study of American trends of thought and action; as a series of specific arguments or other information on problems under investigation; as a series of speeches to be examined in review of the history and criticism of American public speaking; or as materials and methods for the students of extempore speaking. The book, then, is especially applicable to students of communication, extempore speaking, history, social science, debate, and public speaking.

The Introduction of each volume outlines aspects of methods for the criticism of a speech and for speech-making. For comprehensive survey of this editor's approach to the philosophy and technique of the criticism of speaking and for his own principles of selecting "representative" addresses, the student is advised to read the Introduction to each volume.

The Table of Contents of each annual edition and the Cumulated Author Index at the end of this book will serve as a key for review of the individual orators.

The Introductory notes are often based upon information from the speaker himself concerning his methods and speech-training.

A. CRAIG BAIRD

July 1946

CONTENTS

PREFATORY NOTE 3

INTRODUCTION 7

INTERNATIONAL POLICIES

Surrender of Japan. Douglas MacArthur 13
That Men Might Be Free. Roland B. Gittelsohn 16
The Sinews of Peace. Winston Churchill 20
Farewell to England. Edward R. Murrow 33
Common Interests of the United Nations. James F. Byrnes 39
United Nations Assembly: A Report. Arthur H. Vanden-
    berg 45
International Military Tribunal: Opening Address. Robert
    H. Jackson 60

NATIONAL DEFENSE

The Backwash of War. W. Norwood Brigance 75
National Military Strength. George C. Marshall 85

ATOMIC ENERGY

The Atom Bomb and War. Harold C. Urey 95
The Social Implications of Atomic Energy. Arthur H.
    Compton 109
International Control of Atomic Energy. Bernard Baruch.. 120

ECONOMIC CONTROLS

Freedom or Planned Economy: There Is No Middle Road.
    Lewis H. Brown 133
Price Control and Inflation. Chester Bowles 144
Price Control Veto. Robert A. Taft 154

MANAGEMENT AND LABOR

Should Industry Grant Labor's Demands for a Thirty Per Cent Wage Increase? A Debate.   George V. Denny, Jr., Walter Reuther, and George P. Romney 165
United Mine Workers' Demands.   John L. Lewis 180
The Railroad Strike Emergency.   Harry S. Truman 196

NATIONAL ATTITUDES AND IDEALS

Response at a Reception.   Francis Cardinal Spellman 203
The War Isn't Over at Home.   Ben Kuroki 208
What to Do With Life Today.   Joseph Fort Newton 214

EDUCATION

Civil Courage.   James B. Conant 223
New Directions for Higher Learning.   Harold F. Harding 229
The Greatest Lack.   Robert J. Blakely 241
The Issues in Education: 1946.   Robert M. Hutchins 262
APPENDIX: Biographical Notes 273
CUMULATED AUTHOR INDEX 283

INTRODUCTION

SIGNIFICANCE OF THESE SPEECHES

What of the significance of the speeches in this volume? What is their claim for survival? A hasty reading of them will suggest a considerable amount of dated material. They echo, in some cases, a tale that is done; events, important enough in their hour, but of fading memory in the light of the all-pervading present.

A more considered insight into these documents, however, yields an interpretation, some of it deeply moving, of situations and issues of more than casual concern to students of American history and life.

Here, for example, is the voice of America proclaiming with dignity from a battleship in Tokyo Bay the collapse of an ill-gotten Empire. Here is the voice of a Jewish chaplain, a native of Ohio, dedicating a marine cemetary on Iwo Jima, with sentiments not unworthy of the best Gettysburg tradition. Here, surprisingly, is the rare eloquence of a young Nebraska Nisei, who, after many air missions over Europe and Japan, later appeals to his countrymen for national tolerance. Here, too, out of London, a broadcast, the final one in a nine-year series, refers with restraint and discernment to the genius of the Britisher, who is sometimes desperate but always democratic.

From these pages emerge again the speaking presence of Anglo-Saxon's greatest living orator. At a small Missouri college he expounds the issues that give pause to millions of listeners. In these pages, too, are the crowding delegates of the first United Nations assembly in London, with our Secretary of State addressing fifty-one nations on principles of mutual association. This volume, too, unfolds the drab spectacle of Nuremberg, with the American prosecutor voicing new principles of international criminal justice, principles to be weighed again and again as tomorrow's tyrants are brought to retribution.

Here, too, are America's military leaders, decisive not only in their judgments concerning the strategy of war, but potent likewise in their speaking power before civilian audiences. Here also are United States Senators who deliberate with their colleagues on high political policies; America's elder statesman, with his reasons and formula for the disposition of the atomic bomb; educators who would adjust instruction to the new age and combine wisdom with knowledge; clergymen who relate the current problems to religious faith and leadership.

These then are the documents of the last twelve months. Some of them, I am sure, speak not only of the past but of the present and the future.

These speeches, I have tried to make clear, are to be salvaged not primarily because they are literature. Beauty and emotional-imaginative depth, when present, are secondary. These spoken discourses are unique in their sensitivity to the immediate occasion and audience—the integration of a personality, an audience, and a message. As Dr. Harold Harding suggests, citing John Morley: [1]

> The great political speech, which for that matter is a sort of drama, is not made up by passages for elegant extracts or anthologies, but by personality, movement, climax, spectacle, and the action of the time.

Subject Matter of These Speeches

What mostly provoked speech-making in the United States from July 1945, to July 1946? Out of the scores of themes and partial topics for radio speeches, sermons, university lectures, and congressional debates, four or five chief issues emerged.

First, how could international peace be secured? More specifically, how could Russia and the United States get on together? Could the United Nations be made to work?

Second, should we extend the draft? And should we have permanent military training?

Third, what should be done about the atomic bomb?

Fourth, how should maximum production be secured? How could inflation be put down? Should OPA be abandoned?

[1] See page 229.

Fifth, how could strikes be averted? Or, when they were under way, how could they be stopped? What wage increases should labor receive?

These perplexities underlay most of the talking and furnished the bulk of the ideas contained in the present volume.

CLASSIFICATION OF THESE SPEECHES

To facilitate the use of this book for study, the selections are arranged under the representative topics of International Policies, National Defense, Atomic Energy, Economic Controls, Management and Labor, National Attitudes and Ideals, and Education. The previous volumes have also used a topical plan of arrangement.

These categories, as I have pointed out previously, are tentative only. Some overlapping occurs.

For the student who wishes a classification according to speech types, I suggest an arrangement somewhat as follows:

I. Congressional: Arthur H. Vandenberg's "United Nations Assembly: A Report," Robert A. Taft's "Price Control Veto."

II. Executive Speech: Harry S. Truman's "The Railroad Strike Emergency."

III. Eulogy: Roland B. Gittelsohn's "That Men Might Be Free."

IV. Speeches of Introduction: George Denny's introduction to the speakers in the Town Hall programs; Virgil Hancher's introduction of Joseph Fort Newton.

V. Professional Lecture: Arthur H. Compton's "The Social Implications of Atomic Energy"; W. Norwood Brigance's "The Backwash of War."

VI. Radio Debate: Walter Reuther and George P. Romney's "Should Industry Grant Labor's Demands for a Thirty Per Cent Wage Increase?"

VII. Dedication: Roland B. Gittelsohn's "That Men Might Be Free."

VIII. Farewell: Edward R. Murrow's "Farewell to England."

IX. Judicial Speech: Robert H. Jackson's "International Military Tribunal."

X. Sermon: Joseph Fort Newton's "What to Do with Life Today."

XI. Speech Before a Business Group: Lewis H. Brown's "Freedom or Planned Economy."

XII. Narrative: Ben Kuroki's "The War Isn't Over at Home."

XIII. Military Addresses: Douglas MacArthur's "Surrender of Japan"; George C. Marshall's "National Military Strength."

XIV. Political Speech: Winston Churchill's "The Sinews of Peace."

XV. Response and Reply: Francis Cardinal Spellman's "Response at a Reception."

XVI. Deliberative Speeches: James F. Byrnes' "Common Interests of the United Nations"; Bernard Baruch's "International Control of Atomic Energy."

XVII. Addresses Before Popular Audiences: Harold C. Urey's "The Atom Bomb and War"; Chester Bowles' "Price Control and Inflation."

XVIII. Educational Addresses: W. Norwood Brigance's "The Backwash of War"; James B. Conant's "Civil Courage"; Harold F. Harding's "New Directions for Higher Learning"; Robert J. Blakely's "The Greatest Lack"; Robert M. Hutchins' "The Issues in Education: 1946."

XIX. Baccalaureate Address: Joseph Fort Newton's "What to Do with Life Today."

These divisions obviously overlap. Most of these presentations were also "Radio Talks." The grouping is suggestive and should aid the student in preparing his own addresses according to "speech type" or "occasion."

ACKNOWLEDGMENT

The editor of this collection is heavily indebted to the various authors of these speeches, for permission to use and reprint their addresses, and to the cooperating publishers and organizations. Specific acknowledgment is made in the footnotes ac-

companying each speech. The editor is also grateful to Lillie
Cilley, Sarah Scott Edwards, Mary Brown Humphrey, Sylvia
Noffsinger, and Aletia Redman, librarians at the State University
of Iowa, who since this annual series was projected, have gra-
ciously cooperated.

A. CRAIG BAIRD

June 26, 1946

We stand in Tokyo today reminiscent of our countryman, Commodore Perry, ninety-two years ago. His purpose was to bring to Japan an era of enlightenment and progress by lifting the veil of isolation to the friendship, trade and commerce of the world. But alas the knowledge thereby gained of Western science was forged into an instrument of oppression and human enslavement. Freedom of expression, freedom of action, even freedom of thought were denied through suppression of liberal education, through appeal to superstition and through the application of force. We are committed by the Potsdam Declaration of Principles to see that the Japanese people are liberated from this condition of slavery. It is my purpose to implement this commitment just as rapidly as the armed forces are demobilized and other essential steps taken to neutralize the war potential. The energy of the Japanese race, if properly directed, will enable expansion vertically rather than horizontally. If the talents of the race are turned into constructive channels, the country can lift itself from its present deplorable state into a position of dignity.

To the Pacific basin has come the vista of a new emancipated world. Today, freedom is on the offensive, democracy is on the march. Today, in Asia as well as in Europe, unshackled peoples are tasting the full sweetness of liberty, the relief from fear.

In the Philippines, America has evolved a model for this new free world of Asia. In the Philippines, America has demonstrated that peoples of the East and peoples of the West may walk side by side in mutual respect and with mutual benefit. The history of our sovereignty there has now the full confidence of the East.

And so, my fellow countrymen, today I report to you that your sons and daughters have served you well and faithfully with the calm, deliberate, determined fighting spirit of the American soldier and sailor, based upon a tradition and historical trait, as against the fanaticism of an enemy supported only by mythological fiction. Their spiritual strength and power has brought us through to victory. They are homeward bound—take care of them.

THAT MEN MIGHT BE FREE [3]

ROLAND B. GITTELSOHN [4]

Chaplain Roland B. Gittelsohn delivered this memorial address at the dedication of the Fifth Marine Division Cemetary on Iwo Jima, in March 1945. Iwo Jima is a volcanic island in the North Pacific, seven hundred miles southeast of Tokyo, and about the same distance north of Saipan. This island was the best available airbase for direct attack on Japan, and furthermore was a radar center to warn Tokyo of the approaching United States bombers.

Twenty thousand Japanese held the island and made the most of the natural defenses, the volcanic caves with which the hills were honeycombed. The Nipponese had constructed more than 800 pillboxes, with an interlocking network of tunnels to connect pillboxes and caves. Weeks of intensive bombing had failed to weaken these defenses.

On February 19 and 21, 1945, three marine divisions under General H. M. Smith landed. The Japanese fire on the beaches was accurate and devastating. The fighting during the ensuing month was close up, without cessation, and without quarter. Meat Grinder Hill at the north end of the island was taken and retaken five times. Especially bloody was the struggle for Mt. Suribachi, 546 feet above sea level at the southern end. The raising of the American flag over Mt. Suribachi was one of the dramatic episodes of the Pacific war. Hundreds of thousands of copies of that photo-picture were distributed in the United States and around the world.

Iwo Jima officially fell on March 16, 1945. Practically all Japanese defenders were wiped out. The United States reported 4,287 dead and missing and 19,540 wounded. The Japanese commander, General Tadamichi, who had said, "This island is the front line, it defends our mainland; I will die here," fell leading a charge.

Commentator Robert St. John, over the N.B.C. network, on May 31, 1945, prefaced his own reading of Chaplain Gittelsohn's address by the following introduction:

"Well, that's the news. And now I want to do something unusual, but when I get through, I'm sure you'll understand why I've done it. I want to read to you a memorial address, delivered over the graves of some Fifth Marine Division dead, on the Island of Iwo Jima, by Chaplain Roland B. Gittelsohn, of Rockville Centre, Long Island, New York.

"I think that the words I am about to read to you should be printed in every history book, that millions of copies of the address should be distributed across the land. When I get through, you tell me what you think of it. Here are the words of the Chaplain, as he stood at the side of those American graves on the Island of Iwo Jima."

[3] Text supplied by Rabbi Gittelsohn, Rockville Centre, Long Island, New York. Permission to reprint the speech granted through the courtesy of the author.
[4] For biographical note see Appendix.

Rabbi Gittelsohn attended Cleveland Heights High School, Cleveland, Ohio, where he was trained in speech under Mr. Clinton Drury, a former intercollegiate debater of Bates College. At Western Reserve University, Gittelsohn had speech courses and participated in intercollegiate debate under Professor Howard Woodward, leader in the field of speech and former President of the National Association of Teachers of Speech. These teachers both "emphasized that one should not be a slave to a manuscript. My usual procedure, in keeping with their teaching, is to be thoroughly familiar with my subject and with the organizational outline of the material, but to feel free to add extemporaneous remarks in keeping with the occasion or with the previous speakers." [5] He is a member of Phi Beta Kappa and of Delta Sigma Rho, honorary intercollegiate debate fraternity.

This is perhaps the grimmest, and surely the holiest, task we have faced since D-day. Here before us lie the bodies of comrades and friends. Men who until yesterday or last week laughed with us, joked with us, trained with us. Men who were on the same ships with us, and went over the sides with us, as we prepared to hit the beaches of this island. Men who fought with us and feared with us. Somewhere in this plot of ground there may lie the man who could have discovered the cure for cancer. Under one of these Christian crosses, or beneath a Jewish Star of David, there may rest now a man who was destined to be a great prophet; to find the way, perhaps, for all to live in plenty, with poverty and hardship for none. Now they lie there silently in this sacred soil, and we gather to consecrate this earth in their memory.

It is not easy to do so. Some of us have buried our closest friends here. We saw these men killed before our very eyes. Any one of us might have died in their places. Indeed, some of us are alive and breathing at this very moment only because men who lie here beneath us had the courage and strength to give their lives for ours. To speak in memory of such men as these is not easy. Of them, too, can it be said with utter truth, "The world will little note nor long remember what we say here. It can never forget what they did here."

No; our poor power of speech can add nothing to what these men and the other dead of our Division have already done. All that we can even hope to do is follow their example. To show the same selfless courage in peace that they did in war.

_____
[5] Letter to the editor of this volume, June 6, 1946.

To swear that by the grace of God and the stubborn strength and power of human will, their sons and ours shall never suffer these pains again.

These men have done their job well. They have paid the ghastly price of freedom. If that freedom be once again lost, as it was after the last war, the unforgivable blame will be ours, not theirs. So it is we the living who are here to be dedicated and consecrated.

We dedicate ourselves first to live together in peace the way they fought and are buried in this war. Here lie men who loved America because their ancestors generations ago helped in her founding, and other men who loved her with equal passion because they themselves or their own fathers escaped from oppression to her blessed shores. Here lie officers and men, Negroes and whites, rich men and poor—together. Here are Protestants, Catholics, and Jews—together. Here no man prefers another because of his faith or despises him because of his color. Here there are no quotas of how many from each group are admitted or allowed. Among these men there is no discrimination. No prejudice. No hatred. Theirs is the highest and purest democracy.

Any man among us, the living, who fails to understand that will thereby betray those who lie here dead. Whoever of us lifts his hand in hate against a brother or thinks himself superior to those who happen to be in the minority makes of this ceremony and of the bloody sacrifice it commemorates an empty, hollow mockery. Thus, then, do we, the living, now dedicate ourselves to the right of Protestants, Catholics, and Jews, of white men and Negroes alike, to enjoy the democracy for which all of them have here paid the price.

To one thing more do we consecrate ourselves in memory of those who sleep beneath these crosses and stars. We shall not foolishly suppose, as did the last generation of America's fighting men, that victory on the battlefield will automatically guarantee the triumph of democracy at home. This war, with all its frightful heartache and suffering, is but the beginning of our generation's struggle for democracy. When the last battle has been won there will be those at home, as there were the last time, who will want us to turn our backs in selfish isolation on the rest of organized humanity, and thus to sabotage the very peace for which we fight. We promise you who lie here: We will not do that. We will join hands with Britain, China, Russia in peace, even as we have in war, to build the kind of world for which you died.

When the last shot has been fired, there will still be those whose eyes are turned backward, not forward, who will be satisfied with those wide extremes of poverty and wealth in which the seeds of another war can breed. We promise you, our departed comrades: This, too, we will not permit. This war has been fought by the common man; its fruits of peace must be enjoyed by the common man. We promise you, by all that is sacred and holy, that your sons, the sons of miners and millers, the sons of farmers and workers, will inherit from your death the right to a living that is decent and secure.

When the final cross or star has been placed in the last cemetery, once again there will be those to whom profit is more important than peace, who will insist, with the voice of sweet reasonableness and appeasement, that it is better to trade with the enemies of mankind than, by crushing them, to lose their profit. To you who sleep here silently, we give our promise: We will not listen. We will not forget that some of you were burnt with oil that came from American wells, that many of you were killed by shells fashioned from American steel.

We promise that when once again men seek profit at your expense, we shall remember how you looked when we placed you reverently, lovingly, in the ground.

Thus do we consecrate the living to carry on the struggle you began. Too much blood has gone into this soil for us to let it lie barren. Too much pain and heartache have fertilized the earth on which we stand. We here solemnly swear: This shall not be in vain. Out of this, and from the suffering and sorrow of those who mourn this, will come—we promise—the birth of a new freedom for the sons of men everywhere.

THE SINEWS OF PEACE [6]

WINSTON CHURCHILL [7]

Winston Churchill gave this address at Westminster College, Fulton, Missouri, on March 5, 1946, his first important speech in the United States since his retirement from office as British Prime Minister.

President Truman accompanied Churchill from Washington.

The occasion was a special convocation at the College. The lecture was given as one of the Green Foundation series. Some 3,000 heard the address as given in the College Gymnasium; 20,000 others listened through loud speakers in Fulton churches or on the streets. President Franz McCluer presided. President Truman introduced the distinguished Britisher. At the conclusion of his address, the President and Mr. Churchill were each given honorary degrees. The address was broadcast by the major networks and by short wave throughout the world.

The speaker, although careful to remind his audience of his unofficial status, was nevertheless the voice of Britain from 1940 through 1945, and his words continued to have vast import in world events. At Fulton, he bluntly criticized Russia for her apparent hostile purposes and programs; therefore he suggested a continuation of the close wartime accord between United States and Great Britain, in a "fraternal association." The visible audience applauded repeatedly.

As usual, the oration was couched in original and lively Churchillian prose, rich in allusion, invective, personal proof, vigorous appeals to motives of fear, duty, patriotism, and loyalty to the Allied cause.

The delivery was in this Parliamentary leader's best form. Despite his seventy-one years, the orator had the fire, variety of pitch, rate, and intensity characteristic of the performances of his prime. Here were appropriate pauses and voice quality that well expressed the intellectual-emotional activity of the speaker. Here was that rare event in contemporary America—a supreme orator presenting an important theme to a vast audience (seen and unseen) in an attempt to change or confirm their attitudes and action.

No other speech of 1945-46 probably evoked so much worldwide comment. Hardly had the broadcast ceased until the opinion of the nations began to register decisively. Most of the criticism was probably unfavorable. President Truman, when immediately afterwards invited to express his opinion of the ideas, was silent; but observers pointed out that when Churchill in the speech declared, that it would be "criminal madness to give the atomic bomb to the UNO [United Nations Organization] in this still agitated and ununified world," the President

[6] Text supplied by the British Information Services, 30 Rockefeller Plaza, New York.

[7] For biographical note see Appendix.

joined in hearty applause. The *Wall Street Journal* thought it brilliant with a "hard core of indisputable fact." *PM* called it an "idealogical declaration of war against Russia." The *New York Times* concluded: "Whether all of Mr. Churchill's proposals are acceptable to the United States or not is not the main point now. The American people have long since realized that the United States and Great Britain are governed by a common destiny which brought them together in two world wars and would inevitably do so in any future war. Sharing Mr. Churchill's anxieties about the future, they will give a sympathetic hearing to his proposals for averting a new catastrophe." Secretary Wallace, Senator Pepper, and others called it "shocking."

On March 15, the British orator spoke at a dinner given in his honor by the City of New York. This final appearance before departure threw further light on the Westminister College argument and was an extemporaneous reply to criticism of him. He stated, for example; "I have never asked for an Anglo-American military alliance or treaty. I asked and I ask for something different, and in a sense I asked for something more. I asked for fraternal association, free voluntary fraternal association." Most of the hostile American comment had assumed that Churchill was asking for an outright treaty of alliance. The facts were that Churchill had adopted the same vein as had Senator A. H. Vandenberg, John Foster Dulles, Secretary of State Joseph Byrnes, and the British Foreign Secretary Ernest Bevin, in their veiled or open criticism of Russia.

I am glad to come to Westminster College this afternoon and am complimented that you should give me a degree. The name "Westminster" is somehow familiar to me. I seem to have heard of it before. Indeed it was at Westminster that I received a very large part of my education in politics, dialectic, rhetoric and one or two other things.

It is also an honor, perhaps almost unique, for a private visitor to be introduced to an academic audience by the President of the United States. Amid his heavy burdens, duties and responsibilities—unsought but not recoiled from—the President has travelled a thousand miles to dignify and magnify our meeting here today and give me an opportunity of addressing this kindred nation, as well as my own countrymen across the ocean and perhaps some other countries too. The President has told you that it is his wish, as I am sure it is yours, that I should have full liberty to give my true and faithful counsel in these anxious and baffling times. I shall certainly avail myself of this freedom and feel the more right to do so because any private ambitions I may have cherished in my younger days have been satisfied beyond my wildest dreams. Let me, however, make it clear that I have no official mission or status of any kind and that I speak only for myself. I can therefore allow my mind, with the experience of a life-time, to play over the problems which beset us on the morrow of our absolute victory in arms; and try to make sure that what has been gained with so much sacrifice and suffering shall be preserved for the future glory and safety of mankind.

The United States stands at this time at the pinnacle of world power. It is a solemn moment for the American democracy. With primacy in power is also joined an awe-inspiring accountability to the future. As you look around you, you must feel not only the sense of duty done but also feel anxiety lest you fall below the level of achievement. Opportunity is here now, clear and shining, for both our countries. To reject it or ignore it or fritter it away will bring upon us all the long reproaches of the after-time. It is necessary that constancy of mind, persistency of purpose and the grand simplicity of decision shall guide and rule the conduct of the English-speaking peoples in peace as they did in war. We must and I believe we shall prove ourselves equal to this severe requirement.

When American military men approach some serious situation they are wont to write at the head of their directive, the words, "Overall Strategic Concept." There is wisdom in this as it leads to clarity of thought. What, then, is the overall strategic concept which we should inscribe to-day? It is nothing less than the safety and welfare, the freedom and progress of all the homes and families of all the men and women in all the lands. And here I speak particularly of the myriad cottage or apartment homes, where the wage-earner strives amid the accidents and difficulties of life, to guard his wife and children from privation and bring the family up in the fear of the Lord or upon ethical conceptions which often play their potent part.

To give security to these countless homes they must be shielded from the two gaunt marauders—war and tyranny. We all know the frightful disturbance in which the ordinary family is plunged when the curse of war swoops down upon the breadwinner and those for whom he works and contrives. The awful ruin of Europe, with all its vanished glories, and of large parts of Asia, glares in our eyes. When the designs of wicked men or the aggressive urge of mighty states dissolve, over large areas, the frame of civilized society, humble folk are confronted with difficulties with which they cannot cope. For them all is distorted, broken or even ground to pulp.

When I stand here this quiet afternoon I shudder to visualize what is actually happening to millions now and what is going to happen in this period when famine stalks the earth. None can compute what has been called "the unestimated sum of human pain." Our supreme task and duty is to guard the homes of the common people from the horrors and miseries of another war. We are all agreed on that.

Our American military colleagues, after having proclaimed the "Overall Strategic Concept" and computed all available resources, always proceed to the next step, namely the method. Here again there is widespread agreement. A world organization has already been erected for the prime purpose of preventing war. UNO, the successor of the League of Nations, with the decisive addition of the United States and all that that means, is already at work. We must make sure that its work is fruitful, that it is a reality and not a sham, that it is a force for action and not merely a frothing of words, that it is a true temple of peace, in which the shields of many nations can someday be hung and not merely a cockpit in a Tower of Babel. Before we cast away the solid assurances of national armaments for self-preservation, we must be certain that our temple is built not upon shifting sands or quagmires, but upon the rock. Anyone with his eyes open can see that our path will be difficult and also long, but if we persevere together as we did in the two World Wars,—though not alas in the interval between them—I cannot doubt that we shall achieve our common purpose in the end.

I have however a definite and practical proposal to make for action. Courts and magistrates cannot function without sheriffs and constables. The United Nations Organization must immediately begin to be equipped with an international armed force. In such a matter we can only go step by step; but we must begin now. I propose that each of the powers and states should be invited to dedicate a certain number of air squadrons to the service of the world organization. These squadrons would be trained and prepared in their own countries but would move around in rotation from one country to another. They would wear the uniform of their own countries with different badges. They would not be required to act against their own nation but in other respects they would be directed by the world organization. This might be started on a modest scale and grow as confidence grew. I wished to see this done after the First World War and trust it may be done forthwith.

It would nevertheless be wrong and imprudent to entrust the secret knowledge or experience of the atomic bomb, which the United States, Great Britain and Canada now share, to the world organization, while it is still in its infancy. It would be criminal madness to cast it adrift in this still agitated and ununited world. No one in any country has slept less well in their beds because this knowledge and the method and the raw materials to apply it are at present largely retained in American hands. I do not believe we should all have slept so soundly had the positions been reversed and some Communist or neo-Fascist state monopolized, for the time being, these dread agencies. The fear of them alone might easily have been used to enforce totalitarian systems upon the free democratic world, with consequences appalling to human imagination. God has willed that this shall not be, and we have at least a breathing space before this peril has to be encountered, and even then, if no effort is spared, we should still possess so formidable a superiority as to impose effective deterrents upon its employment or threat of employment by others. Ultimately, when the essential brotherhood of man is truly embodied and expressed in a world organization, these powers may be confided to it.

I now come to the second danger which threatens the cottage home and ordinary people, namely tyranny. We cannot be blind to the fact that the liberties enjoyed by individual citizens throughout the British Empire are not valid in a considerable number of countries, some of which are very powerful. In these states, control is enforced upon the common people by various kinds of all-embracing police governments, to a degree which is overwhelming and contrary to every principle of democracy. The power of the state is exercised without restraint, either by dictators or by compact oligarchies operating through a privileged party and a political police. It is not our duty at this time, when difficulties are so numerous, to interfere forcibly in the internal affairs of countries whom we have not conquered in war. But we must never cease to proclaim in fearless tones the great principles of freedom and the rights of man, which are the joint inheritance of the English-speaking world and which, through Magna Carta, the Bill of Rights, the Habeas Corpus, Trial by Jury and the English Common Law, find their most famous expression in the Declaration of Independence.

All this means that the people of any country have the right and should have the power by constitutional action, by free, unfettered elections, with secret ballot, to choose or change the character or form of government under which they dwell, that freedom of speech and thought should reign, that Courts of Justice independent of the Executive, unbiased by any party, should administer laws which have received the broad assent of large majorities or are consecrated by time and custom. Here are the title deeds of freedom, which should lie in every cottage home. Here is the message of the British and American peoples to mankind. Let us preach what we practice and practice what we preach.

I have now stated the two great dangers which menace the homes of the people. I have not yet spoken of poverty and privation which are in many cases the prevailing anxiety. But if the dangers of war and tyranny are removed, there is no doubt that science and cooperation can bring in the next few years to the world, newly taught in the hard school of war, an expansion of material well-being beyond anything that has yet occurred in human experience. Now, at this sad, breathless, moment, we are plunged in the hunger and distress which are the aftermath of our stupendous struggle; but this will pass and may pass quickly, and there is no reason except human folly or sub-human crime which should deny to all the nations, the inauguration and enjoyment of an age of plenty. I have often used words which I learned fifty years ago from a great Irish-American orator, Mr. Bourke Cockran, "There is enough for all. The earth is a generous mother; she will provide in pentiful abundance food for all her children if they will but cultivate her soil in justice and in peace." So far we are evidently in full agreement. Now, while still pursuing the method of realizing our overall strategic concept, I come to the crux of what I have travelled here to say.

Neither the sure prevention of war, nor the continuous rise of world organization will be gained without what I have called the fraternal association of the English-speaking peoples. This means a special relationship between the British Commonwealth and Empire and the United States. This is no time for generalities. I will venture to be precise. Fraternal association requires not only the growing friendship and mutual understanding between our two vast but kindred systems of society but the continuance of the intimate relationships between our military advisers, leading to common study of potential dangers, similarity of weapons and manuals of instruction and interchange of officers and cadets at colleges. It should carry with it the continuance of the present facilities for mutual security by the joint use of all naval and Air Force bases in the possession of either country all over the world. This would perhaps double the mobility of the American Navy and Air Force. It would greatly expand that of the British Empire Forces and it might well lead, if and as the world calms down, to important financial savings. Already we use together a large number of islands; more may well be entrusted to our joint care in the near future. The United States already has a Permanent Defense Agreement with the Dominion of Canada, which is so devotedly attached to the British Commonwealth and Empire. This agreement is more effective than many of those which have often been made under formal alliances. This principle should be extended to all the British Commonwealths with full reciprocity. Thus, whatever happens and thus only we shall be secure ourselves and able to work together for the high and simple causes that are dear to us and bode no ill to any. Eventually there may come the principle of common citizenship, but that we may be content to leave to destiny whose outstretched arm so many of us can clearly see.

There is however an important question we must ask ourselves. Would a special relationship between the United States and the British Commonwealth be inconsistent with our overriding loyalties to the world organization? I reply that, on the contrary, it is probably the only means by which that organization will achieve its full stature and strength. There are already the special United States relations with Canada and between the United States and the South American Republics. We also have our Twenty-Years Treaty of Collaboration and Mutual Assistance with Soviet Russia. I agree with Mr. Bevin that it might well be a Fifty Years Treaty. We have an alliance with Portugal unbroken since 1384. None of these clash with the general interest of a world agreement. On the contrary they help it. "In my father's house are many mansions." Special associations between members of the United Nations which have no aggressive point against any other country, which harbor no design incompatible with the charter of the United Nations, far from being harmful, are beneficial and, as I believe, indispensable.

I spoke earlier of the temple of peace. Workmen from all countries must build that temple. If two of the workmen know each other particularly well and are old friends, if their families are intermingled and if they have faith in each other's purpose, hope in each other's future and charity towards each other's shortcomings, to quote some good words I read here the other day, why cannot they work together at the common task as friends and partners? Why cannot they share their tools and thus increase each others' working powers? Indeed they must do so or else the temple may not be built, or, being built, it may collapse, and we shall all be proved unteachable and have to go and try to learn again for a third time, in a school of war, incomparably more rigorous than that from which we have just been released. The dark ages may return, the stone age may return on the gleaming wings of science, and what might now shower immeasurable material blessings upon mankind, may even bring about its total destruction. Beware, I say; time may be short. Do not let us take the course of letting events drift along till it is too late. If there is to be a fraternal association of the kind I have described, with all the extra strength and security which both our countries can derive from it, let us make sure that that great fact is known to the world, and that it plays its part in steadying and stabilizing the foundations of peace. Prevention is better than cure.

A shadow has fallen upon the scenes so lately lighted by the Allied victory. Nobody knows what Soviet Russia and its Communist international organization intends to do in the immediate future, or what are the limits if any to their expansive and proselytizing tendencies. I have a strong admiration and regard for the valiant Russian people and for my wartime comrade, Marshal Stalin. There is sympathy and goodwill in Britain—and I doubt not here also—towards the peoples of all the Russias and a resolve to persevere through many differences and rebuffs in establishing lasting friendships. We understand the Russian needs to be secure on her Western frontiers from all renewal of German aggression. We welcome her to her rightful place among the leading nations of the world. Above all we welcome constant, frequent and growing contacts between the Russian people and our own people on both sides of the Atlantic. It is my duty, however, to place before you certain facts about the present position in Europe.

From Stettin in the Baltic to Trieste in the Adriatic, an iron curtain has descended across the continent. Behind that line lie all the capitals of the ancient states of Central and Eastern Europe. Warsaw, Berlin, Prague, Vienna, Budapest, Belgrade, Bucharest and Sofia, all these famous cities and the populations around them lie in the Soviet sphere and all are subject in one form or another, not only to Soviet influence but to a very high and increasing measure of control from Moscow. Athens alone, with its immortal glories, is free to decide its future at an election under British, American and French observation. The Russian-dominated Polish Government has been encouraged to make enormous and wrongful inroads upon Germany, and mass expulsions of millions of Germans on a scale grievous and undreamed of are now taking place. The Communist parties, which were very small in all these Eastern States of Europe, have been raised to preeminence and power far beyond their numbers and are seeking everywhere to obtain totalitarian control. Police governments are prevailing in nearly every case, and so far, except in Czechoslovakia, there is no true democracy. Turkey and Persia are both profoundly alarmed and disturbed at the claims which are made upon them and at the pressure being exerted by the Moscow Government. An attempt is being made by the Russians in Berlin to build up a quasi-Communist party in their zone of Occupied Germany by showing special favors to groups of left-wing German leaders. At the end of the fighting last June, the American and British Armies withdrew Westwards, in accordance with an earlier agreement, to a depth at some points of 150 miles on a front of nearly 400 miles to allow the Russians to occupy this vast expanse of territory which the Western Democracies had conquered. If now the Soviet Government tries, by separate action, to build up a pro-Communist Germany in their areas, this will cause new serious difficulties in the British and American zones, and will give the defeated Germans the power of putting themselves up to auction between the Soviets and the Western Democracies. Whatever conclusions may be drawn from these facts—and facts they are—this is certainly not the liberated Europe we fought to build up. Nor is it one which contains the essentials of permanent peace.

In front of the iron curtain which lies across Europe are other causes for anxiety. In Italy the Communist party is seriously hampered by having to support the Communist-trained Marshal Tito's claims to former Italian territory at the head of the Adriatic. Nevertheless the future of Italy hangs in the balance. Again one cannot imagine a regenerated Europe without a strong France. All my public life I have worked for a strong France and I never lost faith in her destiny, even in the darkest hours. I will not lose faith now. However, in a great number of countries, far from the Russian frontiers and throughout the world, Communist fifth columns are established and work in complete unity and absolute obedience to the directions they receive from the Communist center. Except in the British Commonwealth and in the United States, where Communism is in its infancy, the Communist parties or fifth columns constitute a growing challenge and peril to Christian civilization. These are sombre facts for anyone to have to recite on the morrow of a victory gained by

so much splendid comradeship in arms and in the cause of freedom and democracy, and we should be most unwise not to face
them squarely while time remains.

The outlook is also anxious in the Far East and especially in
Manchuria. The agreement which was made at Yalta, to which
I was a party, was extremely favorable to Soviet Russia, but it
was made at a time when no one could say that the German war
might not extend all through the summer and autumn of 1945
and when the Japanese war was expected to last for a further
eighteen months from the end of the German war. In this country you are all so well-informed about the Far East, and such devoted friends of China, that I do not need to expatiate on the
situation there.

I have felt bound to portray the shadow which, alike in the
West and in the East, falls upon the world. I was a Minister at
the time of the Versailles Treaty and a close friend of Mr. Lloyd
George. I did not myself agree with many things that were done,
but I have a very strong impression in my mind of that situation,
and I find it painful to contrast it with that which prevails now.
In those days there were high hopes and unbounded confidence
that the wars were over, and that the League of Nations would
become all-powerful. I do not see or feel the same confidence or
even the same hopes in the haggard world at this time.

On the other hand I repulse the idea that a new war is inevitable; still more that it is imminent. It is because I am sure
that our fortunes are in our own hands and that we hold the
power to save the future, that I feel the duty to speak out now
that I have an occasion to do so. I do not believe that Soviet
Russia desires war. What they desire is the fruits of war and the
indefinite expansion of their power and doctrines. But what we
have to consider here to-day while time remains, is the permanent
prevention of war and the establishment of conditions of freedom
and democracy as rapidly as possible in all countries. Our difficulties and dangers will not be removed by closing our eyes
to them. They will not be removed by mere waiting to see what
happens; nor will they be relieved by a policy of appeasement.
What is needed is a settlement, and the longer this is delayed,
the more difficult it will be and the greater our dangers will be-

come. From what I have seen of our Russian friends and Allies during the war, I am convinced that there is nothing they admire so much as strength, and there is nothing for which they have less respect than for military weakness. For that reason the old doctrine of a balance of power is unsound. We cannot afford, if we can help it, to work on narrow margins, offering temptations to a trial of strength. If the Western Democracies stand together in strict adherence to the principles of the United Nations Charter, their influence for furthering those principles will be immense and no one is likely to molest them. If however they become divided or falter in their duty, and if these all-important years are allowed to slip away, then indeed catastrophe may overwhelm us all.

Last time I saw it all coming and cried aloud to my own fellow-countrymen and to the world, but no one paid any attention. Up till the year 1933 or even 1935, Germany might have been saved from the awful fate which has overtaken her and we might all have been spared the miseries Hitler let loose upon mankind. There never was a war in all history easier to prevent by timely action than the one which has just desolated such great areas of the globe. It could have been prevented without the firing of a single shot, and Germany might be powerful, prosperous and honored today, but no one would listen and one by one we were all sucked into the awful whirlpool. We surely must not let that happen again.

This can only be achieved by reaching now, in 1946, a good understanding on all points with Russia under the general authority of the United Nations Organization and by the maintenance of that good understanding through many peaceful years, by the world instrument, supported by the whole strength of the English-speaking world and all its connections.

Let no man underrate the abiding power of the British Empire and Commonwealth. Because you see the forty-six millions in our island harassed about their food supply, of which they only grow one half, even in wartime, or because we have difficulty in restarting our industries and export trade after six years of passionate war effort, do not suppose that we shall not come through these dark years of privation as we have come through the glorious years of agony, or that half a century from now, you will not see 70 or 80 millions of Britons spread about the world and united in defense of our traditions, our way of life and of the world causes we and you espouse. If the population of the English-speaking Commonwealths be added to that of the United States, with all that such cooperation implies in the air, on the sea and in science and industry, there will be no quivering, precarious balance of power to offer its temptation to ambition or adventure. On the contrary, there will be an overwhelming assurance of security. If we adhere faithfully to the Charter of the United Nations and walk forward in sedate and sober strength, seeking no one's land or treasure, or seeking to lay no arbitrary control on the thoughts of men, if all British moral and material forces and convictions are joined with your own in fraternal association, the highroads of the future will be clear, not only for us but for all, not only for our time but for a century to come.

FAREWELL TO ENGLAND [8]

Edward R. Murrow [9]

Edward R. Murrow, the representative in England of the Columbia Broadcasting System, gave this commentary on Sunday, March 10, 1946. It marked the conclusion of his nine years' service in Britain. During that time, he had established a reputation as an outstanding radio reporter. His delivery was calm and precise. His reports were accurate, vivid. He singled out and described characteristic experiences "helpful to future students of history."

Three times bombs had destroyed the London C.B.S. offices.[10] He had flown twenty sorties with United States and British pilots. He had sailed the channel on a minesweeper, broadcast the sound of an air raid as he lay in a London gutter. This talk of March 10th was an eloquent summing up of his experiences and interpretation of "the soul of Britain."

He was recalled to New York to serve as vice president of Columbia Broadcasting System in charge of correspondents. The *London Morning Telegraph* called him, "America's unofficial ambassador." Other British papers, including the *Manchester Guardian*, also paid tribute to him.

The broadcast, to provide a specimen of the complete continuity of such a program, is here printed in full.

ANNOUNCER: [*Big Ben*] . . . Big Ben tolls out the hours as history writes a new chapter. Columbia's Edward R. Murrow, now at a microphone in London, is ready with his comments on the week's developments. . . . [Commercial]. . .

Now, here's Edward R. Murrow.

MURROW: This is London. During the past week the voice from Fulton, Missouri, was the loudest in the land. Mr. Churchill's speech has been digested, interpreted, and commented upon. The reactions have fallen into an altogether predictable pattern. The extreme left accuse him of advocating an anti-Russian alliance. The extreme right give a warm welcome to the speech. And the majority, in the middle, continue in a state of confusion.

[8] Text and permission to print supplied through the courtesy of the Columbia Broadcasting System.

[9] For biographical note see Appendix. For further comment on Mr. Murrow see *Representative American Speeches: 1940-1941*, p. 157-62 ; and *Representative American Speeches: 1943-1944*, p. 37-45.

[10] See *Time*. 47:59. March 18, 1946.

Britain's leading government spokesmen have been careful to refrain from comment, but that should not be taken to mean that they had advance knowledge of the contents of the speech, or that it had in any sense government sanction or approval. It did not.

There appears to be a tendency on both sides of the Atlantic to regard the solution of the ideological, economic and geographical conflict between Russian and the western world as being soluble only by creating a world in the image of Mr. Churchill, or in the image of Mr. Stalin. In this connection, it is useful to remember that Mr. Churchill and his party were decisively beaten and turned from office by the ballots of the British people. After full and free debate, they decided that their gratitude to the great wartime leader was not sufficient to cause them to return him and his party to power.

The British, in common with many peoples on the Continent, sought for middle ground between the conservatism of Mr. Churchill and the suppressive collectivism of Mr. Stalin. It was true, of course, that since the Labor Government assumed office in this country, the Russians have laid down their almost ceaseless barrage against it. They have missed no opportunity to launch diplomatic offensives. And the language employed, both in press and radio, has been such as would have caused careful reporters ten years ago to speak of the imminence of war. There is no question that Mr. Churchill uttered many of the dark thoughts and apprehensions that have occupied the minds of people in this country. It is equally true to say that Russia during the last three months has lost a great deal of the sympathy, admiration and allegiance that she once enjoyed in this country.

It would appear, from official statements in London and in Washington, that it is the desire of both countries to limit the expansion of Communist influence, and the dominance by Moscow of neighbor nations. If that is true, then the question arises as to whether this can best be done by a powerful coalition of the English-speaking world, sharing bases around the world, and saying to Russia "thus far, and no farther," or whether the limitation of the expansion of communism can best be achieved by eliminating as rapidly as may be those economic, social and political inequalities, the desire for land and security, which represent Russia's greatest asset in her appeal to the peoples of the Middle East, India, and Asia.

It is evident that the unity produced by the threat of a common foe is in jeopardy, if it has not, in fact, already been destroyed. The prospect of famine, dissension and fear provides ample ammunition for the pessimists. Already before the end of the first year of peace there is talk of another war. It becomes increasingly clear that victory, purchased at such a price, secured nothing more than the opportunity for statesmen to devise methods and means whereby nations may live together in peace. And it is equally clear that many, if not most, Europeans doubt that the statesmen are doing a very good job of it.

It was customary during the war to say that democracy was on trial—as indeed it was. It survived, but the trial is not yet ended. The outcome will be determined, not by dollars—not by American battleships showing a flag in the Mediterranean—not by luxury or productivity at home. It will, I think be determined by the degree to which Americans understand the role in world affairs that has been thrust upon them. And the importance, not only of our decisions, but of our examples.

We have, whether we like it or not, come into our full inheritance, our full strength. The rest of the world knows it, if we do not. We can no longer mediate, or non-intervene. Our influence and our interests spread round the world. That seems to me to have been a rapid development. I remember 1938 in Vienna when the Germans marched in. A man cut his throat with a butcher knife. That night there were shots in the dark, and then screams. An Austrian friend said, "Surely the Americans will do something about this." The following summer in Warsaw, Polish friends saying, "America will not permit the Germans to destroy us again." The French in '40 appealing for help. The British in '40 and '41. Mr. Churchill looking to the West, where the land was bright. It is true enough to say that there has not been such procrastination in Britain, such dissension in France; and if Mr. Baldwin, instead of proclaiming that Britain's frontier was on the Rhine had done something to keep it there; if the low countries had realized their peril; if the clock over the speaker's chair in the House of Commons had not ticked away so many wasted minutes and lost opportunities; then all that has happened might not have happened.

People here, and on the Continent, might not have died in old buildings. It might not have been necessary to bury all that was mortal of so many American boys along the roads from Omaha Beach to Osterbrook. It might have been possible to save the lives of those starving, stinking people who were later freed from Belsen, Buchenvald, and Dachau. And to save, too, the lives and the hopes of the gay and gallant youngsters, who went down in streaming flames, as though pushed earthward by a finger of dark smoke, over Berlin, Hamburg, and hundreds of other targets. But it didn't happen. They went out and bought—bought with their lives the chance to prevent this happening again, on a vaster and more terrible scale.

We may say that this slaughter and degradation was due to the malice and mismanagement of these Europeans. That can be left to history. Whatever causes, they have paid, and will continue to pay a frightful price. The important thing would seem to be that any future war will walk down our streets, enter our houses, and is unlikely to spare any.

We have emerged from this war into a precarious peace with great power. Indeed, with a power which fills our friends with a mixture of admiration and fear. And the victory has placed upon us a responsibility which we have never before borne. It is true that the new world came to the rescue of the old. It is true that the old world looks to us for continuing assistance and the means of averting starvation and chaos, but there's something more. There's a heavier obligation we bear—which is to demonstrate that our power is not devoid of tolerance; that we can apply at home and abroad the principles we profess.

We have been accustomed for many decades to look upon Europe as a place of continuing quarrel and dissension, from which our ancestors were glad to escape. Now much of Europe looks to the West with a mixture of hope and anxiety to see what, if anything, we shall do with our power. For what happens in America is vastly more important than anything that happens over here. And the thing that is important is not what we say, but what we do. It is no exaggeration to say that now, as never before, the eyes of the world are upon us. What we eat, what we wear, the movies we make, the broadcasts we do, the actions of our statesmen at conference are news to that part of Europe which still has access to information and opinions. The senator who speaks or votes may have regard only for his constituents, but his actions would have influence from London to Chungking. That is the price of power.

It's difficult to get any idea of size, the dimensions of a sky-scraper or a powerhouse, if you're inside it. I spent the past several years looking at America from the outside. Tomorrow I'm coming home to stay. That is why I have ventured to speak as I have about how America appears from Europe. If I have been wrong, then most of the people I know over here have been wrong, too. For it would seem that we are confronted with a choice—a choice between leadership and isolation; not isolation of our own choice, but the isolation which will be imposed upon us if we travel in one direction and the rest of the world in another.

During the last few years I have seen a considerable number of people die with great dignity, but the thing that impressed me most was not the demonstration of physical courage. That's been a chief commodity in this war. Many people of many nations, the Spaniards, the Poles, the Dutch, the British, and the Germans, were brave under the bombs. I doubt that the most important thing was Dunkirk, or the Battle of Britain, El Alemain, or Sta-lingrad. Not even the Limeys in Normandie, or the great blows struck by British and American bombers—perhaps not even the arrival of the American troops and American power in Europe. Historians may decide that any one of these events was decisive. But I am persuaded that the most important thing that happened in Britain was that this nation chose to win or lose the war under the established rules of parliamentary procedure. It feared nazism, but did not choose to imitate it. Mr. Churchill remained the servant in the House of Commons. The government was given dictatorial power, but it was used with restraint. And the House of Commons was ever vigilant.

I remember that while London was being bombed in the daylight, the House of Commons devoted two days to discussing conditions under which enemy aliens were detained on the Isle of Man. Though Britain fell, there were to be no concentration camps here. I remember that two days after Italy declared war an Italian citizen, convicted of murder in the lower court, appealed successfully to the highest court in the land, and the original verdict was set aside. There was still in the land, regardless of race, nationality, or hatred, representative government. Equality before the law survived. Future generations, who bother to read the official record of proceedings in the House of Commons, will discover that the British Army retreated from many places, but that there was no retreat from the principles for which our ancestors fought.

The record is massive evidence of the flexibility and toughness of the principles and traditions we share with the people who live in this island. It will, I think, inspire and lift men's hearts long after the names of most of the great sea and land engagements have been forgotten.

This reporter, who has not always been right, and who on occasion had the high privileges of sharing the dangers and discomforts of the American Army under the British people, saw Americans and Britains give the reply to tyranny that their history, their traditions, and their ancestors demanded of them. It would be foolish for any reporter to leave this land without acknowledging his debt to the many people who have given him tea, hospitality and information—and—on occasion, inspiration. It would be equally unmannerly to fail to acknowledge the debt to those people at home who have written or cabled praise, condemnation or condolences. And now for the last time—this is Edward R. Murrow in London.

COMMON INTERESTS OF THE
UNITED NATIONS [11]

JAMES F. BYRNES [12]

The Honorable James F. Byrnes, Secretary of State, delivered this address before the United Nations Assembly, in Central Hall, London, on January 14, 1946.

The Assembly convened on January 10th, when Paul-Henri Spaak, the Belgium foreign minister, was elected President. On the preceding evening, King George had given a dinner and had officially greeted the delegates.

Secretary Byrnes, the first speaker of the day, urged the General Assembly to adopt the atomic energy resolution of the Big Four (Russia, Great Britain, China and the United States). The speech aimed to reassure the delegates concerning the attitude of the United States toward the purposes of the United Nations. The seven hundred and fifty delegates from the fifty-one nations applauded the speech roundly and "sincerely" (according to the *Manchester Guardian*), especially at the mention of the names of Roosevelt, Churchill, and Stalin.

The address should be viewed in the light of the divergent philosophies and policies at work in the Assembly. Byrnes was attempting to help get the organization on its feet. Almost all countries, especially the small ones, were clamoring to push forward their individual problems. Byrnes appealed to the Turks, the Iranians, and other groups waiting to argue their cases, to hold their thunder until problems of organization, jurisdiction, trusteeships, and similar matters were safely taken care of.

The American representative was soft-spoken but firm in his presentation. According to one observer, Captain Halbert Gulley, in charge of the speech program at Shrivenham University, England, "the delivery was more after the manner of the modern American business tradition with its forthrightness" than after that of the "grand manner" of Parliamentary debate or after that of the Franklin D. Roosevelt eloquence." [13]

Commented the *Manchester Guardian* of January 15, on the Byrnes address: "When all the speeches at the General Assembly are concerned with such things as raising the standard of living, abolishing poverty, hunger, and unemployment throughout the world, then—and only then—we may be getting somewhere near the vision of universal peace."

[11] Text is from the *New York Times*, January 15, 1946.

[12] For biographical note see Appendix.

[13] For further comment on Byrnes, see *Representative American Speeches: 1942-43*, p. 189ff.

We have met here today to consider the report of the Preparatory Commission. This report is the result of painstaking and devoted labor by the delegates on the executive committee and the Preparatory Commission.

This preparatory work has made it possible for the United Nations to begin its work at the very start of the first year of peace after six successive years of devastating war and less than five months after the surrender of Japan.

For this prompt beginning the world owes an immeasurable debt to many who are not here today. We are particularly indebted to Franklin Delano Roosevelt, Winston Churchill and Joseph Stalin.

It was they who four years ago this month, at one of the darkest moments of the war, joined with their allies to proclaim the United Nations Declaration. Even as they exerted every effort to mobilize and unite at that late and critical moment the forces of freedom for survival, they knew that military survival, military victory was not enough.

The vision of those nations large and small which joined in the United Nations Declaration was not restricted to a wartime alliance. Their determination was to bind together in peace the free nations of the world so that never again would they find themselves isolated in the face of tyranny and aggression. Their resolve was to see that military victory was not a mere armistice to allow time for aggressor nations to choose their victims and enslave them one by one.

The purpose of these nations which united in the defense of their freedom was not to escape but to face the realities of the world in which we live. They recognized, as the peace-loving nations failed to recognize after the last war, that in this modern world nations, like individuals, cannot live with themselves alone.

They realized the lives and treasure which might have been saved if the free nations of the world had heeded in time the practical idealism of Woodrow Wilson, Lord Robert Cecil, Aristide Briand and Maxim Litvinoff.

They realized the lives and the treasure which might have been saved if the free nations of the world had united to preserve the peace before the peace of any of them was broken instead of waiting until aggression had engulfed the whole world in flames and compelled them to unite or perish.

So the nations which were compelled to unite in a war for survival resolved even before victory was attained that they would take steps to preserve a free and a united world. They resolved to keep faith with the millions who were fighting and dying to give the world the chance which it so tragically missed after the first World War.

At Moscow, in 1943, a start was made by Mr. Hull, Mr. Molotoff and Mr. Eden. On that occasion a pledge was undertaken by the United States, the United Kingdom and the Soviet Union, in which China joined, to work for the creation of an effective international organization. Then came the Dumbarton Oaks proposals, the Yalta decision to call the San Francisco Conference and finally the United Nations Charter, which fifty-one nations joined in writing.

The Charter is now part of the law of nations. It has been ratified by all the countries which are represented here. The preparatory work has been completed. The Assembly of the United Nations is no longer a plan on paper. It is a living reality, the representatives are here in this hall. The Security Council and the Economic and Social Council have been elected.

The functioning of the United Nations will depend not merely upon the words of its Charter or the rules or procedures we adopt here or upon the individuals we elect to hold office. It will depend upon the support it receives from the governments and the peoples of the nations which have created it and which must sustain it.

If the United Nations lives in the minds and the hearts of our peoples, it will be able to adapt itself to the changing needs of a changing world and it will endure. If it lacks broad popular support, no charter, however perfect, will save it.

I believe the United Nations will live. I believe it because it springs from the impelling necessities of the age in which we live. It has been born out of the indescribable pain and suffering of many peoples in many lands.

It must live because in this atomic age the common interests which should unite free nations in maintaining a friendly, peaceful world far outweigh any possible conflict in interest which might divide them.

The United Nations does not threaten any people. It comes into conflict with no real or vital interest of any of its members.

It is not interest, it is fear and suspicion, which in turn breed fear and suspicion, that cast a shadow upon the path of peace.

As the late President Roosevelt said, "We have nothing to fear but fear itself." We must dedicate ourselves to the task of exposing and eliminating blind and unreasoning fears and the unnecessary difficulties which they create.

Nothing can help dispel fear and suspicion so much as co-operation in common tasks and common problems. The opportunities afforded for working together within the United Nations can help to break down habits of thinking in national isolation and go far to bring about understanding and tolerance.

The United Nations is not a mere pact among its members, it is an institution or a series of institutions capable of life and growth.

Let us use the institutions that we have created to help one another rebuild a shattered world in which there can be real security. Let us not be unduly concerned about possible shortcomings of the Charter before we have even tried to operate under it.

No charter that must be acceptable to all of us can be regarded as perfect by any one of us. But it is a great tribute to the framers of the charter that it has been accepted by all the United Nations, large and small.

It is argued that the great states may abuse the rights given them under the Charter. There are risks in any human undertaking. But I have confidence that the great states will respect their obligations. As President Truman stated in his opening address at the San Francisco Conference:

While these great states have a special responsibility to enforce the peace, their responsibility is based upon the obligations resting upon all states, large and small, not to use force in international relations except in the defense of law. The responsibility of great states is to serve, and not to dominate, the world.

Great states as well as small states must come to view their power as a sacred trust to be exercised not for selfish purposes but for the good of all peoples.

If the United Nations becomes a working institution with broad popular support, devoted to the development of peace, security and human well-being, whatever defects there may be in its lettered provisions will not be beyond practical remedy. Institutions that come to live in the minds and the hearts of the people somehow manage to meet every crisis.

But I offer a word of warning. Let us not expect feats of magic overnight from the institutions we have created. Let us beware of the diehard enthusiasts as well as the diehard unbelievers. Let us not think that we can give over any and every problem to the United Nations and expect it to be solved. Let us avoid casting excessive burdens upon the institutions of the United Nations, especially in their infancy.

I recall to you the clear provisions of the Charter, which obligate member nations to make every effort to settle their disputes by peaceful means of their own choice before calling upon the United Nations to intervene. The primary responsibility of the United Nations is to build a lasting system of peace and security capable of meeting the stresses and strains of the future and to promote through more effective international cooperation the economic and social well-being of the peoples of the world.

In the months ahead we must concentrate upon these tasks. We have first to provide the Security Council with the military force it needs to maintain peace. This must be done by special agreements which remain to be worked out between the Security Council and the member states. We should begin upon this task immediately.

We have another task of transcending importance. The establishment of a commission to deal with the problems raised by the discovery of atomic energy is inseparably linked with the problem of security. It is a matter of primary concern to all nations. We must not fail to devise the safeguards necessary to insure that this great discovery is used for human welfare and not for more deadly human warfare.

I hope that this Assembly will approve promptly the solution proposed by my government in association with the United Kingdom, the Soviet Union, China, France and Canada so that this commission may begin its work without delay.

The United Nations must be a cooperative effort upon the part of all peace-loving nations. Our fighting men have given us this opportunity. A great responsibility now rests upon all of us. Upon the meeting of that responsibility depends the future of civilized humanity.

Twenty-five years ago we in the United States were not fully aware of our responsibility. But, with others, we have learned from experience. This time both the United States and its people are deeply conscious of their responsibility. This time, on their behalf, I pledge full and wholehearted cooperation.

UNITED NATIONS ASSEMBLY: A REPORT [14]

ARTHUR H. VANDENBERG [15]

Senator Arthur H. Vandenberg gave this report before his fellow Senators, on February 27, 1946. He summed up his experiences as American delegate to the first meeting of the General Assembly of the United Nations Organization in London, and added his notions of a proper policy toward Russia. His was the voice of the Republican party in foreign affairs.

Although he did not mention James F. Byrnes, Secretary of State, Vandenberg implied that strong American leadership was lacking. In the Security Council proceedings he felt that Russia too frequently proposed and disposed, with the United States either trailing along indecisively, or speaking up with "too little and too late."

At the end of his one-hour address, the Senate stood and applauded. Colleagues swarmed about him enthusiastically.

One day later Secretary Byrnes, before the Overseas Press Club in New York City, gave a well-prepared and vigorous speech that fully satisfied those who had criticized him for his mild handling of the Russian-American issues.

These two addresses were generally interpreted as marking the inception of a firmer stand toward the Soviet Republics. The areas of friction included (1) Manchuria, (2) Iran, (3) Central and Southeastern Europe, and (4) Germany. In Manchuria Russian troops were still present in large numbers despite promises to leave. Moreover they were removing much of that country's industrial plant. Russia proposed to remain in Azerbaijan Province, Iran, again despite the Big Three agreement of evacuation. In Austria, Russia again held up plans for withdrawal; the Russian pressure for Mediterranean bases continued; she backed the Yugoslav demand for Trieste; refused to support free elections in Bulgaria; demanded large reparations from Italy; allegedly helped block any satisfactory unified administration in Germany; and continued to support a policy of communistic penetration into France, and absolute domination of Poland and the other countries bordering directly on prewar Russia.

The immediate background of the Vandenberg-Byrnes speeches dated from the Yalta Conference of February 4-12, 1945. There the Big Three agreed on principles of peace and underwrote the United Nations as the agency for international peace-keeping.[16]

[14] Text is from *Congressional Record*, 79th Congress, *Second Session*, 92:1726-29, February 27, 1946 (daily edition).

[15] For biographical note see Appendix.

[16] See *Representative American Speeches: 1944-1945*, p. 15 ff.

At the Potsdam Conference, July 17-August 6, 1945, hopes for agreement and progress toward peace brightened. But in the Conference of Foreign Ministers at London, September 11-October 2, 1945, Russia apparently stifled almost every effort toward framing peace treaties. Secretary Byrnes, on October 5th, back in this country, charged the Stalin spokesmen as largely responsible for the failures. In December 1945, another meeting of the Big Three Foreign Ministers was held in Moscow. It, too, bogged down. The meeting of the United Nations First Assembly in London, January 10-February 15, 1946, accentuated the differences. In the Security Council, Mr. Vishinsky, the Russian delegate, opposed almost every move by Britain and America. Such was the general situation, familiar at first hand to Mr. Vandenberg when he spoke in the Senate.

The speech was typical of Vandenberg's style. He was methodical and direct in his reporting; was accurate in his use of facts. He fell into an alliterative and rhythmical pattern of composition. It was the expression of an orator, with here and there colorful analogies or metaphors. In delivery the Senator was aggressive, somewhat florid, pedantic. He is a large man, with dark, heavy eyes that flash beneath his heavy brows. He dominates easily his audience, persuades them by his earnestness, his physical animation and his oratorical inflections.

As this paragraph is written, many a political prophet is pointing to this Senate leader as one of the leading candidates for the Republican presidential nomination in 1948.[17]

At the conclusion of the address, Senator Wiley of Wisconsin, said:

"Mr. President, when our distinguished associate who has just addressed the Senate, the Senator from Michigan [Mr. Vandenberg] left for Europe, it was my privilege to say a few words on the floor of the Senate about his voyage into a far country. At that time it was the wish and the prayer of all his associates in the Senate that God would speed him, and give him the health and the strength and the vision to carry through.

"History is a record of great men. We have heard a great American report to us on one of the great events in world history. He has done a great job. I wish that every person in America could read his address. I think it will rank as one of the great addresses of all time delivered in this chamber.

"The Senator from Michigan has done several things which are of utmost importance. He has brought to America a great hope. He has shown that the meeting in London was not a failure, as so many have said. He has demonstrated to us clearly, by a factual recital of what took place there, that to a large extent judgment, common sense, and reason were in the saddle in London. I have stated that history is the record of great men, and I believe that the record here established indicates that great men were in action in London."

[17] For further comment on Vandenberg as a speaker, see *Representative American Speeches: 1937-1938*, p. 39.

Mr. President: I am presenting a brief report to my Senate colleagues regarding the recent meeting of the United Nations in London, where, thanks to your generous confirmation of the President's appointment I sat as an American delegate in the first General Assembly.

I had expected to postpone this statement until the return of the Senate's other representative at London, the distinguished chairman of the Senate Foreign Relations Committee, the Senator from Texas [Tom Connally]. But events seem to recommend these observations now. The Senator from Texas will be back in the near future. I compliment him in the highest possible terms for his sterling services in London. He filled important and often difficult assignments with wisdom, vigor, tenacity and success. He was distinctly a credit to the Senate, to his country and to the great cause which he embraced with typical earnestness and zeal.

Mr. President, I say frankly at the outset that I return from London with mixed emotions. I return with no illusions that automatic peace awaits the world just because the machinery of the United Nations is now in gear. But I return also with an overriding conviction, even more emphatic than before, that the world's only hope of organized peace and security is inseparably linked with the evolution and the destiny of the United Nations enterprise. I return in the convinced belief that the more complex or ominous the world's international relations may become, in that same degree the greater becomes the critical need that the peace-loving peoples of the earth shall strive to make this enterprise succeed. I return in the belief that it can succeed unless Russia, Britain and the United States, individually or collectively, make it impossible.

I can share your disappointments over some phases of the London record. I can share your anxieties over some of its disturbing trends. I can share your desires that the San Francisco Charter should be improved in certain aspects. I intend to speak frankly about some of these things. But I cannot—and I do not—share the melancholy pessimism heard in some quarters that the United Nations, as a result of this experience, will be unable to cope with world realities as disclosed in current history. It would be silly to ignore the hazards. It would be sillier to ignore vindicated hopes. The amazing thing at London is not that there were areas of disagreements but that the areas of agreement were so vast and so significant.

In my opinion, Mr. President, I repeat—because it is so dreadfully important—that the United Nations must be made to succeed if we are to avoid unspeakable catastrophe in this atomic age when decisive war may be waged in minutes instead of years and when the first casualty list may be the last. To those who are already earnestly suggesting substitutes, I prayerfully suggest that if the UNO compact, as a starter, cannot command the agreement and cooperation essential to success, then any more ambitious program would obviously multiply these obstacles. Any less ambitious program would die of pernicious international anemia.

This Charter clearly has its imperfections. We must be constantly alert to opportunities for its improvement. It is helpful that the earnest friends of peace should press these discussions. But it seems clear to me that we must first learn to live with what we have. It seems clear to me that our challenge is to make the United Nations work. It is particularly a challenge to the so-called five great powers. More particularly, it is a challenge to three of them. Still more particularly, it is an individual challenge to the Union of Soviet Socialist Republics and to our own United States, as I shall presently undertake to demonstrate.

Now, sir, Mr. President, let's look at London. In thirty-seven days the United Nations turned a blueprint into a going concern. It turned an ideal into a reality. On January 10, 1946, we had only a pious dream. On February 16, 1946, we had organized, in working detail, the complete machinery for the General Assembly, for the Security Council, for the Court of International Justice, for the Social and Economic Council, and for the functioning of every instrument of peace which this Senate envisioned when it underwrote this dream last July with but two dissenting votes. On January 10 we had a "scrap of paper." In thirty-seven days we gave it life. The supreme need, in the name of flesh and blood and human hearts and hopes, is that it shall not return to the status of a "scrap of paper."

There was sharp controversy and competition in some of these organizational decisions. But all of them were accepted in good spirit by all concerned. There was not a suspicion of insincerity or sabotage. In other words, the original purpose—and what was intended to be the exclusive purpose—of this first General Assembly was carried out with complete comity and with significant success. There was healthy rivalry. But there was equally healthy agreement. In athletic parlance, the "team" was learning to "play team ball." The temporary quarters of the United Nations is already rising in the United States. The machinery is all in gear. Indeed, they were thirty-seven momentous days.

All this involved great labor and the composition of many differing points of view. For example, I was chairman of the subcommittee which dealt with administration and with budgets. Starting from zero, we had to create the framework for a tremendous institution. Fifty-one nations, spanning the gamut of race, color, language and tradition, had to concur. They did— with ultimate unanimity.

I venture to ask, with great respect, how long, and with what travail, it would have taken Congress to complete a comparable task. Obviously it was possible only with the highest degree of cooperation; with the best of mutual goodwill; and with a common dedication to a common purpose. And it is highly significant that there were no exceptions to this rule.

I should say, at this point, that UNO will be financed from a so-called working capital fund of $25,000,000; and that its provisional budget for 1946, including the Court at the Hague, is $21,500,000. Our provisional share is 25 per cent. In other words, the United States will spend for peace, on this account, far less per annum than it spent per hour on war.

So, Mr. President, let's put this big entry in the credit ledger. When we look at London and at the first General Assembly of the United Nations, let's remember that its organizational phase was a phenomenal success and a vigorous omen of hope for the tolerant cooperations which are the life-blood of this adventure in behalf of the collective security for which men and women pray, in a hundred different tongues, at the war-scarred heathstones of the world. Again in athletic parlance, let's anticipate that when the "team" has played together a little longer it will be invincible.

Let us remember some other things about this first General Assembly.

Let's remember that it initiated the joint studies which should lead to the international control of atomic energy, on a basis requiring adequate and dependable security and inspection arrangements as a mandate prerequisite to any disclosures. This is the way to save civilization from the use of atomic energy as a lethal curse to humankind.

Let's remember that this General Assembly—this vocal conscience of the earth—unanimously offered new hope to dependent peoples everywhere through the expression of our mutual purpose to encourage their self-government.

Let's remember that it pledged itself to encourage a world-wide free press through instrumentalities to be created at its next session in September. Blackouts and iron curtains are not the insignia of liberty nor the trade-marks of peace.

Let's remember that this General Assembly encouraged the hopes of war refugees—the pathetic derelicts of recent conflict—by refusing, on a decisive roll call, to sanction their involuntary repatriation.

Let's remember, Mr. President, that this General Assembly has now put itself in full position to proceed hereafter to implement dynamic Article 14 of the Charter. This means that it can recommend the peaceful adjustment of any situation, regardless of origin, which it deems likely to impair the general welfare or to infringe upon equal rights and self-determination of peoples.

All this, and more, the General Assembly did in thirty-seven days! Let's put this entry into the credit ledger.

No; it is not the whole story. I shall come to that in a moment. But it is enough of the story to hearten men of goodwill to refuse any defeatism in their attitudes and to carry on. We have the greatest encouragements to believe that the United Nations can gather strength and moral power to meet the major issues which may threaten international peace and security; or, as an alternative, to organize the conscience of the world against any aggressor who defies these precepts.

Ah, yes, you say, but how about the Security Council? Well, Mr. President, let's look at the Security Council. By all means, let's look at the Security Council.

First, let's remember that the Security Council was put to unexpected test just six days after it came into being—before it had any of the Charter instruments intended for its use—before it even had any rules for its own procedure. That was like expecting a motor car to run on one wheel. Or, changing the metaphor, it was like asking General Eisenhower to invade the Continent twenty minutes after we declared war on Germany. It took four years to integrate the machine that won the war.

I respectfully submit, to those who are impatient with the London story, that we are entitled to at least a few months of grace in the winning of a lasting peace. Even if it took as long as the winning of the war, still it would be a miracle—in the light of man's dismal failures for 1900 years to follow in the foot-steps of the Prince of Peace or, again changing the metaphor, I would suggest a study of our swaddling days and of the time and travail involved in accommodating ourselves to our own Constitution. The truth is, Mr. President, that the brief, preliminary record made by the Security Council is, under the circumstances, much more notable for what it did than for what it did not do.

Four controversies—each involving the presence of foreign troops in lands other than their own—were submitted to the Security Council upon which sit Britain, China, France, Russia, United States, Egypt, Mexico, the Netherlands, Australia, Brazil and Poland. In each instance, after full hearing, the four controversies were left, on conciliatory American initiative, to further negotiations between the nations in direct concern. But that qualifying phrase—"After full hearing"—is of paramount importance.

Mind you, these were the raw materials out of which wars have sprung in other days. But here the contestants were not meeting on a battlefield. They were meeting at the Council table—in the white light of full publicity—in the presence of their peers—under the searching eyes of a watching world—and under the impulse of a solemn pledge to keep the peace.

Here, words—which would have been fighting words in other days—were the substitutes for guns and swords. Here the frankest imaginable discussions were taking place—eye to eye—cheek by jowl. Here the contestants shook hands at the termination of the jousts. Here there was a clear verdict rendered on the facts by the member nations sitting in their judgment seats, as each representative spoke into the record. It was the "open diplomacy openly arrived at" of which men heretofore have dreamed in vain. It was an epoch in the hopes of mankind. Let's put that in the credit ledger!

To be sure, the ultimate disposition of each case, after full hearing, was a reversion to direct negotiation between the parties involved, instead of some affirmative act of penalty or of enforced restraint. This may have been a disappointment to some of our more impatient direct actionists who would like a god of peace as militant and as relentless as the gods of war.

But I remind you that the United Nations Charter does not contemplate the techniques of the meat-axe. It is not built to hasten sanctions and the use of force. It is built to prevent, if possible, the use of sanctions and the use of force. It is built to stop war, not to make it. It requires the exhaustion of all possibilities of direct negotiations, and of inquiry, and of mediation, and of conciliation, and of arbitration, and of judicial settlement before we turn to grimmer disciplines.

And this, Mr. President, is desperately important. I venture to assert that the renewal of direct negotiations in the instant cases, after these full hearings, is calculated to be quite a different thing than it was before. Now these negotiations will proceed in the presence of the necessity for an ultimate accounting not only to the Security Council but also to the critical opinions of mankind. Now the record, be it good or ill, defies distortion in the future conduct of these events.

In most instances, I dare to believe there will be adequate results. By way of example, I point only to the fact that the Soviet Union immediately opened negotiations with Iran—after months of previous refusal to confer; and that, in the midst of Indonesian discussion, the Netherlands announced new plans for an autonomous Indonesian Commonwealth. This, too, goes on the credit ledger.

I say again that this is the wholesome pattern of a great hope—even as it also has its danger spots. I do not intend to deny the latter, as will presently appear. But neither do I intend to ignore the former, lest we be treacherously misled against our own best destiny. The price of failure is too great.

By way of concrete illustration, Mr. President, let me submit a blow-by-blow account of the final contest before the Security Council. Within it are found all of our hopes and fears—all of the credits and the liabilities—all of the encouragements and all of the warnings for the future.

Lebanon and Syria were asking the simultaneous withdrawal of French and British troops. Just linger for a moment, Senators, upon this unprecedented scene. Two of the newest and the smallest and the humblest of governments were complaining against two of the five great powers—against two of the permanent members of the Security Council. The difference in relative power and authority could scarcely approach greater extremes. Yet little Lebanon and little Syria were invited to temporary seats at the Council table, pursuant to the mandate of the Charter. There they sat, with the mightiest of earth, to have their untrammeled day in this court of world opinion. It was the triumph of an ideal.

They spoke without limitation and without curb. French and British troops had been necessary in Lebanon and Syria once upon a time, particularly the British, who had entered upon invitation and who were staying by request until such time as both the British and the French could retire together. Lebanon and Syria testified that the need for these foreign troops was done, but that negotiations for their withdrawal had been unsuccessful. Frankly, without rancor, they laid their facts upon the table and petitioned for relief. At long last here, indeed, was an approach to the Parliament of Man. Another large entry on the credit ledger!

When Lebanon and Syria had finished, sturdy Ernest Bevin, Foreign Minister of the United Kingdom, promptly announced that he would be willing and glad to withdraw the British troops at once. Monsieur Bidault, the able Foreign Minister for France, immediately followed with a statement in kind. He said that there were technical arrangements to be concluded; but that he would gladly press their speediest possible negotiation.

The controversy gave promise of amicable composition at one sitting of the Council. Our own distinguished Ambassador Stettinius, speaking for the United States, offered a resolution which took note of the record; asserted the Council's general belief that there should be no unwanted troops on foreign soil in time of peace; expressed the Council's confidence that the case could be safely remanded to the parties in interest for final negotiation; and asked that the Council be kept advised of these developments. It appeared to be a prompt and happy and effective composition of the incident. The dove of peace flew in the window. But quickly it flew out again.

At this point the brilliant Soviet Commissar, Vishinsky, intervened. He wanted no such easy peace. He was not satisfied, he said, thus to let the matter rest. Long and bitterly he indicted the action particularly of France in Lebanon and Syria. Instead of being closed, the incident then blazed into two more days of intense and futile debate. He offered amendments to the American resolution which both France and Britain and most members of the Council interpreted as stinging and unwarranted rebukes. This was not oil on troubled waters. It was salt in reopened wounds.

The chairman of the Security Council finally called for a vote. Vishinsky said he too was ready provided the vote was taken under the provisions of the Charter prohibiting the participation of members of the Council who were parties to a dispute which threatens international peace and security. Both Bevin and Bidault hotly protested that this was not a "dispute threatening international peace and security"; that, therefore, they were entitled to vote and that they could not accept the Vishinsky implication. But they then announced that, upon their own responsibility, they would voluntarily abstain.

Vishinsky's amendment was voted down with only its author on its side. The American resolution was then given the seven affirmative votes required by the Charter, the chairman announced that it was carried. But he was wrong. The Charter also required that these seven votes had to include the concurring votes of the permanent members of the Council. This is the famous "veto" of which so much has been heard. Vishinsky promptly challenged the chairman's announcement. He was wholly within his rights—as, indeed, he was from start to finish. The resolution was lost by "veto."

That left little Lebanon and little Syria just where they started. But then came the thrilling climax. Bevin for Britain and Bidault for France magnificently asserted that they would voluntarily accept the terms of the resolution and abide by its terms precisely as though it were the law of the Council. Put that high up on the credit ledger!

Mr. President, I confess that I was proud of Western democracy that night! And the life of the United Nations took on new assurance and new expectancy, in the pattern of their attitudes. On the other hand, I trust I am not unfair in also confessing that it seemed to me the distinguished Soviet delegate— one of the ablest statesmen I have ever seen in action—seemed to be less interested in helping Lebanon and Syria than he was in baiting France and Britain—less interested in peace at this point than he was in friction.

I am certain it posed the same question in all our minds which I am now finding almost every day, in one form or another, in every newspaper I read—"What is Russia up to now?" It is, of course, the supreme conundrum of our time. We ask it in Manchuria. We ask it in Eastern Europe and the Dardanelles. We ask it in Italy, where Russia, speaking for Yugoslavia, has already initiated attention to the Polish legions. We ask it in Iran. We ask it in Tripolitania. We ask it in the Baltic and the Balkans. We ask it in Poland. We ask it in the capital of Canada. We ask it in Japan. We ask it sometimes even in connection with events in our own United States. "What is Russia up to now?" It is little wonder that we asked it at London. It is less wonder that the answer—at London and everywhere else—has a vital bearing on the destiny of the United Nations.

It would be entirely futile to blink the fact that two great, rival ideologies—democracy in the West and communism in the East—here find themselves face to face with the desperate need for mutual understanding in finding common ground upon which to strive for peace for both. In the final analysis this means that the two greatest spokesmen for these rival ideologies—Soviet

Russia and the United States—find themselves face to face with this same need for mutual understanding, both in and out of the United Nations. Indeed, if this does not oversimplify the problem, it might even be said that the future of the United Nations is wrapped up in this equation.

If this be so, I assert my own belief that we can live together in reasonable harmony if the United States speaks as plainly upon all occasions as Russia does; if the United States just as vigorously sustains its own purposes and its ideals upon all occasions as Russia does; if we abandon the miserable fiction, often encouraged by our own fellow-travelers, that we somehow jeopardize the peace if our candor is as firm as Russia's always is; and if we assume a moral leadership which we have too frequently allowed to lapse. The situation calls for patience and goodwill; but not for vacillation.

Let me make it wholly clear that I do not complain because Russia speaks—indeed, Mr. Vishinsky probably spoke in this Security Council more than the spokesmen of all the other powers combined. I am glad she speaks. She ought to speak. That is what this forum is for. But it is for others, too—just as Mr. Bevin used it upon more than one eloquent and courageous occasion. It is, I repeat, for others, too. All should feel an equal freedom, an equal duty and an equivalent responsibility.

The governments of the world suddenly find themselves in the presence of a new technique in international relations. It is in this forum of the United Nations where the most dominant of all debates and decisions are now calculated to occur. It would be impossible to overemphasize the importance of our own role and our own performance in such epochal events, and the need for positive foreign policies as our consistent guide.

Speaking in New York last week at a celebration in honor of the great Red Army which Marshal Stalin certifies will be kept at a progressive peak, our new American Ambassador-designate to Moscow, Lieut. Gen. Walter Bedell Smith, said: "It is imperative that our national temperatures remain normal." I agree. He said that "both nations want nothing so much as peace and security." I not only agree; but, in addition, if what still bothers Russia is really a security fear against resurgent aggression, I would renew my offer of one year ago for a direct treaty of mutual defense, under the United Nations, in the event an aggressor axis ever rises again.

General Smith said that the United States is willing to go a long way in meeting its international associates, but that it must be watchful of its own vital interests and hold to the line beyond which compromise cannot go—even if we once crossed that line under the pressures of the exigencies of war. But how can we expect our alien friends to know where that line is unless we reestablish the habit of saying only what we mean and meaning every word we say? I have the deep conviction that this way is the dependable way to permanent peace and concord between us, with its inevitable effect upon the United Nations. Indeed, I have the feeling it is the best way to win Soviet respect and Soviet trust. Respect must precede trust, and both are indispensable to peace.

General Smith said that "America and the U.S.S.R., given honesty and frankness on both sides, can get along together in the future just as well as they have for almost a hundred and fifty years, in spite of the fact that our governments and our economic systems have been quite different." Again I associate myself with that sentiment. But the honesty and frankness must be mutual.

Sometimes it is a useful, albeit painful, thing to search our own souls in critical hours like these. Was Sumner Welles, the late President Roosevelt's long-time Under Secretary of State, right in a recent statement from which I quote:

If the United States is to exercise any potent influence in promoting world peace and in establishing a better international order, other nations must be confident that this government will abide by our professions. American foreign policy must possess the all-important quality of dependability. . . The United States continues to possess the influence in world affairs which is derived from its potential military might and from its material resources. But the moral influence which it possessed during the war years because of the belief that this government was determined to support those principles which are indispensable to be established is rapidly vanishing. . . . It would be better far to refrain from giving assurances, however noble they may be, than to fail to carry them out. For the United States cannot exercise any specific leadership until all nations know that it means what it says.

Mr. President, this sort of an analysis does not detract for an instant from the notably loyal and richly helpful record which the United States has made to the foundations of the United Nations. I have been privileged to be so placed that I could see these great works of ours at first hand. We have a right to be eternally proud of America's part in launching this new argosy of peace upon the seas of time. The startling fact at London—I cannot repeat too often—is not that it sometimes trembled in the gale but rather that it so staunchly weathered all the storms. But, sir, we would be dubious mariners if we did not look back upon this pioneering journey to assess the dangers that developed and to put up warning signals for journeys yet to come.

Therefore, in addition to what I have already said, I must add two further admonitions.

I confess that in this first meeting of the United Nations I missed the uplifting and sustaining zeals for a great, crusading, moral cause which seemed to imbue the earlier Charter sessions at San Francisco. Perhaps it was because the agenda was so largely confined to the humdrum routine of organizational details. Perhaps it was the burden of anxiety over the misgivings that are inevitable in launching a peace project which never yet has succeeded in the history of civilization; or, on the other hand, perhaps it was the accumulated tiredness which dampens ardor and easily surrenders to the expedient notion that "all's well." Perhaps it was because, in the aftermath of war, we confront too many grim realities that are utterly at odds with the precepts of justice which we presume to defend. In any event, and whatever the cause, we are on notice that the peoples of the earth must never cease to evangelize this struggle for peace if it shall reach full flower.

Again, Mr. President, I sensed at London what seemed to be too great a tendency to relapse into power politics, in greater or less degree, and, as some one has said, to use the United Nations as a self-serving tribune rather than as a tribunal. It will require constant, consistent, courageous guidance to keep the United Nations within the main channel of its obligations—and here again is a clear call to America always to act in its traditional character for liberty and justice.

Mr. President, I have endeavored faithfully to report both the credits and the debits on the United Nations' ledgers. I fear it has been illy and inadequately done. But I want to leave the positive and emphatic conclusion that the credits utterly preponderate with a heavy, a significant, a wholesome and an encouraging balance.

Those, sir, were thirty-seven vital days in London. They are freighted with hope—solidly justified hope—in respect to collective security in this atomic age. In such an age there can be no security which is not collective. With unwavering fidelity we must carry on the great adventure. If there be any failure, let not the blood be upon our hands nor the tragedy upon our souls.

The United States has no ulterior designs against any of its neighbors anywhere on earth. We can speak with the extraordinary power inherent in this unselfishness. We need but one rule. What is right? Where is justice? There let America take her stand.

INTERNATIONAL MILITARY TRIBUNAL:
OPENING ADDRESS [18]

ROBERT H. JACKSON [19]

President Truman, on May 2, 1945, named Associate Justice Robert H. Jackson of the United States Supreme Court as chief United States counsel on the international military tribunal to try Axis war criminals. Justice Jackson stated (July 6th) that the Union of Soviet Socialist Republics, the United States, Great Britain, and France had agreed that the accused would be entitled to a fair trial, the procedure, however, to be unobstructed by merely delaying tactics.

On November 20th, at Nuremberg, Germany, acting as chief prosecutor, Justice Jackson made the opening statement for the prosecution. One section of that charge, several hours in length, is reprinted below.

Justice Jackson indicted the twenty-odd Nazi defendants on trial as responsible for World War II. His statement, heavily documented, was measured, judicial, conclusive. In essence his position was that planning a war of aggression was a crime; and that the planners, individually, could be held responsible for such aggression. The indictment is one of specific organizations and of "specific men."

"Military men are before you," said Jackson, "not because they served their country. They are here because they mastered it, along with these others, and drove it to war."

Justice Jackson's chief problem was not that of amassing evidence of German atrocities, successive invasions, enslavement of Europeans, or even the planning of aggressive war. His problem was to set up law under which the defendants could be condemned. The charter of the Nuremberg tribunal, completed long after V-E Day, was the *ex post facto* law that covered the case. The object of these trials was not simply to punish these defendants, but to create a body of international law for future war criminal trials. To justify his legal position he declared, "And let me make clear that while this law is first applied against German aggressors, the law . . . must condemn aggression by another nation, including these which now sit here in judgment."

Of his speech training Justice Jackson writes:

"I debated in high school, and have always done a good deal of public speaking as well as pretty constant professional work in court.

"My method of preparation varies with the occasion. If the occasion is a formal one, I prepare a written speech. After outlining it I

[18] Text furnished by Timothy A. McInerny, Director of Public Information, Department of Justice, Washington, D.C.
[19] For biographical note see Appendix.

sometimes dictate it and sometimes write it in long hand. If the occasion is an important one, or the subject matter is of special interest to me, I may rewrite it many times. On such occasions I follow the manuscript very carefully and the text to be printed represents exactly what I said, except that I sometimes make informal introductory remarks in response to something that has previously occurred on the program. On informal occasions my preparation consists of notes which are followed as a general outline. I have never written an argument to be made in court, but always made careful preparation of notes to make quite certain that nothing in the excitement of the moment would be overlooked. The only advice that I can give to young speakers is as old as the hills. Certainly no one ought to attempt to speak on a subject unless he has given it careful study so that his words would carry some authority. I know of nothing that would increase one's self confidence and improve his presentation as a thorough knowledge of the subject.

"I am one who believes that public speaking is no less important now than formerly. Techniques must be changed to meet new conditions such as the radio and the amplifier. Certainly there has been no decrease in the influence of a sincere and earnest personality which can best be sensed by the actual presence of the speaker." [20]

May It Please Your Honors: The privilege of opening the first trial in history for crimes against the peace of the world imposes a grave responsibility. The wrongs which we seek to condemn and punish have been so calculated, so malignant and so devastating that civilization cannot tolerate their being ignored because it cannot survive their being repeated. That four great nations, flushed with victory and stung with injury, stay the hand of vengeance and voluntarily submit their captive enemies to the judgment of the law is one of the most significant tributes that Power ever has paid to Reason.

This tribunal, while it is novel and experimental, is not the product of abstract speculations nor is it created to vindicate legalistic theories. This inquest represents the practical effort of four of the most mighty of nations, with the support of fourteen more, to utilize international law to meet the greatest menace of our times—aggressive war. The common sense of mankind demands that law shall not stop with the punishment of petty crimes by little people. It must also reach men who possess themselves of great power and make deliberate and concerted use of it to set in motion evils which leave no home in the world

[20] Letter to the editor, May 9, 1940.

untouched. It is a cause of this magnitude that the United Nations will lay before Your Honors.

In the prisoners' dock sit twenty-odd broken men. Reproached by the humiliation of those they have led almost as bitterly as by the desolation of those they have attacked, their personal capacity for evil is forever past. It is hard now to perceive in these miserable men as captives the power by which as Nazi leaders they once dominated much of the world and terrified most of it. Merely as individuals, their fate is of little consequence to the world.

What makes this inquest significant is that these prisoners represent sinister influences that will lurk in the world long after their bodies have returned to dust. They are living symbols of racial hatreds, of terrorism and violence, and of the arrogance and cruelty of power. They are symbols of fierce nationalisms and of militarism, of intrigue and war-making which have embroiled Europe generation after generation, crushing its manhood, destroying its homes, and impoverishing its life. They have so identified themselves with the philosophies they conceived and with the forces they directed that any tenderness to them is a victory and an encouragement to all the evils which are attached to their names. Civilization can afford no compromise with the social forces which would gain renewed strength if we deal ambiguously or indecisively with the men in whom those forces now precariously survive.

What these men stand for we will patiently and temperately disclose. We will give you undeniable proofs of incredible events. The catalog of crimes will omit nothing that could be conceived by a pathological pride, cruelty, and lust for power. These men created in Germany, under the *Fuehrerprinzip*, a National Socialist despotism equalled only by the dynasties of the ancient East. They took from the German people all those dignities and freedoms that we held natural and inalienable rights in every human being. The people were compensated by inflaming and gratifying hatreds toward those who were marked as "scapegoats." Against their opponents, including Jews, Catholics, and free labor, the Nazis directed such a campaign of arrogance, brutality, and annihilation as the world has not witnessed since the pre-Christian ages. They excited the German ambition to be a "master race," which of course implies serfdom for others. They led their people an a mad gamble for domination. They diverted social energies and resources to the creation of what they thought to be an invincible war machine. They overran their neighbors. To sustain the "master race" in its warmaking, they enslaved millions of human beings and brought them into Germany, where these hapless creatures now wander as "displaced persons." At length bestiality and bad faith reached such excess that they aroused the sleeping strength of imperiled civilization. Its united efforts have ground the German war machine to fragments. But the struggle has left Europe a liberated yet prostrate land where a demoralized society struggles to survive. These are the fruits of the sinister forces that sit with these defendants in the prisoners' dock. . . .

But if it be thought that the charter, whose declarations concededly bind us all, does contain new law I still do not shrink from demanding its strict application by this tribunal. The rule of law in the world, flouted by the lawlessness incited by these defendants, had to be restored at the cost to my country of over a million casualties, not to mention those of other nations. I cannot subscribe to the perverted reasoning that society may advance and strengthen the rule of law by the expenditure of morally innocent lives but that progress in the law may never be made at the price of morally guilty lives.

It is true, of course, that we have no judicial precedent for the charter. But international law is more than a scholarly collection of abstract and immutable principles. It is an outgrowth of treaties and agreements between nations and of accepted customs. Yet every custom has its origin in some single act, and every agreement has to be initiated by the action of some state. Unless we are prepared to abandon every principle of growth for international law, we cannot deny that our own day has the right to institute customs and to conclude agreements that will themselves become sources of a newer and strengthened international law. International law is not capable of development by the normal processes of legislation for there is no continuing international legislative authority. Innovations and revisions in international law are brought about by the action of governments designed to meet a change in circumstances. It grows, as did the common law, through decisions reached from time to time in adapting settled principles to new situations. The fact is that when the law evolves by the case method, as did the common law and as international law must do if it is to advance at all, it advances at the expense of those who wrongly guessed the law and learned too late their error. The law, so far as international law can be decreed, had been clearly pronounced when these acts took place. Hence, I am not disturbed by the lack of judicial precedent for the inquiry we propose to conduct.

The events I have earlier recited clearly fall within the standards of crimes, set out in the charter, whose perpetrators this tribunal is convened to judge and punish fittingly. The standards for war crimes and crimes against humanity are too familiar to need comment. There are, however, certain novel problems in applying other percepts of the charter which I should call to your attention.

A basic provision of the charter is that to plan, prepare, initiate, or wage a war of aggression, or a war in violation of international treaties, agreements, and assurances, or to conspire or participate in a common plan to do so, is a crime.

It is perhaps a weakness in this charter that it fails itself to define a war of aggression. Abstractly, the subject is full of difficulty and all kinds of troublesome hypothetical cases can be conjured up. It is a subject which, if the defense should be permitted to go afield beyond the very narrow charge in the indictment, would prolong the trial and involve the tribunal in insoluble political issues. But so far as the question can properly be involved in this case, the issue is one of no novelty and is one on which legal opinion has well crystalized.

One of the most authoritative sources of international law on this subject is the Convention for the Definition of Aggression signed at London on July 3, 1933 by Rumania, Estonia, Latvia, Poland, Turkey, the Soviet Union, Persia, and Afghanistan. The subject has also been considered by international committees and by commentators whose views are entitled to the greatest respect. It had been little discussed prior to the First

World War but has received much attention as international law has evolved its outlawry of aggressive war. In the light of these materials of international law, and so far as relevant to the evidence in this case, I suggest that an "aggressor" is generally held to be that state which is the first to commit any of the following actions:

(1) Declaration of war upon another state;

(2) Invasion by its armed forces, with or without a declaration of war, of the territory of another state;

(3) Attack by its land, naval, or air forces, with or without a declaration of war, on the territory, vessels, or aircraft of another state;

(4) Provision of support to armed bands formed in the territory of another state, or refusal, notwithstanding the request of the invaded state, to take in its own terriory, all the measures in its power to deprive those bands of all assistance or protection.

And I further suggest that it is the general view that no political, military, economic or other considerations shall serve as an excuse or justification for such actions; but exercise of the right of legitimate self-defense, that is to say, resistance to an act of aggression, or action to assist a state which has been subjected to aggression, shall not constitute a war of aggression.

It is upon such an understanding of the law that our evidence of a conspiracy to provoke and wage an aggressive war is prepared and presented. By this test each of the series of wars begun by these Nazi leaders was unambiguously aggressive.

It is important to the duration and scope of this trial that we bear in mind the difference between our charge that this war was one of aggression and a position that Germany had no grievances. We are not inquiring into the conditions which contributed to causing this war. They are for history to unravel. It is no part of our task to vindicate the European status quo as of 1933, or as of any other date. The United States does not desire to enter into discussion of the complicated prewar currents of European politics, and it hopes this trial will not be protracted by their consideration. The remote causations avowed are too insincere and inconsistent, too complicated and doctrinaire, to be the subject of profitable inquiry in this trial. A familiar example is to be found in the "Lebensraum" slogan, which summarized the contention that Germany needed more living space as a justification for expansion. At the same time that the Nazis were demanding more space for the German people, they were demanding more German people to occupy space. Every known means to increase the birth rate, legitimate and illegitimate, was utilized. "Lebensraum" represented a vicious circle of demand—from neighbors more space, and from Germans more progeny. We do not need to investigate the verity of doctrines which led to constantly expanding circles of aggression. It is only the plot and the act of aggression which we charge to be crimes.

Our position is that whatever grievances a nation may have, however objectionable it finds the status quo, aggressive warfare is an illegal means for settling those grievances or for altering those conditions. It may be that the Germany of the 1920's and 1930's faced desperate problems, problems that would have warranted the boldest measures short of war. All other methods—persuasion, propaganda, economic competition, diplomacy—were open to an aggrieved country, but aggressive warfare was outlawed. These defendants did make aggressive war, a war in violation of treaties. They did attack and invade their neighbors in order to effectuate a foreign policy which they knew could not be accomplished by measures short of war. And that is as far as we accuse or propose to inquire.

The charter also recognizes individual responsibility on the part of those who commit acts defined as crimes, or who incite others to do so, or who join a common plan with other persons, groups, or organizations to bring about their commission. The principle of individual responsibility for piracy and brigandage, which have long been recognized as crimes punishable under international law, is old and well established. That is what illegal warfare is. This principle of personal liability is a necessary as well as logical one if international law is to render real help to the maintenance of peace. An international law which operates only on states can be enforced only by war because the most practicable method of coercing a state is warfare. Those familiar with American history know that one of the compelling reasons for adoption of our Constitution was that the laws of the Confederation, which operated only on constituent states, were found ineffective to maintain order among them. The only answer to recalcitrance was impotence or war. Only sanctions which reach individuals can peacefully and effectively be enforced. Hence, the principle of the criminality of aggressive war is implemented by the charter with the principle of personal responsibility.

Of course, the idea that a state, any more than a corporation, commits crime is a fiction. Crimes always are committed only by persons. While it is quite proper to employ fiction of responsibility of a state or corporation for the purpose of imposing a collective liability, it is quite intolerable to let such a legalism become the basis of personal immunity.

The charter recognizes that one who has committed criminal acts may not take refuge in superior orders nor in the doctrine that his crimes were acts of states. These twin principles working together have heretofore resulted in immunity for practically everyone concerned in the really great crimes against peace and mankind. Those in the lower ranks were protected against liability by the orders of their superiors. The superiors were protected because their orders were called acts of state. Under the charter, no defense based on either of these doctrines can be entertained. Modern civilization puts unlimited weapons of destruction in the hands of men. It cannot tolerate so vast an area of legal irresponsibility.

Even the German Military Code provides that

If the execution of a military order in the course of duty violates the criminal law, then the superior officer giving the order will bear the sole responsibility therefor. However, the obeying subordinate will share the punishment of the participant: (1) if he has exceeded the order given to him, or (2) if it was within his knowledge that the order of his superior officer concerned an act by which it was intended to commit a civil or military crime or transgression. (Reichsgeist platt 1926, No. 37, pg. 278, Art 47)

Of course, we do not argue that the circumstances under which one commits an act should be disregarded in judging its legal effect. A conscripted private or an enlisted man on a firing squad cannot expect to hold an inquest on the validity of the execution. The charter implies common-sense limits to liability just as it places common-sense limits upon immunity. But none of these men before you acted in minor parts. Each of them was entrusted with broad discretion and exercised great power. Their responsibility is correspondingly great and may not be shifted to that fictional being, "the state," which cannot be produced for trial, cannot plead, cannot testify, and cannot be sentenced.

The charter also recognizes a vicarious liability, which is recognized by most modern systems of law, for acts committed by others in carrying out a common plan or conspiracy to which a defendant has become a party. I need not discuss the familiar principles of such liability. Every day in the courts of countries associated in this prosecution, men are convicted for acts that they did not personally commit but for which they were held responsible because of membership in illegal combinations or plans or conspiracies.

Accused before this tribunal as criminal organizations are certain political and police organizations which the evidence will show to have been instruments of cohesion in planning and executing the crimes I have detailed. Perhaps the worst of the movement were the Leadership Corps of the N.S.D.A.P., the Schutzstaffel or "S.S.," the Sturmabteilungen or "S.A.," and the subsidiary formations which these include. These were the Nazi Party leadership, espionage, and policing groups. They were the real government, above and outside of any law. Also accused as organizations are the Reich Cabinet and the secret state police, or Gestapo, which were fixtures of the government but animated solely by the Nazi Party.

Except for a late period when some compulsory recruiting was done in the S.S., membership in all these militarized formations was voluntary. The police organizations were recruited from ardent partisans who enlisted blindly to do the dirty work the leaders planned. The Reich Cabinet was the governmental facade for Nazi Party government and in its members legal as well as actual responsibility was vested for the entire program. Collectively they were responsible for the program in general, individually they were especially responsible for segments of it. The finding which we ask you to make, that these are criminal organizations, will subject members to punishment to be hereafter determined by appropriate tribunals, unless some personal defense—such as becoming a member under threat to person, or family, or inducement by false representation, or the like—be established. Every member will have a chance to be heard in the subsequent forum on his personal relation to the organization, but your finding in this trial will conclusively establish the criminal character of the organization as a whole.

We have also accused as criminal organizations the High Command and the General Staff of the German Armed Forces. We recognize that to plan warfare is the business of professional soldiers in every country. But it is one thing to plan strategic moves in the event war comes, and it is another thing to plot and intrigue to bring on that war. We will prove the leaders of the German General Staff and of the High Command to have been guilty of just that. Military men are not before you because they served their country. They are here because they mastered it, along with these others, and drove it to war. They are not here because they lost the war but because they started it. Politicians may have thought of them as soldiers, but soldiers know they were politicians. We ask that the General Staff and the High Command, as defined in the indictment, be condemned as a criminal group whose existence and tradition constitute a standing menace to the peace of the world.

These individual defendants did not stand alone in crime and will not stand alone in punishment. Your verdict of "guilty" against these organizations will render prima facie guilty, as nearly as we can learn, thousands upon thousands of members now in custody of United States forces and of other armies.

To apply the sanctions of the law to those whose conduct is found criminal by the standards I have outlined is the responsibility committed to this tribunal. It is the first court ever to undertake the difficult task of overcoming the confusion of many tongues and the conflicting concepts of just procedure among divers systems of law, so as to reach a common judgment. The tasks of all of us are such as to make heavy demands on patience and goodwill. Although the need for prompt action has admittedly resulted in imperfect work on the part of the prosecution, four great nations bring you their hurriedly assembled contributions of evidence. What remains undiscovered we can only guess. We could, with witnesses' testimony, prolong the recitals of crime for years—but to what avail? We shall rest the case when we have offered what seems convincing and adequate proof of the crimes charged without unnecessary cumulation of evidence. We doubt very much whether it will be seriously denied that the crimes I have outlined took place. The effort will undoubtedly be to mitigate or escape personal responsibility.

Among the nations which unite in accusing these defendants the United States is perhaps in a position to be the most dispassionate, for having sustained the least injury, it is perhaps the least animated by vengeance. Our American cities have not been bombed by day and by night, by humans and by robots. It is not our temples that have been laid in ruins. Our countrymen have not had their homes destroyed over their heads. The menace of Nazi aggression, except to those in actual service, has seemed less personal and immediate to us than to the European peoples. But while the United States is not first in rancor, it is not second in determination that the forces of law and order be made equal to the task of dealing with such international lawlessness as I have recited here.

Twice in my lifetime, the United States has sent its young manhood across the Atlantic, drained its resources, and burdened itself with debt to help defeat Germany. But the real hope and faith that has sustained the American people in these great efforts was that victory for ourselves and our Allies would lay the basis for an ordered international relationship in Europe and would end the centuries of strife on this embattled continent.

Twice we have held back in the early stages of European conflict in the belief that it might be confined to a purely European affair. In the United States, we have tried to build an economy without armament, a system of government without militarism, and a society where men are not regimented for war. This purpose, we know now, can never be realized if the world periodically is to be embroiled in war. The United States cannot, generation after generation, throw its youth or its resources onto the battlefields of Europe to redress the lack of balance between Germany's strength and that of her enemies, and to keep the battles from our shores.

The American dream of peace-and-plenty economy, as well as the hopes of other nations, can never be fulfilled if those nations are involved in a war every generation so vast and devastating as to crush the generation that fights and burden the generation that follows. But experience has shown that wars are no longer local. All modern wars become world wars eventually. And none of the big nations at least can stay out. If we cannot stay out of wars, our only hope is to prevent wars.

I am too well aware of the weaknesses of juridical action alone to contend that in itself your decision under this charter can prevent future wars. Judicial action always comes after the event. Wars are started only on the theory and in the confidence that they can be won. Personal punishment, to be suffered only in the event the war is lost, will probably not be a sufficient deterrent to prevent a war where the warmakers feel the chances of defeat to be negligible.

But the ultimate step in avoiding periodic wars, which are inevitable in a system of international lawlessness, is to make statesmen responsible to law. And let me make clear that while this law is first applied against German aggressors, the law includes, and if it is to serve a useful purpose it must condemn, aggression by any other nation, including those which now sit here in judgment. We are able to do away with domestic tyranny and violence and aggression by those in power against the rights of their own people only when we make all men answerable to the law. This trial represents mankind's desperate effort to apply the discipline of the law to statesmen who have used their powers of state to attack the foundations of the world's peace and to commit aggressions against the rights of their neighbors.

The usefulness of this effort to do justice is not to be measured by considering the law or your judgment in isolation. This trial is part of the great effort to make the peace more secure. One step in this direction is the United Nations organization, which may take joint political action to prevent war if possible, and joint military action to insure that any nation which starts a war will lose it. This charter and this trial, implementing the Kellogg-Briand Pact, constitute another step in the same direction—juridical action of a kind to insure that those who start a war will pay for it personally.

While the defendants and the prosecutors stand before you as individuals, it is not the triumph of either group alone that is committed to your judgment. Above all personalities there are anonymous and impersonal forces whose conflict makes up much of human history. It is yours to throw the strength of the law back of either the one or the other of these forces for at least another generation. What are the real forces that are contending before you?

No charity can disguise the fact that the forces which these defendants represent, the forces that would advantage and delight in their acquittal, are the darkest and most sinister forces in society—dictatorship and oppression, malevolence and passion, militarism and lawlessness. By their fruits we best know them. Their acts have bathed the world in blood and set civilization back a century. They have subjected their European neighbors to every outrage and torture, every spoliation and deprivation that insolence, cruelty, and greed could inflict. They have brought the German people to the lowest pitch of wretchedness, from which they can entertain no hope of early deliverance. They have stirred hatreds and incited domestic violence on every continent. These are the things that stand in the dock shoulder to shoulder with these prisoners.

The real complaining party at your bar is civilization. In all our countries it is still a struggling and imperfect thing. It does not plead that the United States, or any other country, has been blameless of the conditions which made the German people easy victims to the blandishments and intimidations of the Nazi conspirators.

But it points to the dreadful sequence of aggressions and crimes I have recited, it points to the weariness of flesh, the exhaustion of resources, and the destruction of all that was beautiful or useful in so much of the world, and to greater potentialities for destruction in the days to come. It is not necessary among ruins of this ancient and beautiful city, with untold members of its civilian inhabitants still buried in its rubble, to argue the proposition that to start or wage an aggressive war has the moral qualities of the worst of crimes. The refuge of the defendants can be only their hope that international law will lag so far behind the moral sense of mankind that conduct which is crime in the moral sense must be regarded as innocent in law.

Civilization asks whether law is so laggard as to be utterly helpless to deal with crimes of this magnitude by criminals of this order of importance. It does not expect that you can make war impossible. It does expect that your juridical action will put the forces of international law, its precepts, its prohibitions and, most of all, its sanctions, on the side of peace, so that men and women of goodwill in all countries may have "leave to live by no man's leave, underneath the law."

NATIONAL DEFENSE

THE BACKWASH OF WAR [1]

W. Norwood Brigance [2]

Dr. W. Norwood Brigance, Professor of Speech at Wabash College, delivered this address before the Valley Division of the Illinois Educational Association, at La Salle, Illinois, on October 12, 1945.

This was the forty-second time he had given this speech; the first was before the Shortridge High School in Indianapolis, on November 11, 1943.

The address is here included not simply because it had unusual appeal, nor because it dealt with America's central problems underlying postwar readjustment, but because it furnishes a specimen of excellent speech composition.

Significant is the personal and direct quality of the style, the identification of the speaker with his auditors, the discerning analysis of the soldier's mind, the larger psychological interpretation of the American postwar attitudes, the frequent use of narrative, the effective, if restrained, use of ethical proof (note the speaker's own authority to talk on the GI reflexes and attitudes), the abundant illustrations, the structure of the whole and of the parts, and the constant emotional-imaginative treatment (note, for example, the illustration of Oliver Wendell Holmes).

Dr. Brigance is President (1946) of the Speech Association of America. He has been editor of the *Quarterly Journal of Speech.* He is the author of many texts and learned publications. Notably he was the editor, under the Speech Association of America, of the *History and Criticism of American Public Address.* Many well-known public speakers have been his students. Several of his student orators took high honors in intercollegiate and interstate contests.

Dr. Brigance usually prepares a somewhat detailed outline of his talks. The outline for "The Backwash of War," for example, filled sixteen pages, 6 x 9 size. He uses a full set of notes without further reduction, or abbreviated "speaker's notes."

This speaker states that he does not write a speech. Rather he prepares a full outline, because he wishes to see "in my mind the relationship of each idea to every other one and to the whole speech. An outline shows this; a manuscript does not." Brigance never reads from a manu-

---

[1] Text furnished by the author. Permission to include in this volume, through the courtesy of Dr. Brigance.

[2] For biographical note see Appendix.

script; nor does he memorize a manuscript for presentation. "Rather," as he explains, "my outline is very full. Every fact, reference, and quotation is checked twice and the course noted on the outline margin. This outline I fix in mind and speak extempore without notes or paper of any kind before me. The rare occasions when I deviate from this practice come only when it seems appropriate, or more effective, to read a quotation. This method is not as difficult as it might seem to a beginning speaker. It does require careful basic training." [3]

After nearly four years of war the shooting is over, and now the backwash has begun. I want to inquire what this backwash will do to the emotional responses, the conditioned reflexes, and the behavior patterns of the American people. Let us look first at the effects on the men in the armed forces, then later we shall consider the effect upon American civilians.

From the standpoint of those in armed services, now that the war is over 12,000,000 men and women are being discharged from military duty; 12,000,000 men and women who have been living in uniform under conditions of military regimentation that were necessary to winning a war but irksome to the American spirit of individual initiative; 12,000,000 men and women who have been living in distant parts of America or more distant parts of the world, who will come home knowing that they have been changed by war, knowing also perhaps that those at home have been changed by war.

More significantly, upward of 6,000,000 of these men will have been engaged in battle, and subject not merely to the physical hazards of combat, but also to mental and emotional strain that result in what is now known as "operational fatigue." It is not easy—it is almost impossible—to explain to civilians what living under prolonged battle conditions does to the nervous system and behavior. True, you may read a war book or see a war picture, and get a glimpse of what it is like to live for an hour or a day under fire—but no war book or war picture has ever adequately conveyed the cumulative effect of fatigue that burns itself into the nervous system and exhausts the elasticity of the human mind of men who live day after day in battle, knowing each day that for them there may be no tomorrow.

[3] Letter to the Editor, May 26, 1946.

In the end there comes the accumulated blur and the hurting vagueness of prolonged strain. There comes the strain of ever-lasting alertness to sounds and sources of danger, an alertness that invariably separates the experienced soldier from the inex-perienced, and tragically often separates the quick from the dead. There is the cell by cell exhaustion of the human body as day follows nameless day. There is the thinning of the ranks around you, the disappearance of men who fought by your side, men whose bodies are gone but whose faces linger in the memory. And always, as Ernie Pyle has stated it, there is "the constant march into eternity of your own small quota of chances for survival."

These are the things that add up to what is so smugly defined as "operational fatigue." In reality, it includes more than oper-ational fatigue, for it lingers in the conditioned reflexes and behavior patterns long after the operational fatigue has passed.

This, you will understand, is not peculiar to this war. It is part of the backwash that follows all wars. I would present the testimony of Mr. Justice Oliver Wendell Holmes. Mr. Holmes fought three years in the Civil War, came out still a young man —only twenty-three years of age—entered Harvard Law School, graduated with distinction, became a world authority on *Kent's Commentaries* and on Common Law, then lived to serve exactly fifty years in the Supreme Courts of Massachusetts and the United States. But sixty years after the close of the Civil War, Mr. Holmes said in a moment of complete sobriety, "When the ghosts of dead fifers begin to play in my head, the laws are si-lent." Once again, across the span of sixty years, he stood again at Antietam, or on the Jerusalem Road, and could hear the crack of the skirmishers' muskets, and then the long roll of fire as it came from the main line and the battle was begun. This, after sixty years.

My own experience is considerably short of sixty years. It will be twenty-seven years ago this coming November 11 that I heard the echo of guns die away and it became "All Quiet on the Western Front" of a now almost-forgotten war that caused

21,000,000 casualties and taught us almost nothing. I have not been in or near a battle since that day. But I would suggest that even now, more than a quarter century later, I still carry conditioned reflexes that are more sharp and intense than those produced by experiences of ten years ago, or even five.

For the soldier, a war is not over when the armistice is signed, a war is not over when the treaty of peace is written. Its aftermath lingers on in the mind and behavior patterns. The day comes when this soldier stands his last inspection, snaps his last salute, and is mustered out of service. He is now a civilian again. But his days of marching are not yet over. Ahead lies the longest march he has ever made. It is the march on "The Road Back," the long road that mind and emotion must travel in returning to the ways of civilian life.

Listen to the testimony of two soldiers. The first comes from a man who had been a lawyer in civilian life:

What can you do now? Nothing, nothing. You can't go back to the old petty things without purpose, direction, or unity—defending the railroad for killing a cow, . . . suing someone for money, coping again, all over, with that bright rascal who rehearses his witnesses. You can't go on with that kind of thing 'til you die.

These are the words of William Alexander Percy, a soldier in World War I. Now listen to these words from another soldier:

I have almost a dread of being a citizen, of trying to be sharp and trying to make money. I don't think I dread the work. I don't remember shirking any work I ever attempted, but I am sure that civil life will go sorely against the grain for a time.

These words—almost identical with those spoken in my office by a returning soldier in this war a few weeks ago—were written by a soldier in Sherman's Army on April 15, 1865—six days after the surrender of Lee at Appomatox.

In the other war we sang that well-known song which so genuinely reflected our longing while in military life:

> There's a long, long trail awinding
> Into the land of my dreams,
> Where the nightingale is singing,
> And the white moon beams.

It is a longing that reflects the sentiments of every soldier in every war. Now on "The Road Back" he is groping down that trail of his dreams, wondering how much of it will be real, and how much is only the stuff that dreams are made of.

In the minds of the people at home hovers that inevitable question: "Will he ever get over all this?" I give you the answer in a short and qualified yes. I know that a few psychiatrists got excited two years ago and issued a lot of false warnings to the people back home. I disagree with those psychiatrists, and I think the competent psychiatrists likewise disagree with them. Again I would repeat that this is not a new phenomenon, but is one that has followed all wars. You can trace it through the letters written by friends of soldiers in the American Revolution, through those of the Civil War, and we who fought in World War I can remember it well.

I do not mean to imply that soldiers are not changed by military experience. All experience leads to change. I am rather saying that the operational fatigue which afflicts the returning soldier soon wears off.

I know, of course, that many men entered service who were ill adapted to civilian life. They will not return to civilian life better adapted than when they went away, but the returning soldier who blames his misfitness on his military experience is simply finding a dignified excuse for explaining away the elements of failure that were already in him.

Nevertheless, the typical returning soldier is for the time *numb,* and he will need time to acquire the sense of feeling again. While he is in this state of numbness the woman who married him during the war is likely to discover he is different than before, will want to get a divorce, and ultimately marry someone else. Or many a young woman is likely to discover that that returning soldier, to whom she is engaged, is not the same man he was when he went away; she will break the engagement, and also marry someone else. What I fear is that these women some morning ten years later will look across the breakfast table at the men they married and wonder how they got there! If I were permitted to give advice to these women, my advice would be: "Get no divorce, break no engagement, until after the period of numbness has worn off."

In summary, then, the backwash of war as it affects the returning soldier is primarily one of numbness. You cannot coddle him, or else you may rob him of self-reliance and make it easier for him to look to the governmment for a pension because of imaginary or slight injuries—as too many soldiers did after 1918.

You cannot give him sympathy because brave men do not need sympathy.

He asks two things only: *time* and *understanding*. As Bill Mauldin stated it: "They simply need bosses who will give them a little time to adjust their minds and their hands, and women who are faithful to them, and friends and families who stay by them until they are the same guys who left years ago."

So much for the returning soldier. What about the others of us, those who stayed home, ran the factories, taught the schools, paid the taxes, and bought the bonds? War always affects the people at home. It runs a rather definite pattern, no matter when the war, no matter what the people. Especially do I want to consider three problems as they affect the American people in 1945:

First, now that the war is over *we face the danger of transferring our hatred against the Japanese and Germans to somebody else.* During the war we built up a gigantic hatred of the enemy. They set booby traps. They tortured prisoners. They killed our sons and relatives.

Now suddenly the war is over. They are not our enemies any more. We don't hate them as we once did. Now all of this would be grand if it implied that we had ceased hating. But the point is that when a war is over a people do not stop hating. They merely transfer their hatred from the late enemy to someone else. We are like a high-power electric line. The wires snap loose in the storm. They lie on the ground, loose and flapping in the wind, charged with 10,000 volts of electricity—and a menace to anyone that comes near them. Now that this war is over we don't hate the Japanese and Germans at all, hardly, compared to what we did a year ago. But the pressure of hate is still there, and we are in danger of transferring it to someone else. Do you ask who?

First, the Negro. Unless we are careful there will be an increase of lynchings in the South and race riots in the North.

Second, the Jew. I know we did not like Hitler's persecution of the Jews, but there are some Americans who hate the Jews. There are others who are willing to make financial or political capital out of such hatred. The danger we now face is that tens of millions of Americans, led by these fanatics, will unthinkingly and unknowingly transfer their hatred of the Japanese and Germans over to the Jews.

Third, Catholics and Protestants. These two great religious groups have been living together now for 400 years. They ought to know by this time that they can trust one another. But we had a Ku Klux Klan after the last war, and we can have a new name for this old hate after this war.

Fourth, England. We don't like England. The dead hand of the past has never buried its dead. We still remember 1776. Besides, there are lots of Irishmen in America—and whoever heard of an Irishman liking an Englishman? I am just about three-quarters Irish, you know, and I did not read that out of a book! But I dare suggest that it is unsafe to hate England too much, for if we systematically, politically and economically, push our hatred of England too far, we *can* drive England into an unwilling alliance with Russia. England and the United States today form the strongest military combine in the world. England and Russia tomorrow could form the strongest combine. It is not safe to hate England too much.

Finally, and especially, there is Russia. A year ago Russia was our ally, a nation to whose strength and sacrifice we owed a great debt. Today we hate Russia probably more than we hate either Germany or Japan. I brush aside all the superficial reasons that have been given for that hate. I remind you that big nations who fight wars as allies always hate each other intensely the moment that war is over. The reasons mouthed by speakers and writers are mere plausible excuses. Fundamentally, our hating of Russia is part of the backwash of war.

This, then, is the first problem that we face, the danger of transferring our hatred from the Japanese and Germans over to someone else.

Second, in the backwash of war there is always the danger that you will become like the thing you fight against. This is illogical, but it is true, and it is dangerously true. Now in this war we have not always been sure what we have been fighting for, but we are definitely sure what we have been fighting against. We have been fighting against the militarism of Japan and Germany, a militarism that made them a menace to the world.

But because we have been fighting a war against militarism, we ourselves in this backwash of war are tending to become militaristic. It is an old story. Read your Bible, and you will find where the early Hebrews fought mightily against tribes with pagan gods—and then for a time adopted those gods. Read your history, and you will find that in 1789 the people of France arose against tyranny and began a revolution, having as its aim, "liberty, . . . fraternity, . . . equality"—and ended by having (1) a Reign of Terror, in which thousands of its people were executed, (2) compulsory military training, and (3) a dictator by the name of Napoleon. Now the United States is following this same time-worn paradoxical human pathway. We, who set up liberty in a new world, who gave shelter to emigrants that fled from tyranny in the old world, we are now debating whether we should fasten compulsory military training upon ourselves. I know the argument offered by advocates of conscription. They say that it will protect America against war. Well, Russia in 1941 had military conscription, with a total army and trained reserve of 18,000,000 men—and her conscription did not protect her from assault by Germany. They say it will make us safer in event of war. Well, France had compulsory military training in 1870 and again in 1940. Germany had it in 1914 and in 1939. And Japan had it in 1941. The only two nations in the modern world who have not had compulsory military training are United States and Great Britain—and these are the only nations who have won every war that they have engaged in for the past hundred years.

Obviously, compulsory military training is not the key to national security. But under the postwar psychosis our military leaders speak as though there were no other adequate means of defense for America.

The truth is that military conscription is just about as dangerous to the United States as would be an atomic bomb in case of war. No nation has ever maintained both an aggressive system of compulsory military training and a true democracy. France in 1939 had a decadent democracy and a decadent system of military training. Germany before 1848 had the stirrings of democracy, but in 1815 she had fastened compulsory military training upon her people. Democracy lost. Militarism prevailed. Italy under Garibaldi likewise experienced an impetus toward democracy. But in Italy, too, compulsory military training was fastened upon the people, and democracy died.

The critical danger, then, that we face in this backwash of war is whether we can save ourselves from embarking upon a course that threatens to destroy the democracy that we fought in this war to preserve.

Third, in this backwash of war we face a moral letdown. During this war you women gave up your nylon hosiery. For a time you even gave up cigarettes! We put up with gas rationing and food rationing. We gave our pints of blood to the Red Cross. We bought bonds again until it hurt, and we paid taxes until it did not hurt any longer—for we were numb!

Now that the war is over we will tend to eat, drink, and be merry, for we are free of restrictions. We will tend to drive our automobiles eighty miles an hour—because we were not supposed to drive them more than thirty-five miles an hour during the war. Young people, craving the need of excitement now that peace has come, will seek their own especial ways of excitement; and "when money runs low, or excitement runs high, the automobile offers an easy tempting roadway to the committing of crime." In my own State of Indiana we came out of World War I with approximately 1,900 prisoners in the state penitentiary, and after the war that number promptly rose to more than 3,000. We shall need a penitentiary after this war to house more than 5,000. But perhaps I should not speak of such a delicate thing to people in this state who might have painful memories of Loeb, Leopold, and Al Capone.

Now there will be many who will warn us that we are having a moral collapse. I do not fear a moral collapse. The American people are altogether too vital a people to have a moral collapse. They simply will be taking a moral holiday, and after the manner of Americans will be making it "bigger and better."

These, then, are the especial problems that face us in this backwash of war: First, the problem of the returning soldier adjusting himself to civilian life; second, the danger of transferring our hatred of the Japanese and Germans to other groups; third, the danger that in fighting against militarism, we ourselves shall become militaristic; and finally, the danger of permitting too much of a moral holiday now that we are relieved from the Spartan discipline of war.

We do not face these problems with fear. We do not face them with hesitation. To the timid and faint-hearted who long for security and repose, we quote the answer of Mr. Justice Oliver Wendell Holmes: "Security is an illusion, and repose is not the destiny of man." We shall meet these problems as a people who are conscious of their destiny.

NATIONAL MILITARY STRENGTH [4]

GEORGE C. MARSHALL [5]

General George C. Marshall, Chief of Staff of the United States Army, gave this address on Monday evening, October 29, 1945. The occasion was the opening session of the Fourteenth Annual Forum, conducted in the Grand Ballroom of the Waldorf-Astoria Hotel, New York City, under the auspices of the *New York Herald Tribune.*

The General, dealing with his topic of universal military training with his usual persuasive approach, unfolded his propositions with logical and disarming understanding. His first major syllogism concluded that since the world must be governed by law, the enforcement of that law was essential. His next syllogism, a disjunction, posited that the global order (law) must be enforcible by cooperation or by operation. Then he advanced the proposition that the enforcement by cooperation (United Nations) and the full assumption of American responsibilities require a strong American military force.

General Marshall, especially since August 25, 1944, battled in season and out for peacetime permanent service by all American youth. Before civic groups, at Congressional hearings, and on many other official gatherings, he labored for his cause. His arguments were buttressed by history, statistics, testimony, plausible logic, and by highly effective delivery. He was a master of the spoken word—calm, fluent, tactful, highly extempore when necessary, well qualified not only to direct military policy but to interpret it orally.

His was the attempt to stem the receding tide. The American public and Congress confused the selective service law calling for a continuation of the draft, with a permanent peacetime training program. In May 1946, the Senate and House passed an emergency measure extending the draft to July 1, 1946, but exempting those under twenty years of age. Criticizing alleged military fraternization with former enemies, faith in the atomic bomb, growing pacificism, the feeling that a big army would further antagonize Russia, the rush to cut loose from all wartime conditions, and above all, interest in sending the eighteen-year-old sons to college or into jobs, all made General Marshall's splendid arguments of not much avail. By July 1, 1946, Congress had voted to extend the draft for nine months, but draft no American youths under nineteen years of age.

[4] The text was supplied by Mrs. S. C. Chamberlain, Secretary to General Marshall. Permission to reprint was given through the courtesy of the War Department and of the *New York Herald Tribune.* For full proceedings of the Forum, see Section IX, *New York Herald Tribune,* for November 4, 1945, "Annual Forum on Current Problems."

[5] For biographical note see Appendix.

The subject of this year's Forum discussion is on the minds of men and women the world over. You who have assembled here and those listening on the radio are all conscious, I am sure, of our great responsibility to the hard-won victory. Americans are more keenly aware today than ever before of the responsibility they bear to the destiny of the nation and its responsibility to the world at large.

So complex is the society of mankind that even those who have thought a great deal about it find themselves at a loss for exact conclusions. I question that there is anyone among us who can provide a satisfying answer to even a small number of the searching questions that tax our minds today, and sharpen our fears and weigh on our hearts. I certainly cannot provide the answers. There appear to be no short cuts to a better world. But I do think that if we all make an earnest and devoted effort in a spirit of good faith and of patience and tolerance, somehow or other a formula for the better guidance of mankind may be evolved.

At this moment of history, in a world convulsed by the after effects of the most devastating of all wars, evident signs of moral progress in the human race appear to be lacking. The question can be argued either pessimistically or optimistically: but regardless of whether man in 7,000 years of recorded history has demonstrated social or moral advances, I believe it can be said that throughout the ages men have consistently sought to discover order both in nature and in human relations.

This inherent tendency has been called a "feeling for law." There must be an inherent order in this universe: to deny it is to deny God. We admit advances in scientific thought whereby men recognize and accumulate knowledge of nature, and little by little he understands, predicts and manipulates it. The feeling for order, I believe, can be traced in political thought. From the beginning man has established rules of orderly conduct whenever such rules were a prerequisite of survival. First on a family basis, then on a tribal or community basis, and later on national levels.

Within the national societies, definite rules are laid down whereby men must live. Almost everywhere in the world it is unlawful to commit murder, it is unlawful to rape, and to steal. In our complex society it is unlawful to defraud and gain the advantage of other men by conspiracy.

It is not only unlawful in these matters, but there are established procedures throughout the world for making the rules stick. Here in New York the constabulary, the police force, the prisons and finally the electric chair encourage us to play the game according to man-made rules. For centuries man has been seeking, I believe, to extend this inherent order of the cosmos, toward which he strives, to the level of the entire planet. There are two ways in which this has been manifest; we might say one is by way of cooperation and the other by way of operation, or, better still, domination. Hitler, whether he knew it or not, sought to establish one kind of order in the world when he precipitated the recent holocaust. This would be by way of domination. The League of Nations, on the other hand, sought to establish a global order by cooperation. There were many examples of both kinds of effort prior to this century, but I cite these two because they are easy to recognize. It would appear that one or the other of these methods will prevail. Time and space have been so shrunken that the world must, I believe, establish definite global rules. Community and national rules no longer suffice. They by themselves are no longer realistic.

Basically, then, the question in my opinion is: which one of the two methods is to prevail—global order by cooperation, or by domination? Since the United States is one of the senior partners in this world, we have a powerful interest in the formulation of these rules. That is how I would define our responsibility of the victory.

It seems quite clear to me that the determining factor in whether we have order by cooperation or order by operation will depend on who are the stronger, the operators or the cooperators. That seems to be natural law. The cooperators are, quite logically, usually those people who control their own affairs. For the purposes of simplification let us say the democracies. Democracy certainly is government by cooperation. The operators or dominators are the autocracies. Among the democracies the United States has clearly been the strongest. The strength of the cooperators, therefore, at the present moment is tied directly to the strength of the United States.

And we and our allies have recently advanced the structure of the United Nations organization as a vehicle to promote the cooperative idea of global order. Nations which subscribe to this principle, this system, do not propose to establish order by conquering everybody else as Hitler did, nor do they propose to control for their own profit the domestic affairs of the peoples of the earth. What they do propose is a set of rules for global conduct, principally rules against aggression or international violence. They themselves are to resort to violence only to enforce these rules, just as does the State of New York, and every other state in this nation, to enforce its rules.

If the vehicle of the United Nations organization is to be effective, it will be because those who advocate it choose to make it so. Those who oppose it certainly will not make it effective, and I personally am convinced that the organization has not even a remote chance of success unless it is nourished by the strength and fiber of the United States. Obviously, if we have no manifest strength, the nourishment of the United Nations organization will be too lean.

We are still strong today, but we won't be so a few months hence unless we take very positive and definite measures to give some degree of permanence to the strength for which we have just spent so much of human life and money to develop.

We are currently engaged in the demobilization of our wartime forces at the fastest possible rate. That, to my mind, is precisely as it should be. The machinery that we built to fight this war has been eating into our national resources for years. The sooner we reconvert it to peaceful production and ways of life, the more likely is this nation to survive the economic storms that may quite easily follow this great world disturbance.

It is certain, however, that the military establishment cannot hope to insure the safety of the United States very much longer at the present rate of demobilization unless some permanent peacetime program is established and at an early date.

For the moment, in a widespread emotional crisis of the American people, demobilization has become, in effect, disintegration, not only of the armed forces but apparently of all conception of world responsibility and what it demands of us. If we are to nourish the infant United Nations organization and thus establish some possibility of a future decent world order, definite measures must be taken immediately to determine at least the basic principles for our postwar military policy. I have never felt so certain of anything in my life.

There has been much discussion about holding what we have fought so desperately to win. What is it that we have fought to win? We fought to prevent Germany and Japan from imposing their kind of order on the world. That certainly was but a negative return for our tremendous investment of blood and money. Did we win anything of a more positive nature? Well, to my mind we did. We won the healthy respect of the peoples of the earth, and therefore a reasonable chance of negotiating a world order that would fit ideals of decency and justice. Respect, it is true, is an intangible, but consider what it would have meant to us in tangibles had we commanded the military respect of Germany, Italy and Japan in 1939. Recently we demonstrated to the world our capability, I might even say our invincibility, in the air, on the seas and wherever our armies fought on the ground. Germany and Japan were surprised, actually startled, by our willingness to fight, and by our ability and overwhelming success in the actual business of fighting. Incidentally, they were not the only ones who had their doubts about us in this matter.

On the day of final victory, no such doubts existed anywhere in the entire world. Yet need I remind you that respect, like all intangibles, is fleeting, unless we bend our efforts to preserve it.

Just a few months ago the world was completely convinced of the strength and courage of the United States. Now they see us falling back into our familiar peacetime pattern. They witness the tremendous enthusiasm with which we mount demobilization and reconversion, but they see as yet no concrete evidence that we are determined to hold what we have won—permanently. Are we already at this early date inviting that same international disrespect that prevailed before this war? Are we throwing away today what a million Americans died or were mutilated to achieve? Are we already shirking the responsibility of the victory?

This business of dissipating the political benefits that a nation may derive from victory is in the American tradition. It is quite understandable in a nation that runs its own affairs, because there is no easy way to get big things done on this earth. The victory was hard won. It will require a great deal of effort and sacrifice to fulfill our responsibilities of that victory, to achieve the future we recently talked about so freely.

We must somehow get it clear in our thinking that the fulfillment of our responsibilities is not some vague mumbo jumbo. It requires positive active effort and sacrifice, and above all it is a continuing process. We cannot do it in one step and then have done with it. Even if the United States now adopts a sound program in its relationships with the rest of the world, the program will be worthless unless we continue to support it year in and year out.

For example, after the last war the Congress enacted the defense act of 1920. It was not the best program we could have found, but it was generally sound and would have been a long forward step had it been implemented through the years. It wasn't.

Hardly before the President's signature on the defense act had dried, the act was emasculated by an appropriation measure which reduced the strength of the army from the 297,000 men just authorized to 160,000 men. The following year this appropriation was further cut by 25 per cent to a little more than a quarter of the sum recommended by the War Department at the conclusion of World War I. Within a few years, Congress had thus completely reversed itself on the policy of maintaining a respectable military posture, not by meeting the issue head-on but by refusing to appropriate the money necessary to carry it out. The army at home and abroad fell to the woefully inadequate strength of 130,000 men.

It was argued then and it will soon be argued again that the nation's economy could not stand such military expenditures. Is not that absurd if you consider that the country's economy can better stand expenditures for national security than it can stand defeat, or even a victory with a consequent debt of more than three hundred billions?

As late as the spring of 1940, when Hitler was about to complete the domination of the continent of Europe, we actually spent about one and three-quarter billions on our entire defense establishment, military and naval. It is true that the Congress, as France fell, actually appropriated more money, but the wheels of mobilization were just commencing to turn and it was impossible to realize much of this program in the remaining months of the year.

The year that France fell, gate receipts for amusements and sporting events in the United States totaled a billion and a half, nearly as much as our entire outlay for the army and navy. We spent five and a half billion more on tobacco and alcoholic drinks—about three times the sum we devoted to our precious national security, even in that most critical hour of world history. Do not misunderstand me. I have no quarrel with such expenditures. They are a part of our freedom of life that I myself enjoy. The point is that if we would cheerfully expend seven billion dollars in this manner as civilization crashed down in Europe, we should at the very least be willing to accept the expenditures in normal times that are necessary to the peace and the security of our homes and our freedom.

In 1937, when the world was becoming a powderbox, we spent but 1.6 per cent of our national income for our military and naval establishment. In that year of clearly impending disaster the United States spent five billion, or 7 per cent of its income, for the incidental pleasures I have referred to.

As late as 1937 we might have convinced the Axis gangsters of the complete futility of their preparations by simply matching our "cigarette money"—using the term figuratively—with expenditures on our national security.

Viewed in this light, it would seem that the tragedy of our unwillingness to maintain what Washington called a respectable military posture becomes monstrous.

I sincerely believe that if we had given our security its proper attention the Axis nations would not have started the war. Millions of men and women, Europeans, Asiatics and Americans, who perished in battle by disease, starvation and brutality in the last five years might be alive today had we faced the world in righteous strength instead of careless weakness. The enemy counted on us to go ahead with our pleasures, ignoring the threat to our lives and our very freedom. We proved them wrong, but in the end it cost us a million casualties and astronomical sums of money to restore our security and rightful position in the world. Had we not had Allies to buy us time, our own efforts, great as they finally were, might easily have been too late.

The War Department has made several recommendations to Congress on how we can best go about maintaining our strength in the future at a cost within our financial means. These recommendations have been questioned, usually by groups looking for an easy way out. I have opposed dogmatism all my life and think for a military man it can be a fatal mental disease, but I must say here tonight with all the emphasis I can command—there is no easy way. The American people will do well to give sober thought to their fateful problem.

In the current emotionalism of the hour we turn for relief from positive action to new theories, new discoveries—the supersonic rocket, or atomic power or explosion. If these remarkable products of our science are merely to turn us from action to inaction on one plea, one theory or another, they may well have a more tragic influence on the destiny of the United States than the most pessimistic fear they will have on civilization. I have been considering the military ramifications of atomic explosion for more than two years since my job placed me in the middle of the grim race towards this scientific power. I think I have—if only because of my head start—spent much more time than most Americans thinking about such bombs and what they will mean to military operations as well as to civilization at large.

I cannot escape the conclusion that the possibilities of atomic explosion make it more imperative than ever before that the United States keep itself militarily strong and use this strength to promote cooperative world order.

No one can see unerringly into the future, but it is not hard to predict that supersonic atomic rockets will have a profound influence on any war that ever again has to be fought. But, rather than decrease the necessity for our preparation both in manpower and materiel, this terrible new weapon will tremendously increase it.

The present public apathy regarding our military obligations for the future comes as no surprise to me. Three years ago here in New York at a meeting of the Academy of Political Science, just twenty-four hours after our landing in Africa in the first step toward liberation of Europe, I closed my remarks with this comment, which seems even more appropriate to this day and hour:

> My particular interest at this time in your affairs rests on the fact that after a war, a democracy like ours usually throws to the wind whatever scientific approach has been developed in the conduct of the war. This is an historical fact. It is the result of the immediate postwar aversion of the people to everything military, and of the imperative demand of the taxpayer for relief from the burden imposed by the huge war debt.

> We are in a terrible war, and our every interest should be devoted to winning the war in the shortest possible time. However, in view of your interest in the science of government and the intimate relationship that it bears to military requirements, I would ask your very careful consideration of these related military factors in whatever studies you make regarding the readjustments which must follow this war. The theories on the subject will have to be compressed into the realities. The attitude of the taxpayer is human and inevitable. The differing reactions of the people in the center of the country, of those along the coasts, of the people who face the Pacific and the people who face the Atlantic, must be considered. The extreme distaste for things military, to which I have already referred and which always follows an exhausting war, will have to be taken into account. Then, with all of these reactions, how can we so establish ourselves that we will not be doomed to a repetition of the succession of tragedies of the last thirty years? We must take the nations of the world as they are, the human passions and prejudices of peoples as they exist, and find some way to secure for us a free America in a peaceful world.

That statement was made three years ago, while our troops were still pouring ashore at Casa Blanca and Algiers. I submit that it represents rather accurately the emotional state of mind of articulate America at this particular moment.

Are we once more to seek the easy way out, to heed only the voice of the minor objector, the critics of so-called militarism, the proponent of the selfish motive? Are we to waste the victory and doom our children's children to more years of horror and destruction?

I beg of you to analyze carefully for yourselves all that is said on this subject against the background of our history, to give critical thought to all proposals and objections, to sift the wheat from the chaff and then to act—and act before it is again too late.

ATOMIC ENERGY

THE ATOM BOMB AND WAR [1]

HAROLD C. UREY [2]

Dr. Harold C. Urey gave this speech at a mass meeting in Orchestra Hall, Chicago, Illinois, on Monday evening, February 25, 1946, sponsored by the Midwest Independent Citizens' Committee of the Arts, Sciences, and Professions. ⟨ The purpose of the address was chiefly to inform the American public concerning the power of atomic energy, and to bring home to them the possibilities of destruction of civilization through an atomic war.

This conversion of matter into energy by the atomic transformation through nuclear fission and the production of the bomb marked one of the most important dates, perhaps the most important one, in the world's history. The first atom bomb dropped on July 16, 1945, had more power than 20,000 tons of TNT. In this test in the desert 120 miles southeast of Albuquerque, New Mexico, a tall steel tower was completely destroyed. A crater marked the spot of the explosion. A dense cloud billowed forty thousand feet. The spectacle instantly became world news.

On August 6th, the atomic bomb fell on Hiroshima, Japan, a city of 340,000. Some 60,00 died, 100,000 were wounded, and the rest were homeless. The city was practically wiped out. On August 9th, an atomic bomb, again flown by a B-29, was dropped on Nagasaki. Again the destruction, although not so great as at Hiroshima, was appalling. A great crater marked the immediate spot of explosion. On August 14th Japan surrendered. Winston Churchill declared that the use of the atomic bomb thus saved the lives of 1,000,000 Americans and 250,000 British.

The actual development of the bomb for war purposes was a joint undertaking by United States, Great Britain, and Canada. The United States provided the two billion dollars that were invested in the gamble and the four years of highly complicated planning and labor. President Roosevelt is credited with much courage for approving a venture involving such huge stakes and such uncertain outcome.

There were vast plants, thousands of workers, overall directors, civilian scientists and industrialists, and military personnel. The proj-

---

[1] Text furnished and permission to reprint, through the courtesy of Dr. Harold C. Urey.
[2] For biographical note see Appendix.

ect was under the Office of Scientific Research and Development, with Professor Vannevar Bush as director. President J. B. Conant, of Harvard, represented Dr. Bush in the project itself. Drs. A. H. Compton and Dr. Urey were program chiefs. Included in the program were the Manhattan District, the Chilton Engineering Project, at Knoxville, Tennessee, the Columbia River Pasco Works, and the Hanford Engineering Works, near Santa Fe.

In October 1945, Congress began consideration of the problem, what should be done with the atomic bomb? Should it be shared with all nations? With Russia and our other World War II Allies? If so, what methods of inspection of all nations would be practicable? Should it be placed under the control of the United Nations? Or should it be kept as a "secret"? Or should all bombs thus far produced be destroyed as well as the means of production? If none of these plans were carried out, what policy of governmental control over the development of atomic energy should be adopted? Should the control be exclusively in the hands of the military? Or of civilians? Or would it be possible to envolve some sort of joint control that would leave civilians largely free for experimentation in this area? American public opinion lined up in sharp divisions concerning the answer to most of these questions. The scientists, at any rate, were determined that no legislation should hamper their freedom in the laboratory. These issues were still under debate and unsettled in June 1946.

Dr. Urey, although not especially trained as a debater or general public speaker, took the lead in interpreting the scientists' position in this matter, just as he took a strong lead in the discovery or development of the bomb itself. Because of his scientific reputation as well as his leading role in the development of atomic energy, he was widely listened to. After October 1945, he spoke repeatedly at governmental hearings, before large and small community groups, and engaged in a number of radio discussions or similar programs. His skillful organization of his materials, his animated voice, especially acceptable over the radio, made him fully effective as spokesman for the scientists.

On December 2, 1942, under the West Stand of Stagg Field at the University of Chicago, there occurred an event which marks a turning point of first magnitude in history. This was the generation of heat at a constant, steady level from atomic reactions. This was a first miniature power unit, a prototype of power units which may be developed in the years to come and which may have enormous industrial importance.

On July 16, 1945, in the deserts of New Mexico, occurred another event in which atomic energy was liberated in the form of an explosive chain reaction. This event also marks a transition from the past in the use of atomic energy for destructive purposes. These events will influence our lives for years to come, and in fact, will influence all of history in the future. If the former of these is predominant in the future, we may expect increased well-being for men; while if the latter becomes predominant in the future, we may expect that civilization as we know it today may be destroyed, never to rise again. In view of these spectacular events of the last years, it is well for thoughtful people to consider carefully what the future may bring, and to exercise if possible some choice in regard to future events.

During the first years of this century, there was another great development, though I believe not so important as the release of atomic energy. I refer to the invention of the airplane, by which invention man conquered a new element. During the forty-odd years since that discovery, the airplane has been used both for peaceful and war purposes. Today, if we try to assess the good and the evil which has been done by the airplane, I think we must conclude that the net effect has been a curse to humanity. The destruction which it has wrought in the world cannot be compensated by its peacetime uses. If we allow events to take the same course in the future as they have taken in the past forty years, we may expect that a similar appraisal of the merits of atomic energy will be made forty years from now; and I think the conclusion undoubtedly will be that the evil of atomic energy will have been far greater than its contribution for good. At this time, we are at the turning of the ways, and it is therefore of first importance that we consider carefully what the future holds with respect to this new form of energy, a form of energy which was stored in the nuclei of atoms from the beginning of the earth, the solar system, or perhaps the beginning of the sidereal universe.

These discoveries of nature's laws and the inventions based upon them are not in themselves evil, for it is only the use which men make of these things that leads to constructive or destructive results. Perhaps man has no free will that enables him to make a free choice in regard to such matters, and history must roll on its inevitable course. And then again, perhaps man can make a choice, and since all of us behave as though this were the case, we should attempt to make a proper decision in regard to the use of atomic energy. To us at this time the most important problem facing all humanity is the problem of proper control and proper development of atomic energy. Our decisions which we make in this very year will influence the course of history for many years to come. Very seldom does the opportunity and the responsibility come to man that we face in this critical year of 1946.

The problem of the atomic bomb is not primarily the problem of that instrument of warfare. The problem is war itself. It is war that drove men to produce this weapon against their wishes and desires and better judgment, for there were few men working on this weapon who did not realize that it was wholly evil, that it would lead to the death of many men, and that it would be a constant threat over all men for all future time. It is war that drives men and women in all walks of life to pervert their constructive instincts to destructive purposes. It is war that is the real problem of this year, and the decision in regard to this problem is the one which will determine whether it is to be a solution of the atomic energy problem.

The problem of war is a very old problem, and has been with man from the time that he first organized his kind into societies; and this age-old problem is one which perhaps cannot be solved at all. However, the present situation results from a very special kind of war, one in which the destructive powers of men have increased to such an extent because of the application of science to technical problems, particularly in this century. I wish to review briefly the situation as it has developed in recent years.

During the twentieth century a revolution has occurred in our methods of production which had its roots in the nineteenth century, as all important revolutions of this kind have their roots in the past. During this century we have learned to make use of mass production methods for the production of peacetime goods. These methods depend upon a scientific and engineering background, but they also depend upon a purely economic invention, namely, the limited liability corporation which first made possible enormous accumulation of capital, and upon management techniques that have developed along with these corporations and the scientific and engineering foundation for manufacturing processes. At about the year 1900, a very large fraction of all the materials which people used were manufactured or produced near the points at which they lived, mostly by hand manufacturing methods. (I myself as a boy in Indiana saw a barn built from hewn timbers.) At the present time, nearly everything which is used by people in the United States is the product of mass production techniques. This revolution has occurred in the brief span of this last half-century, and our high standard of living today is due to these methods of production. Also, with their use it is possible to bring a high standard of living to all the peoples of the world, providing natural resources and other local conditions are at all favorable.

During this same time, we had two brief periods during which we were able to apply these same methods of production to the arts of war. During World War I the machine gun, tanks, airplanes, and submarines were first used on a large scale, and their methods of mass production explored in what is today a rather minor way. By the aid of such weapons, a narrow strip across the north of France and Belgium was laid waste, and a very considerable number of ships were destroyed. Those of us who lived during the last war recall vividly our reaction to the destruction wrought in that war, though today it seems to be only minor in importance. The airplane particularly was given a considerable impetus for its development during that war, though it did not contribute greatly to the destruction wrought.

During the years between the two World Wars, but minor development of war weapons took place, especially in this country, where the arts of mass production have been developed to the greatest extent. But during World War II these methods were applied on a vast scale to the mass production of weapons of the last war and the methods of research and development were applied to introduce new weapons of great magnitude. Among these we may mention radar, the proximity fuse, many details for the detection and destruction of submarines, and finally, the invention of the atomic bomb; and in the hands of our enemies, the pilotless airplane, the so-called V-1 weapon, and long-range rockets or the so-called V-2 weapon. The extent of destruction accomplished by these means is very vast indeed. The cities of Germany and Japan lie in nearly total ruin. Those of Russia, England, France and the Balkan countries suffered serious damage. Among the major combatants, only the United States escaped such destruction.

It is of interest to consider what could possibly be the future development in a possible third world war. Such a war may start with atomic bombs, or it may start with other mass destruction weapons and finish with atomic bombs. It is almost certainly to be expected that the scientific foundations for other weapons of war will be discovered in the years ahead, and their development on a large scale will again occur in another world war. Of course, it is not clear as to how such a war would start, because of course we do not know what conditions may obtain at such a time; but just as World War I ended with the airplane and World War II started with it, so we may expect that World War III may start with the atomic bomb which was developed at the end of World War II. It is surely to be expected that such a war would again result in a vastly increased destruction over that which we have witnessed in this war. It is to be expected that all the large cities of all the industrialized countries of the world will lie in ruins at the end of such a conflict. This statement would probably be true even if the atomic bomb had never been invented, but the atomic bomb certainly dramatizes the situation and gives us perhaps a more realistic picture of what such a future war would do. One could only conclude that the chance of survival of our civilization would be small, and it is possible that even the survival of the dominant races of the earth would be in doubt.

Had the development of atomic energy occurred in peacetime, the development of peacetime uses would have been predominant, and the development of the atomic bomb might have been delayed until later. Had this occurred, it would be far more difficult to convince people in regard to the danger of a future world war; and in this case, the world would almost certainly have drifted toward another conflict, with all the combatants securing atomic weapons at approximately the same time and using them against their enemies. There is just a possibility that because atomic weapons were developed in this war, and used only at the very end, we can use the spectacularly destructive character of these weapons to warn the peoples of the world in regard to the dangers of such another conflict. In this way, it may be that the development of these weapons during this war may be a positive benefit to the world. Those of us who contributed in one way or another to the solution of this weapon hope that our efforts may in fact in the long run contribute to the ultimate well-being of men, and not to their destruction.

It is well to review again some of the features of atomic bombs, for they present a compelling reason for the solution of political problems of greatest magnitude. The atomic bomb is a very great weapon, even at its present stage of development. Recently the War Department has released detailed statistics on the destruction caused by a single bomb exploding over the Japanese city of Hiroshima: 78,150 persons were killed; 13,000 persons were missing, and 305,000 were casualties. Of 300 doctors in the city, 240 were casualties. Of 2400 nurses and hospital orderlies, 1800 were casualties. The general and his staff, stationed in the city, were all killed. Out of a garrison of 8,000, 5,000 were killed. Twenty-six fire stations out of thirty-three were useless. All hospitals were useless. All buildings within a radius of one and a half miles were down, and something like half of the buildings at distances of three to four miles were wrecked. Fires burned uncontrolled for ten hours.

These figures leave no doubt as to the destructive character of this bomb. It remains to state, however, that they can be made relatively cheaply and in relatively large numbers. Granting reasonable improvements in processes which are largely foreseen at the present time, these bombs probably could be made more cheaply than equivalent amounts of any other explosive known. They could be delivered by a variety of methods which we now know of, including airplanes, the V-2 weapon, as well as mining of our cities by enemy agents.

Scientific men who have worked on the atomic bomb state they know of no defense against the atomic bomb, and they state categorically that none can ever be invented. This is a very broad statement, one which many will question, and there are two points of view in regard to this which I wish to present briefly. In the first place, we might consider detailed mechanisms by which these bombs might be delivered, and then attempt to devise methods to prevent their delivery. Such studies lead to the conclusion that it would be very difficult indeed to devise defensive measures that would be adequate, and lead to the conclusion that so far as present developments go, none could be devised that would meet the necessary tests for adequacy. In a more general way, we can see that if defenses against atomic bombs are no more effective than defenses against other types of weapons such as airplanes carrying ordinary bombs, submarines, machine guns, and other weapons, these new weapons will also be able to produce an amount of destruction commensurate with their capacities for destruction. It is to be expected that at least some of the atomic bombs, and perhaps a large fraction of all atomic bombs that are launched in the future, will arrive at their destinations, and produce a destruction of the order of magnitude or greater than that produced at Hiroshima. In this way, we may conclude that atomic bombs will destroy the industrial cities of the entire world, and probably do so in a very short time.

In another way, it is impossible to expect a defense against the atomic bomb. It is a saturation weapon. One single bomb dropping on a fair-sized city completely paralyzes all possible defensive methods that may be used against others which might be launched against that city. Statistics on Hiroshima again show that no adequate defense could possibly have been put up by that city against any further bombs being launched against it. In one single blow, all the natural resources of the population, and all its technical methods of defense are completely paralyzed. The V-1 weapon was a slow-flying plane which could easily be seen and which could be shot down by airplanes. This was all known before the weapon was first used against London. Yet in the first attack only some 10 per cent of these bombs were shot down, and it was some six weeks before 95 per cent were destroyed. Had they been loaded with atomic bombs, the city of London would have disappeared in a matter of minutes, and there would have been no opportunity to become proficient against the delivery of other bombs. The V-1 could then have been directed against another city, which would have suffered the same fate. Never, during the course of the war did we succeed in intercepting a V-2 bomb. These traveled at a velocity higher than that of sound. They cannot be heard and they could not be seen even with the aid of radar. They arrived without warning, and had they been loaded with atomic bombs, the city of London would have disappeared without the people ever having realized that any weapon was being directed against the city until the blinding flash of atomic bombs appeared in the sky. There is no defense against the atomic bomb, and there never will be any defense. It is well to remember this in thinking of the possible solution of the problems of modern war.

Accepting these statements—and so far as I know, all the informed atomic scientists on the entire Manhattan Project accept them without question—it is necessary to review other methods for the defense of a country such as the United States, or any other large country of this kind, than those which have been considered in the past. The problem, in fact, moves beyond even the problems of major strategy of military forces. The problem moves into the realm of the fundamental organization of modern society, and the ultimate causes of armed conflict. But before going on to such questions, let us ask a few questions in regard to the possible uses of traditional methods of defense of a country such as our own. What means can a navy use to prevent the effects of atomic bombs? How would a land army prevent these effects, and what means would an air force exert to accomplish these same ends? These armed forces must develop means for intercepting airplanes, V-2 weapons, or perhaps other delivery vehicles before delivering their atomic bomb loads. One can imagine a large circle of defense far from the shores and boundaries of this country, which must keep up its vigilance night and day, year in and year out, against the possible undeclared attack of another country against ours. The tragic story of Pearl Harbor illustrates the difficulty of being constantly on the alert, even in a limited area, and leads us to the conclusion that such a constant alert over a long period of time could not possibly be maintained. Even if these various vehicles of delivery could be detected with certainty, the problem of complete, decisive interception of those weapons to a very high degree of effectiveness would be impossible on the basis of our experience in past wars. There is no military way to intercept the delivery of atomic bombs in adequate numbers to prevent the total destruction of the military effort of a country such as the United States.

We turn from the possibility of defense to the possibility of offense. The United States has the atomic bomb, is manufacturing them and storing them, according to the latest public information which we have. We may be able to produce a large stockpile of these bombs before any other country has them, and a possible method of solution of our problems is to attack. At that time, we probably could destroy the entire industrial potential of all the other industrial countries of the world, and prevent them from attacking the United States for some years to come. In order to prevent in such conquered countries the development of atomic bombs, it would then be necessary to police those countries, or perhaps to periodically destroy all their industries. The policing of the world by some 7 per cent of its population is a very big problem indeed, and one which would convert this country from a peace-loving people to a nation of warriors, on a permanent basis. Such a solution would change our lives and those of our children for generations to come.

It is difficult for me to imagine that the people of the United States would choose such a course of their own free will. I am quite sure that this program can only be carried out by first destroying completely the democratic form of the government of the United States, and completely eliminating all of the freedoms which the people of this country enjoy. It must be converted into a totalitarian, military machine of the type that ruled Germany from 1933 until the defeat of the country in World War II. Only in this way can we expect that the people of the United States could be induced to take on the onerous burden of such an aggressive war. We must remember that this might be done. This solution might be imposed upon the people of the United States if they do not watch from this moment on every tendency to destroy the liberties of our people. I reject this solution.

In the second place, there is the possibility of dependence upon strongly armed nations all around the world, all of us depending upon the threat of the destruction of future war to prevent anyone from undertaking such a war. This type of security has never worked in the past. Under these conditions, all the peoples of the world would live in constant fear of atomic bombs which might be delivered without warning from unknown enemies. There certainly could be no feeling of security in such a world. I am sure that all our traditional liberties will disappear under those conditions. Our country, down to the smallest hamlet and the most remote farm, will be an armed camp living under rigid military control. It seems to me that there is no solution to this problem except one where war is abandoned by all nations. In 1928, the Kellogg-Briand Pact attempted to outlaw war as an instrument of national policy. It was unsuccessful. The present situation requires that the ideals expressed in this Pact must succeed if we are to have any peace in the future. The only questions are, how shall this be accomplished? The problem is essentially a political one, and not at all a scientific one, and hence is a more proper one to be discussed by our political leaders. However, the scientific men who helped to produce the atomic bomb have exhausted all possible technical methods of solving this problem, and hence they must turn to fields which are strange to them, and in which they can claim no particular competence over their fellow citizens. The old adage says that need and fear are the mothers of invention. Need and fear are with us, to a degree never before experienced on such a vast scale in all of history. We of the scientific group are trying to bring home to our colleagues and our fellow citizens the intense fear that we have experienced for years. We have recognized for years that the product of our minds and hands would become the greatest threat to ourselves, our children and our fellow citizens.

Today, it seems inescapable that within a relatively short time a world government must be established if we are to avoid the major catastrophe of a third world war. It seems that this must occur by one method or another, by conquest or by agreement. That it is difficult to accomplish this must be admitted by all of us, since there are so many divergent interests and points of view between the principal countries of the world. There is the great difficulty of the Communist and capitalist systems, and the perhaps even greater difficulty of our different ideas in regard to personal freedom. There is also the great problem of the large disparity in education and economic well-being in the various parts of the world. But today, even oceans cannot be regarded as adequate barriers against the invader. It seems very doubtful indeed if in another world conflict this country can emerge with the small amount of destruction that we have experienced in this war; it seems nearly certain that as great or greater destruction as that of Europe in this war will be our lot.

Many proposals have been made in regard to accomplishing this end result of world government. There is the United Nations, where at least the difficulties arising between states are now for the first time discussed openly for all the world to note and hear, which is indeed an important step forward, for we at least have a public debating society to help form public opinion. The United Nations as it is at present organized, however, cannot be regarded as a world government, for such a government must be expected to have sovereignty in at least certain limited fields, and it must have legislative, executive and judicial functions, none of which it possesses at the present time. However, the problem of atomic energy has at least formally been given to it. This may be the beginning of complete disarmament of the nations of the world, as has been called for by Senator Tydings in a resolution presented to the Senate. The complete disarmament of the nation-states and the reservation to the United Nations of the right to maintain a military force armed only with rifles, does not in itself solve the problem of a world government. There must be in addition to this an adequate organization for settling the disputes which arise between the states of the world.

But over and beyond all of these things, we must establish a consciousness on the part of all the peoples of the world that the old methods of settling disputes can no longer be used. Behind any government of any kind there must be the consent of the governed in a very real sense. The peoples of the world must have confidence in the United Nations, and must believe that it will act justly and fairly with respect to their interests. This is a general statement of the solution to these problems. It is not easy to attain, but in these matters something of the genius which entered into the development of our modern industrial civilization and finally into the invention of the atomic bomb must be put to work if we are to survive in this modern world.

I have said little in regard to the peace uses of atomic energy because they are of little value unless the threat of the atomic bomb is exorcised. In fact the peace uses of anything else will be of short duration unless this problem of technological war is solved. But we can hardly secure all our motivation from negative incentives and therefore some discussion of the peacetime uses of this new energy should be presented.

We at this time do not know how great the industrial uses of atomic energy will be, and it seems probable that any estimate we make will be on the conservative side. Could anyone have foreseen the industrial development of steam, electricity, the radio, internal combustion engine, to mention only a few examples?

First of all let us consider the possibility of power from atomic energy. The present piles are generating large amounts of heat but at such low temperatures that it is useless for power purposes. Technically it is feasible to produce power at high temperatures though it is not possible at present to say that such power can be produced at such costs that it can compete with power from coal, oil, or waterpower. It is my expectation that it will be some time before power at such price levels can be secured because of the extensive development which must still be done. Such power plants so far as we can see will be very large because enormous amounts of radio activity are produced in such piles and they must be shielded by thick concrete walls. Thus power plants will be large and massive and therefore can be used only for stationary power plants or for large ships. They present the possibility of smokeless power though the radioactivity must be disposed of in some manner.

These large amounts of radioactivity are now available for work on cancer. Progress on the control of this disease has been made during recent decades by a variety of methods including the use of radium. Further progress will be made because of the inexpensive radioactive substitutes for radium that are now available.

Atomic energy plants also produce large quantities of radioactive tracers which are research tools of the greatest importance. In the future our metals, plastics, and other materials of construction will be better because of the use of atomic energy biproducts in our studies.

At the present time there is a great tendency to justify science on the basis of its practical utility—a tendency against which I wish to protest. The greatest accomplishment of the Manhattan Project was neither the production of the atomic bomb, which is wholly evil, or the possible peacetime industrial use of atomic energy. The great accomplishment, in which all scientists who worked on this project take great pride, was the unlocking of nature's secrets and the production of events which never took place anywhere else in all the universes of the heavens. Nuclear chain reactions of the controlled kind or of the explosive kind are probably novelties of this earth and do not occur anywhere in the billions of stars of the milky way unless some other particle of dust such as our earth is inhabited by intelligent beings such as ourselves. Science, literature, art and all the intellectual pursuits of man are particularly those of our species. It is these of which we are all proud. It is the contribution to these things of which scientists of the atomic bomb project are proud. We ask your help and offer ours to you for a united effort toward making this a safe and secure world in which man's constructive genius in all lines of human endeavor may expand. We ask your help and offer ours to the end that the destructive uses of science shall not destroy its constructive uses and all else of value in this civilization.

THE SOCIAL IMPLICATIONS OF
ATOMIC ENERGY [3]

ARTHUR H. COMPTON [4]

Dr. Arthur H. Compton, chancellor of Washington University, St. Louis, gave this address before a thousand scientists at the annual meeting of the American Physical Society and the American Association of Physics Teachers, at the McMillin Theater, Columbia University, New York, on January 24, 1946. Dr. Harvey Fletcher, president of the American Physical Society, presided.

On the same day, Washington sources announced that atomic bomb tests would be made against a hundred floating targets, including some thirty-five warships, at the Bikini Atoll in the Marshall Islands, during July 1946. On January 24, 1946, also was announced the creation of an atomic energy commission, by vote of the United Nations Assembly, in London. Dr. Compton was one of the committee, under Dr. Bush, active in the development of the project during 1941-45.

Dr. Compton is highly effective as a speaker, before both technical and popular audiences. He has addressed many educational groups, has spoken frequently before religious organizations, and has been an acceptable radio speaker. He ranks in the upper group of scientists who are also popular speakers. He can simplify for listeners complicated materials, and he expresses his ideas with vocal warmth, clean cut articulation and enunciation, and with tonal flexibility, indicating conversational ease and audience adjustment. Of his methods of preparation for speaking, Dr. Compton states:

"During preparatory school and college I took the usual part in student debating clubs and other public and semi-public occasions to address audiences. My public speeches are always carefully outlined, frequently, and in the case of radio addresses nearly always, written. For radio speeches such as that which I sent you, I ordinarily follow the manuscript closely. For addresses to an audience I rarely use a manuscript. Having outlined the address beforehand, I find that this outline remains in mind and it is rarely necessary to refer to it during the address." [5]

[3] Text furnished by the author. Permission to reprint was given through the courtesy of Dr. Compton and of Dr. Duane Roller, of Wabash College, editor of the *American Journal of Physics,* in which publication this address (with the text somewhat changed from the version here inserted) was printed, Vol. 14:173-85. May-June 1946.

[4] For biographical note see Appendix.

[5] Letter to editor May 24, 1940. For further comment on Dr. Compton, see *Representative American Speeches: 1939-1940,* p. 421.

The release of atomic energy means that wars must cease. This is by all odds the most important direct social implication of the ability to release the energy of the atomic nucleus. There are other social implications also, resulting from applications of atomic power to industry, of radioactive materials to medicine, and of tracer atoms to the solving of scientific problems. The development of the nucleonics industry from new basic discoveries in science is another step toward making mankind a socially minded world community with resulting major effects on education, social attitudes, and objectives of life. But first and foremost is the fact that wars are on their way out, and in order to keep them out some form of world government is on its way in.

Mr. Bethe has helped us understand how the energy of the atomic nucleus is released, and how the nuclear chain reaction occurs. The atomic power piles operating under smooth control at Chicago, Clinton, Richland, and Los Alamos show that the energy of the atomic nucleus is harnessed. The explosions in New Mexico dramatically followed by those at Hiroshima and Nagasaki seem perhaps like the recollections of a frightful dream. But they are convincing demonstrations that if we let another war come the destruction on the receiving end will be terrific.

I shall not delve into the problem of how the world is to organize itself to prevent the recurrence of war. This question is in the much more able hands of Mr. Shotwell. I must rather speak of the effect on our society of the adjustment to the realities of atomic bombs, describe as well as I can the significance of the peaceful applications of atomic energy, and point out the social trends that are being accentuated by the whole development of nucleonics.

In speaking of the adjustment to the realities of atomic bombs I shall make certain assumptions. I shall suppose first that the nations of the world seeing the prohibitive cost of war will work vigorously and determinedly toward a situation in which international war is virtually impossible. Second, recognizing that this stable situation cannot be reached at once, I shall assume an interim period during which each nation must continue to prepare itself to ward off or resist attack. How long this interim period will last Mr. Shotwell can estimate much better than I. But I cannot see how the necessary world adjustments needed for stability can be made before 1950, and if they are not made before 1970 they will probably be too late to avert catastrophe. My own thinking is based on a ten-year period ending in 1955, by which time the nations will see that their safety is better served by placing all major war powers in international hands. I hope the time may be shorter.

With this picture in mind, I doubt whether we should attempt now to disperse our cities or place our key industrial plants under ground. If the indications become clear that no insurance of peace will come from international agreements, such extreme measures will then become a necessity for survival. Now we should rather assume success, and provide for our own protection in other ways. We can, I think, safely assume that no nation will attack us if we are known to be prepared for a reply with devastating power. This retaliatory power we can maintain, using a combination of modern military developments including atomic bombs, without undue strain on our national economy. Thus we can avoid the disruption of our life that would follow, for example, from spreading the activities now centered in New York throughout the Catskills and the Allegheny mountains.

Thus, more than ever before, society can now afford to become peace minded, so long as we make sure that there is adequate provision to take care of the renegade nation or group that wants to prey upon a peaceful world. The maintenance somewhere of adequate police power, armed with the most modern weapons, can provide this precaution. Until an international organization is prepared to function in this police capacity, we ourselves must at least maintain the partial assurance of peace that our own armed strength can provide. Other nations will have to do the same.

Our outlook thus becomes world-wide. No longer is this world interest for cultural and commercial reasons alone. More significantly now it is because our only assurance of continued peace is in reliance on agreements with other nations. The whole civilized world is perhaps for the first time convinced that war is too destructive to be considered as the alternative to the unpleasantnesses that cause quarrels, and that hence these quarrels must be solved by peaceful means. Atomic bombs are thus an important factor in forcing all men to become world-minded. The effect of such world-mindedness on education, industry, culture and religion is sure to be great.

Let me now turn to the peacetime practical applications of atomic energy and their effects on society. Atomic energy can be released either explosively or so gradually that the resulting heat is carried away as rapidly as it is produced. So far no one has proposed any important peacetime use of atomic explosions. Being equivalent to from 1000 to 100,000 tons of TNT, they are too big for the ordinary jobs of industry. The cost per unit of energy released by present atomic methods is not greatly different from that of TNT. Though this might be reduced by ten-fold or more by future developments, we do not now see any important engineering tasks that can profitably use such mighty explosions.

The controlled release of nuclear energy is, however, of great practical importance. While there are several other possibilities, the most obvious method of producing power from atomic fission is to heat a cooling agent such as air or steam or liquid metal in the chain reactor unit, and pass this heated coolant through a heat exchanger which heats the steam for driving a turbine. Beyond the heat exchanger of such a plant everything would be done according to standard practice. Up to the heat exchanger all the design requires new features, among them protection against the extreme radioactivity of everything, including the coolant, that has been exposed to the neutrons.

The chain reacting unit itself can assume many forms. The one essential is that it shall contain a fissionable substance such as uranium, either in its natural state, or if a small unit is desired, enriched with additional U-235 or plutonium. H. D. Smyth, in his official report, has described in some detail how this active material can be combined with a moderator such as carbon or beryllium or heavy water so as to bring about the chain reaction.

The large atomic power plants now used for producing plutonium have in them many tons of natural uranium and graphite.

By using uranium containing more than the usual fraction of U-235, chain reacting units have been built that are of much smaller size.

There is, however, a lower limit to the size and weight of an atomic power plant that is imposed by the massive shield needed to prevent the photons and neutrons and other dangerous radiations from getting out. Next to cosmic rays, these radiations are the most penetrating that we know, and for a plant designed to deliver for example no more than 100 horsepower, are enormously more intense than the rays from a large supply of radium or an x-ray tube. To reduce them to a harmless level of intensity a shield equivalent in weight to at least three feet of solid steel is needed. The principles underlying the absorption of photons are such as to rule out any lighter shield if protection against the rays is necessary. This means that there is no reason to hope that atomic power units for normal uses can be built that will weigh less than perhaps 100 tons. Driving motor cars or airplanes of ordinary size by atomic power must thus be counted out.

Prominent among the advantages of atomic power are the extraordinary low rate of fuel consumption and consequent low cost of fuel, the wide flexibility and easy control of the rate at which power is developed, and the complete absence at the power plant of smoke or noxious fumes. With regard to fuel consumption, when completely consumed, the fission energy available from a pound of uranium is equivalent to burning over a thousand tons of coal. With the prewar price of uranium oxide at roughly $3 per pound and of coal at $3.00 per ton, this would mean the economical use of uranium as fuel if only one part in a thousand of its available energy is used. Actually we should expect the first plants built for producing atomic power to be considerably more efficient than this in their use of the fission energy, which would mean a substantial cost advantage in favor of uranium. One must consider also, however, the need to purify and fabricate the uranium into the desired form. For certain types of power plants under consideration, some separated U-235 is required, and this is expensive. Attempting to consider all such factors, it appears that the fuel cost of the atomic power plant of the future will nevertheless be small as compared with the corresponding fuel cost of a coal burning plant.

In considering the economic aspects there are, however, many other factors. It is not really possible for these to be explored until we have actual experience with atomic power plants. First is the capital cost. Clearly if one must charge against the capital cost what is spent in research and development, this cost is very high indeed. If, however, one looks down the line to a billion dollar a year national industry based on atomic power, the nation can afford a considerable investment in the research and development required to bring this industry into being. When this development is completed, it appears not unlikely that the cost of building and maintaining a large scale atomic power plant may compare favorably with that of a coal consuming plant of the same capacity.

The terrific blasts produced by the atomic bombs have led to unwarranted fear of accidental explosions resulting from the normal use of atomic power. Explosions such as destroyed Hiroshima cannot occur accidentally. Such explosions must be carefully planned for. The dangers of explosions of the "boiler" type with an atomic power plant are about the same as with a steam plant, which is to say they are practically negligible if the plants are designed and handled by competent engineers.

There is, nevertheless, real possibility of damage to health of the operating personnel from ionizating rays emitted by the plant itself and by all materials that are taken out of the plant. These materials could also become a public hazard. This is the problem of the health of radium and x-ray workers on a grand scale. That the problem can be solved is shown by the fact that in all of the operations of the existing half dozen or more such plants, some of which have now been working for years, not a single serious exposure has occurred. This safety, however, is due to the thorough inspection and vigilant care given by a competent health staff. In some of the experimental work we have not been so fortunate. Until we become much more familiar with nucleonics than we are at present, atomic power plants can be safely operated and serviced only with the help of health supervisors who are familiar with radiological hazards.

All of this points toward using atomic power first in relatively large units where careful engineering and health supervision can be given. An obvious suggestion is its application to the power and heat supply of cities and of large industrial plants. Within ten years it is not unlikely that the power companies designing new plants for city service will be considering favorably the use of uranium instead of coal for purely economic reasons.

This of course does not mean that atomic power will put coal out of business. Each will have its own field. For small heating units, such as the kitchen stove, atomic power has no place. If our national economy grows as it should, coal as a chemical agent, as for example in blast furnaces and preparation or organic chemicals, will increase in importance.

From the point of view of the national economy the introduction of such a new source of power is a clear gain. If it will lessen the cost of heat and power to our cities, it will be a stimulus to every industry. If it reduces the pall of winter smoke, it will be a boon to us all. If it gives cheap power where industry and agriculture need it but cannot now get it, it will extend our economic frontiers. These are possibilities that lie immediately before us.

I have discussed the place of power production thus in some detail because it is one of the most obvious and definite of the practical applications of nuclear energy. It is however not the most distinctive. We have many other sources of power. Much more distinctive is the use of nuclear fission as a source of neutrons. Neutrons in turn are useful for transmuting atoms from one isotope into another, and for a variety of scientific tasks. Of the transmutation processes the most important one at present is that of making plutonium out of uranium. Previous to the fission chain reaction, the most abundant source of neutrons was the cyclotron. Per kilowatt of power, fission of uranium gives some 10,000 times as many neutrons as a cyclotron, and it is not difficult to make a chain reaction that delivers 100 times as much power as is used by a cyclotron. This means that we are now using large amounts of atomic power, many times more efficiently for the particular job of producing neutrons than the best electrical machine we have been able to devise.

Looking to the future we may expect the use of neutrons for transmutation to become of increasing importance. Thus plutonium will presumably be produced for peaceful purposes as a concentrated source of energy. Per unit of available energy it could be produced using present methods at a cost comparable with that of gasoline. Since a pound would do the work of a thousand tons of coal, this cost would be justified if fuel weight was important.

It is impossible to predict just what radioactive substances will be found of industrial importance. In the fifty years since their discovery radioactive materials have not come to play an important part in industrial chemistry. Perhaps now that these materials will be cheaper and in a much wider variety of chemical forms, more uses for them will be found; but I do not foresee here any revolutionary industrial developments.

Similarly in the field of radiation therapy. The value of radiation in the treatment of certain tumors is well established. There is nothing however that would lead us to expect a difference in kind between the effect of the rays from these artificial materials and those that occur in nature. Nevertheless there will be some advantages in the case of treatment with these new substances.

The most important new field opened to us by transmuted substances now seems to be that of scientific exploration. By the use of "tagged atoms," identifiable because of their distinctive radioactivity, chemists see new ways of studying molecular structure. Biochemists hope for advance in understanding the living cell. Physiologists hope to learn more of the nature of the process of life. We can well imagine such studies leading to an understanding of the nature of abnormal cell division, leading perhaps to a cure for cancer. Whether in pure science, in industry or in medicine, such applications may become of far-reaching importance indeed.

Fifty years ago it was evident that x-rays were useful for "seeing" through objects, such as the human body, which are opaque to ordinary light. It could not be predicted that x-rays would become a powerful weapon in the fight against cancer, or that researches made possible by x-rays would reveal the electron and with it give us the radio and a host of electronic devices. Such unforeseen developments are the result of every great discovery. It would be surprising similarly if the really important consequences of the release of atomic energy are not in directions as yet unpredicted.

I am inclined to believe, however, that the most important social consequences of the release of atomic energy are not those that are unique to this discovery but are those which it shares with the innumerable other advances of science and technology. I refer to such matters as the fact that the atomic energy development has made the world acutely aware of the importance of highly specialized knowledge. Because we had the physicists and chemists who understood atomic nuclei, the very name of which was unknown to most of the educated world, we were able to put a sudden stop to a tragic war. The case of atomic energy has thus accentuated the trends already clearly recognizable as a result of centuries of growing science and technology. I should fail to answer truly the question as to the social implications of atomic energy if I did not describe these trends.

Let me mention three directions in which science is forcing us to change our social customs. The first is toward increasing education and specialized training. The second is toward improved cooperation and coordination of effort between individuals and groups. The third is toward finding and establishing common objectives toward which to strive. All of these trends are strikingly illustrated in the atomic energy project, and its success gives accordingly added impetus to the trends.

Consider the fact that the only ones who could outline the atomic program and do the studies needed to get it started were men whose training in science went far beyond that of the usual four year technical school. The value of thorough training and the intimate knowledge of a field that comes only from research becomes strikingly evident to all connected with the project. Here is just one more example showing how the individual can do his part better with a thorough training and how the social group is strengthened by having within it specialists in many diverse fields.

Similarly the second trend, namely that toward cooperation. This is an obvious corollary of specialization, for the specialist can live only if he shares the product of his efforts with those who follow other specialties. As in the other war projects, cooperation in the atomic program was well organized and whole hearted. Specially worthy of note, however, was the fact that those who were working together were of the most diverse types. I do not refer to the fact that there were Europeans and Americans, Jews and non-Jews, white and colored. Those were all there, working together without a thought of differences. The differences that were difficult were such as these. The scientist couldn't understand the industrialist's insistence on careful preliminary planning. The army found the scientist undisciplined in taking and giving orders. The mechanics as well as the scientists found the health rules irksome. Differences continually arose—sometimes violent. But these were as to the best method of doing the job. And because all were determined to get the job done well and fast, the differences were forgotten, agreements were reached, and the work went ahead. Everyone wanted to work with the others in the most effective manner. In this will to cooperate we see the basic principle of a smoothly working society. It is a hard lesson to learn. But by and large the trend is there, nation-wide strikes notwithstanding, and the experience and requirements of atomic energy cannot but hasten this trend.

The third trend is harder to establish by reference to what we see going on. It is, however, one necessitated above all others by atomic energy. This trend is that toward the development of common objectives.

In the atomic program the great objective which all accepted was to make good atomic bombs as quickly as possible. United as to goal, cooperation and coordination of effort came willingly. Now we find that we have unprecedented war powers. If people are not to do themselves great damage they must find a goal which all the world can seek. This is the goal of eliminating war. Failure to unite on this goal will be severely punished.

Success will bring a rich human reward. Other goals may be questioned, but here is one that all mankind must recognize.

In the long run, the laws of evolution which demand the survival of the best adapted will mean the replacement of any social system which fails to bring out the full strength of a people. Thus we look with confidence to more and better training of our citizens, to more cordial cooperation, and to the development of objectives that will challenge every man to do his best. The experience of the atomic project, the great powers that the release of atomic energy has put in men's hands, and the unity of all peoples in the dread of further destructive wars all are emphasizing these trends.

In summary, therefore, I would note that by far the most significant direct social effect of the release of atomic energy is to unite the world in an effort to eliminate war. We have reason to hope that this effort may be successful.

The anticipated peacetime consequences of atomic energy are significant, but far from revolutionary within the visible future. Atomic power used in large units is a promising development. The scientific use of radioactive tracers may well open us to new levels of understanding of chemical and biological processes.

Most significant of the social implications of atomic energy may be perhaps the indirect effects of the program in accelerating the social trends toward increased education and training, toward a more complex and hence more cooperative society, and toward finding common objectives for which people will willingly devote their efforts. These are constructive trends which add to the richness of human life.

INTERNATIONAL CONTROL OF
ATOMIC ENERGY [6]

BERNARD M. BARUCH [7]

Mr. Bernard Baruch, United States Representative to the Atomic Energy Commission of the United Nations, gave this address at the opening session of the Commission at Hunter College, New York City, on June 14, 1946.

The speaker, seventy-five years old, American's "Elder Statesman," read slowly and distinctly and with striking earnestness.

Immediate comment was wide-spread and favorable. The Soviet delegate, Andrei A. Gromyko, stated that the speech as "well written and well delivered. I have no comment on the substance." Dr. Quo Tai-Chi of China pronounced it "inspiring" and said that it "presented a challenge to the world and a way of salvation." Sir Alexander Cadogan of Great Britain said that "it was a good speech—just right." Dr. Eelco van Kleffens of the Netherlands commented, "I thought it a marvelous speech."

Immediately after the commission session adjourned, a group of American scientists, including Arthur Compton and Harold H. Urey, issued a statement endorsing the address and the American plan. Said they:

"We were especially stirred by Mr. Baruch's insistence on the supreme issue of the international control of atomic energy to the survival of civilization."

Many commentators regarded the speech as one of the most significant to be given in recent history. Acceptance of the Baruch plan implied a full-fledged world government, backed by law and military enforcement of the law. The issue was immediately drawn, however, when the Communist newspaper *Daily Worker*, of London, denounced the proposal as "paving the way for world dictatorship." [8]

My Fellow Members of the United Nations Atomic Energy Commission, and My Fellow Citizens of the World: We are here to make a choice between the quick and the dead. That is our business.

[6] Text and permission for this reprinting furnished through the courtesy of Mr. Baruch.

[7] For biographical note see Appendix.

[8] The comments above were from the Associated Press dispatches as quoted in the *Des Moines Register*, p. 6, June 15, 1946.

Behind the black portent of the new atomic age lies a hope which, seized upon with faith, can work our salvation. If we fail, then we have damned every man to be the slave of fear. Let us not deceive ourselves: We must elect world peace or world destruction.

Science has torn from nature a secret so vast in its potentialities that our minds cower from the terror it creates. Yet terror is not enough to inhibit the use of the atomic bomb. The terror created by weapons has never stopped man from employing them. For each new weapon a defense has been produced, in time. But now we face a condition in which adequate defense does not exist.

Science, which gave us this dread power, shows that it *can* be made a giant help to humanity, but science does *not* show us how to prevent its baleful use. So we have been appointed to obviate that peril by finding a meeting of the minds and the hearts of our peoples. Only in the will of mankind lies the answer.

It is to express this will and make it effective that we have been assembled. We must provide the mechanism to assure that atomic energy is used for peaceful purposes and preclude its use in war. To that end, we must provide immediate, swift and sure punishment of those who violate the agreements that are reached by the nations. Penalization is essential if peace is to be more than a feverish interlude between wars. And, too, the United Nations can prescribe individual responsibility and punishment on the principles applied at Nuremberg by the Union of Soviet Socialist Republics, the United Kingdom, France and the United States—a formula certain to benefit the world's future.

In this crisis, we represent not only our governments but, in a larger way, we represent the peoples of the world. We must remember that the peoples do not belong to the governments but that the governments belong to the peoples. We must answer their demands; we must answer the world's longing for peace and security.

In that desire the United States shares ardently and hopefully. The search of science for the absolute weapon has reached fruition in this country. But she stands ready to prescribe and destroy this instrument—to lift its use from death to life—if the world will join in a pact to that end.

In our success lies the promise of a new life, freed from the heart-stopping fears that now beset the world. The beginning of victory for the great ideals for which millions have bled and died lies in building a workable plan. Now we approach fulfillment of the aspirations of mankind. At the end of the road lies the fairer, better, surer life we crave and mean to have.

Only by a lasting peace are liberties and democracies strengthened and deepened. War is their enemy. And it will not do to believe that any of us can escape war's devastation. Victor, vanquished and neutrals alike are affected physically, economically and morally.

Against the degradation of war we can erect a safeguard. That is the guerdon for which we reach. Within the scope of the formula we outline here, there will be found, to those who seek it, the essential elements of our purpose. Others will see only emptiness. Each of us carries his own mirror in which is reflected hope—or determined desperation—courage or cowardice.

There is a famine throughout the world today. It starves men's bodies. But there is a greater famine—the hunger of men's spirit. That starvation can be cured by the conquest of fear, and the substitution of hope, from which springs faith—faith in each other; faith that we want to work together toward salvation; and determination that those who threaten the peace and safety shall be punished.

The peoples of these democracies gathered here have a particular concern with our answer, for their peoples hate war. They will have a heavy exaction to make of those who fail to provide an escape. They are not afraid of an internationalism that protects; they are unwilling to be fobbed off by mouthings about narrow sovereignty, which is today's phrase for yesterday's isolation.

The basis of a sound foreign policy, in this new age, for all the nations here gathered, is that: anything that happens, no matter where or how, which menaces the peace of the world, or the economic stability, concerns each and all of us.

That roughly, may be said to be the central theme of the United Nations. It is with that thought we begin consideration of the most important subject that can engage mankind—life itself.

Let there be no quibbling about the duty and the responsibility of this group and of the governments we represent. I was moved, in the afternoon of my life, to add my effort to gain the world's quest, by the broad mandate under which we were created. The resolution of the General Assembly, passed January 24, 1946, in London reads:

Section V. Terms of Reference of the Commission

The Commission shall proceed with the utmost dispatch and inquire into all phases of the problem, and make such recommendations from time to time with respect to them as it finds possible. In particular the Commission shall make specific proposals:

A. For extending between all nations the exchange of basic scientific information for peaceful ends;

B. For control of atomic energy to the extent necessary to insure its use only for peaceful purposes;

C. For the elimination from national armaments of atomic weapons and of all other major weapons adaptable to mass destruction;

D. For effective safeguards by way of inspection and other means to protect complying states against the hazards of violations and evasions.

The work of the Commission should proceed by separate stages, the successful completion of each of which will develop the necessary confidence of the world before the next stage is undertaken.

Our mandate rests, in text and in spirit, upon the outcome of the Conference in Moscow of Messrs. Molotov of the Union of Soviet Socialist Republics, Bevin of the United Kingdom, and Byrnes of the United States of America. The three foreign ministers, on December 27, 1945, proposed the establishment of this body.

Their action was animated by a preceding conference in Washington, on November 15, 1945, when the President of the United States, associated with Mr. Attlee, Prime Minister of the United Kingdom, and Mr. MacKenzie King, Prime Minister of Canada, stated that international control of the whole field of atomic energy was immediately essential. They proposed the formation of this body. In examining that source, the Agreed

Declaration, it will be found that the fathers of the concept recognized the final means of world salvation—the abolition of war. Solemnly they wrote:

> We are aware that the only complete protection for the civilized world from the destructive use of scientific knowledge lies in the prevention of war. No system of safeguards that can be devised will of itself provide an effective guarantee against production of atomic weapons by a nation bent on aggression. Nor can we ignore the possibility of the development of other weapons, or of new methods of warfare, which may constitute as great a threat to civilization as the military use of atomic energy.

Through the historical approach I have outlined, we find ourselves here to test if man can produce, through his will and faith, the miracle of peace, just he he has, through science and skill, the miracle of the atom.

The United States proposes the creation of an International Atomic Development Authority, to which should be entrusted all phases of the development and use of atomic energy, starting with the raw material and including:

1. Managerial control or ownership of all atomic energy activities potentially dangerous to world security.

2. Power to control, inspect, and license all other atomic activities.

3. The duty of fostering the beneficial uses of atomic energy.

4. Research and development responsibilities of an affirmative character intended to put the Authority in the forefront of atomic knowledge and thus to enable it to comprehend, and therefore to detect, misuse of atomic energy. To be effective, the Authority must itself be the world's leader in the field of atomic knowledge and development and thus supplement its legal authority with the great power inherent in possession of leadership in knowledge.

I offer this as a basis for beginning our discussion.

But, I think the peoples we serve would not believe—and without faith nothing counts—that a treaty, merely outlawing possession or use of the atomic bomb constitutes effective fulfillment of the instructions to this Commission. Previous failures have been recorded in trying the method of simple renunciation, unsupported by effective guarantees of security and armament limitation. No one would have faith in that approach alone.

Now, if ever, is the time to act for the common good. Public opinion supports a world movement toward security. If I read the signs aright, the peoples want a program not composed merely of pious thoughts but of enforceable sanctions—an international law with teeth in it.

We of this nation, desirous of helping to bring peace to the world and realizing the heavy obligations upon us, arising from our possession of the means of producing the bomb and from the fact that it is part of our armament, are prepared to make our full contribution toward effective control of atomic energy.

When an adequate system for control of atomic energy, including the renunciation of the bomb as a weapon, has been agreed upon and put into effective operation and condign punishments set up for violations of the rules of control which are to be stigmatized as international crimes, we proposed that:

1. Manufacture of atomic bombs shall stop.

2. Existing bombs shall be disposed of pursuant to the terms of the treaty, and

3. The Authority shall be in possession of full information as to the know-how for the production of atomic energy.

Let me repeat, so as to avoid misunderstandings: My country is ready to make its full contribution toward the end we seek, subject of course to our constitutional processes, and to an adequate system of control becoming fully effective, as we finally work it out.

Now as to violations: In the agreement, penalties of as serious a nature as the nations may wish and as immediate and certain in their execution as possible, should be fixed for:

1. Illegal possession or use of an atomic bomb;

2. Illegal possession, or separation, of atomic material suitable for use in an atomic bomb;

3. Seizure of any plant or other property belonging to or licensed by the Authority;

4. Wilful interference with the activities of the Authority;

5. Creation or operation of dangerous projects in a manner contrary to, or in the absence of, a license granted by the international control body.

It would be a deception, to which I am unwilling to lend myself, were I not to say to you and to our peoples, that the matter of punishment lies at the very heart of our present security system. It might as well be admitted, here and now, that the subject goes straight to the veto power contained in the Charter of the United Nations so far as it relates to the field of atomic energy. The Charter permits penalization only by concurrence of each of the five great powers—Union of Soviet Socialist Republics, the United Kingdom, China, France and the United States.

I want to make very plain that I am concerned here with the veto power only as it affects this particular problem. There must be no veto to protect those who violate their solemn agreements not to develop or use atomic energy for destructive purposes.

The bomb does not wait upon debate. To delay may be to die. The time between violation and preventive action or punishment would be all too short for extended discussion as to the course to be followed.

As matters now stand several years may be necessary for another country to produce a bomb, de novo. However, once the basic information is generally known, and the Authority has established producing plants for peaceful purposes in the several countries, an illegal seizure of such a plant might permit a malevolent nation to produce a bomb in twelve months, and if preceded by secret preparation and necessary facilities perhaps even in a much shorter time. The time required—the advance warning given of the possible use of a bomb—can only be generally estimated but obviously will depend upon many factors, including the success with which the Authority has been able to introduce elements of safety in the design of its plants and the degree to which illegal and secret preparation for the military use of atomic energy will have been eliminated. Presumably no nation would think of starting a war with only one bomb.

This shows how imperative speed is in detecting and penalizing violations.

The process of prevention and penalization—a problem of profound statecraft—is, as I read it, implicit in the Moscow statement, signed by the Union of Soviet Socialist Republics, the United States and the United Kingdom a few months ago.

But before a country is ready to relinquish any winning weapons, it must have more than words to reassure it. It must have a guarantee of safety, not only against the offenders in the atomic area, but against the illegal users of other weapons— bacteriological, biological, gas—perhaps—why not?—against war itself.

In the elimination of war lies our solution, for only then will nations cease to compete with one another in the production and use of dread "secret" weapons which are evaluated solely by their capacity to kill. This devilish program takes us back not merely to the Dark Ages, but from cosmos to chaos. If we succeed in finding a suitable way to control atomic weapons, it is reasonable to hope that we may also preclude the use of other weapons adaptable to mass destruction. When man learns to say "A" he can, if he chooses, learn the rest of the alphabet, too.

Let this be anchored in our minds: Peace is never long preserved by weight of metal or by an armament race. Peace can be made tranquil and secure only by understanding and agreement fortified by sanctions. We must embrace international cooperation or international disintegration.

Science has taught us how to put the atom to work. But to make it work for good instead of for evil lies in the domain dealing with the principles of human duty. We are now facing a problem more of ethics than of physics.

The solution will require apparent sacrifice in pride and in position, but better pain as the price of peace than death as the price of war.

I now submit the following measures as representing the fundamental features of a plan which would give effect to certain of the conclusions which I have epitomized.

1. *General*: The Authority should set up a thorough plan for control of the field of atomic energy, through various forms of ownership, dominion, licenses, operation, inspection, research and management by competent personnel. After this is provided for, there should be as little interference as may be with the economic plans and the present private, corporate and state relationships in the several countries involved.

2. *Raw Materials*: The Authority should have as one of its earliest purposes to obtain and maintain complete and accurate

information on world supplies of uranium and thorium and to bring them under its dominion. The precise pattern of control for various types of deposits of such materials will have to depend upon the geological, mining, refining, and economic facts involved in different situations.

The Authority should conduct continuous surveys so that it will have the most complete knowledge of the world geology of uranium and thorium. Only after all current information on world sources of uranium and thorium is known to us all can equitable plans be made for their production, refining and distribution.

3. *Primary Production Plants*: The Authority should exercise complete managerial control of the production of fissionable materials. This means that it should control and operate all plants producing fissionable materials in dangerous quantities and must own and control the product of these plants.

4. *Atomic Explosives*: The Authority should be given sole and exclusive right to conduct research in the field of atomic explosives. Research activities in the field of atomic explosives are essential in order that the Authority may keep in the forefront of knowledge in the field of atomic energy and fulfill the objective of preventing illicit manufacture of bombs. Only by maintaining its position as the best informed agency will the Authority be able to determine the line between intrinsically dangerous and non-dangerous activities.

5. *Strategic Distribution of Activities and Materials*: The activities entrusted exclusively to the Authority because they are intrinsically dangerous to security should be distributed throughout the world. Similarly, stockpiles of raw materials and fissionable materials should not be centralized.

6. *Non-Dangerous Activities*: A function of the Authority should be promotion of the peacetime benefits of atomic energy.

Atomic research (except in explosives), the use of research reactors, the production of radioactive tracers by means nondangerous reactors, the use of such tracers, and to some extent the production of power should be open to nations and their citizens under reasonable licensing arrangements from the Authority. Denatured materials, whose use we know also requires suitable safeguards, should be furnished for such purposes by the Authority under lease or other arrangement. Denaturing seems to have been over-estimated by the public as a safety measure.

7. *Definition of Dangerous and Non-Dangerous Activities*: Although a reasonable dividing line can be drawn between dangerous and non-dangerous activities, it is not hard and fast. Provision should, therefore, be made to assure constant reexamination of the questions, and to permit revision of the dividing line as changing conditions and new discoveries may require.

8. *Operations of Dangerous Activities*: Any plant dealing with uranium or thorium after it once reaches the potential of dangerous use must be not only subject to the most rigorous and competent inspection by the Authority, but its actual operation shall be under the management, supervision and control of the Authority.

9. *Inspection*: By assigning intrinsically dangerous activities exclusively to the Authority, the difficulties of inspection are reduced. If the Authority is the only agency which may lawfully conduct dangerous activities, then visible operation by others than the Authority will constitute an unambiguous danger signal. Inspection will also occur in connection with the licensing functions of the Authority.

10. *Freedom of Access*: Adequate ingress and egress for all qualified representatives of the Authority must be assured. Many of the inspection activities of the Authority should grow out of, and be incidental to, its other functions. Important measures of inspection will be associated with the tight control of raw materials, for this is a keystone of the plan. The continuing activities of prospecting, survey and research in relation to raw materials will be designed not only to serve the affirmative development functions of the Authority, but also to assure that no surreptitious operations are conducted in the raw materials field by nations or their citizens.

11. *Personnel*: The personnel of the Authority should be recruited on a basis of proven competence but also so far as possible on an international basis.

12. *Progress by Stages*: A primary step in the creation of the system of control is the setting forth, in comprehensive terms

of the functions, responsibilities, powers and limitations of the Authority. Once a Charter for the Authority has been adopted, the Authority and the system of control for which it will be responsible will require time to become fully organized and effective. The plan of control will, therefore, have to come into effect in successive stages. These should be specifically fixed in the Charter or means should be otherwise set forth in the Charter for transitions from one stage to another, as contemplated in the resolution of the United Nations Assembly which created this Commission.

13. *Disclosures*: In the deliberations of the United Nations Commission on Atomic Energy, the United States is prepared to make available the information essential to a reasonable understanding of the proposals which it advocates. Further disclosures must be dependent, in the interests of all, upon the effective ratification of the treaty. When the Authority is actually created, the United States will join the other nations in making available the further information essential to that organization for the performance of its functions. As the successive stages of international control are reached, the United States will be prepared to yield, to the extent required by each stage, national control of activities in this field to the Authority.

14. *International Control*: There will be questions about the extent of control to be allowed to national bodies, when the Authority is established. Purely national authorities for control and development of atomic energy should to the extent necessary for the effective operation of the Authority be subordinate to it. This is neither an endorsement nor a disapproval of the creation of national authorities. The Commission should evolve a clear demarcation of the scope of duties and responsibilities of such national authorities.

And now I end. I have submitted an outline for present discussion. Our consideration will be broadened by the criticism of the United States proposals and by the plans of the other nations, which, it is to be hoped, will be submitted at their early convenience. I and my associates of the United States Delegation will make available to each member of this body books and pamphlets, including the Acheson-Lilienthal report, recently made by the United States Department of State, and the McMahon Committee Monograph No. 1 entitled "Essential Information on Atomic Energy" relating to the McMahon Bill recently passed by the United States Senate, which may prove of value in assessing the situation.

All of us are consecrated to making an end of gloom and hopelessness. It will not be an easy job. The way is long and thorny, but supremely worth traveling. All of us want to stand erect, with our faces to the sun, instead of being forced to burrow into the earth, like rats. The pattern of salvation must be worked out by all for all.

The light at the end of the tunnel is dim, but our path seems to grow brighter as we actually begin our journey. We cannot yet light the way to the end. However, we hope the suggestions of my government will be illuminating.

Let us keep in mind the exhortation of Abraham Lincoln, whose words, uttered at a moment of shattering national peril, form a complete text for our deliberation. I quote, paraphrasing slightly:

We cannot escape history. We of this meeting will be remembered in spite of ourselves. No personal significance or insignificance can spare one or another of us. The fiery trial through which we are passing will light us down in honor or dishonor to the latest generation.

We say we are for peace. The world will not forget that we say this. We know how to save peace. The world knows that we do. We, even we here, hold the power and have the responsibility.

We shall nobly save, or meanly lose, the last, best hope of earth. The way is plain, peaceful, generous, just—a way which, if followed, the world will forever applaud.

My thanks for your attention.

ECONOMIC CONTROLS

FREEDOM OR PLANNED ECONOMY: THERE IS NO MIDDLE ROAD [1]

LEWIS H. BROWN [2]

Mr. Lewis H. Brown, President of the Johns Manville Corporation, gave this address at the Lake Forest Commencement Exercises on May 26, 1945. The address reflects the business leader's philosophy and program for dealing with private enterprise in the postwar United States.

During this period of 1945-46, the issues of wage increases, strikes, lowering of corporation and individual taxes, balancing of the federal budget, stimulation of production, abandonment of the Office of Price Administration, controls of money supply, abandonment of subsidies, loans to Great Britain, and similar problems confronted Congress and the American public. Behind these more specific questions lay the recurrent issue, to what extent should the government limit or control competitive enterprise in order best to safeguard the interests of all the people? Mr. Brown spoke frequently on this subject. Before numerous business groups, he presented carefully prepared discourses delivered with highly acceptable public speaking skill. He is tall and impressive, dominates partly by his personality, employs successfully organization, concrete illustration, logical unfolding of problem and solution.

The address here inserted illustrates his approach to a college audience.[3]

What of Mr. Brown's methods of preparing and delivering speeches? For informal speeches before small groups of company employees and others, he will often speak extemporaneously without notes or other preparation (providing he is thoroughly familiar with the subject).

For larger gatherings he will often prepare a simplified outline and will use that as notes in delivering the address. In this way the delivery is largely extemporaneous, yet he is sure to bring in all the points he regards as important.

[1] By permission of President Brown. Text supplied through the courtesy of the author. See also variation of this text as found in Mr. Brown's "America Tomorrow, a Country of Free Enterprise or State Planned Economy," *Dun's Review.* 16:37-46, September 1945

[2] For biographical note see Appendix.

[3] For further comment on Mr. Brown, see *Representative American Speeches: 1942-1943,* p. 203.

On still other occasions, perhaps less frequently, he will prepare and use as notes a rather detailed outline, in full or almost full sentence form, with illustrations and data noted. In all cases these outlines to be used as notes are carefully redrafted as many times as may seem necessary.

For his formal appearances, which are covered by the press, Mr. Brown writes his speeches in full. For such types he works from a simplified outline and rewrites the full speech until he is completely satisfied with it. On these occasions he will read from manuscript, never attempting to memorize the address. He likes to interpolate and does so frequently unless prevented by a strict time schedule such as is required for radio broadcasts.[4]

Mr. President, Members of the Faculty, Distinguished Guests, Members of the Class of 1945, Ladies and Gentlemen: When someone once asked Aristippus what should be the content of the education of youth, he replied: "Those things which they will use when men."

Amplified to fit the requirements of modern times the statement of this Greek philosopher might say: "The purpose of education is to prepare men and women to live, to think, to see, to be happier and better members of the family, better neighbors in the community, and better citizens of the state."

For two years now, the company with which I am associated has been engaged with Lake Forest College in an experiment in education. We are attempting to fuse the study of the liberal arts with practical business training so that at the end of four years of college work the graduate will have actual business experience sufficient not only to make a living but also for the proper exercise of responsibility and leadership both as an employee and as a citizen.

Experience has made it evident that being trained merely to make a living is not enough to meet the requirements of this day and age. We must also as individuals and as a nation have a clear understanding of how we propose cooperatively to create the political, economic and social atmosphere in which we as civilized beings can work together for our own general welfare.

History tells us that people have always lived and worked together under some form of cooperative and protective organi-

[4] Letter from Mr. Howard W. Allen, of the Johns Manville Corporation, to the editor, May 23, 1946.

zation. One common characteristic of almost all these early forms of organization was the fact that each was headed by a master with great power over his subjects.

Plato in *The Republic* attempted to develop an ideal state. After the dark days of the Middle Ages other men raised their voices in an effort to escape from the compulsions of despotic government.

Among them were More in his *Utopia*; Campanella in his *City of the Sun*; Bacon in his *New Atlantis*; and Rousseau in his *Social Contract*. All were seeking some way to escape the despotism, tyranny and domination of the individual by the government. All dreamed of bettering the condition of mankind.

Out of the American and French revolutions came the basic philosophy that the state is the servant not the master of the people. This brought to the world not a utopia but a practical philosophy and system of organizing our political, economic and social life.

The republic of the United States of America was based upon the belief in the supremacy of the individual citizen, the inherent value and dignity of man, and his inalienable rights which protect him from subservience to the state except by consent of individuals acting collectively.

The economic plan of our republic was based upon individual ownership of property and upon the citizen's right to determine in the market place what should be produced and sold. The government's role in economic life was to protect, to help and to administer justice for all citizens, but not to provide for them.

For over a hundred and fifty years this system that came out of the American Revolution was the beacon light to the rest of the world. Like the Statue of Liberty it held aloft a torch of hope and freedom. As this nation grew from 4,000,000 to more than 130,000,000 people, our political and economic system, implemented by the marvels of modern technology, enabled us to produce the highest standard of living for all the people that had ever been developed in any country in the entire history of the world.

In the decade prior to World War I we in America had come to accept the fruits of the American Revolution and our plan of economic life as a commonplace fact, like the air we breathe. We failed to realize that this system under which we had so greatly prospered had to be understood and defended if it were to survive. We became lax in teaching each new generation the fundamentals of our American heritage.

Instead it became fashionable to point out and exaggerate mistakes and excesses. This was the era of the "muckrakers." They raked in the gutters for mud and muck—the 10 per cent of life that was unsatisfactory or corrupt—and held it up before the eyes of the public as if this were *all* of life. The 90 per cent that was clean, that was good, that was the *real* America, was ignored. Similar internal attacks were being directed against the economic systems of the British Empire and France.

But there was an even greater conflict brewing and it exploded violently with World War I. In addition to its economic causes, this war resulted from a conflict between two basic ideas of government. Few people realized that this clash of political philosophies would lead to a second and perhaps a third world struggle.

Let us pause a moment to examine these conflicting conceptions of government. If we study the pages of history we shall find, I believe, that basically there are only *two* kinds of government that have ever been made to work in our complex civilization. In one, the ruler or the ruling class is the master—the people are the servants. In the other, the people are the masters and the state is the servant.

When Karl Marx in 1867 wrote *Das Kapital*, he challenged the system which gave freedom to the individual in the economic arena. Eventually, his tenets were also to challenge the individual's freedom in the political arena. This book signalled the beginning of socialism and of its extreme form, communism. From 1867 until World War I neither socialism nor communism made much practical headway, although the growing agitation gradually brought fear to those who were the masters of the people and who intended to remain so. Among these masters were the militant Prussian nobility. Determined to prevent the spread of democracy and to stamp out communism and social-ism, this Prussian group turned its thoughts to foreign conquest and the "Drang nach Osten" took on renewed momentum.

When Germany struck in 1914 she was ready. The Allied democracies were not. Germany and the Prussian scheme of domination were almost victorious.

Out of the chaos and bankruptcy of that war there came three significant developments. They were:

1. The Russian Revolution of 1917 that established communism in Russia—its first practical application.
2. The Italian Revolution of 1921 that established a form of planned economy under Mussolini's socialistic government.
3. The Hitler beer-hall *putsch* of 1923 that started Germany on the road to national socialism.

In all three countries socialism or communism was sold to the common people as a means of providing them with a higher standard of living than they could attain under capitalism. There would be a planned economy but the people were never told how greatly their freedoms were to be restricted. The promise was that, in spite of government domination in the economic field, there would be no interference with the freedom and rights of the individual in the political field. As we have since learned, however, this involved a fatal contradiction and the inevitable happened. Step by step, the planned economies became ever more dictatorial and there evolved before our eyes the full-blown totalitarian state.

The emergence of this appalling Frankenstein was entirely contrary to the theories of all socialists, and only a few thinkers and philosophers had clearly foreseen this consequence. For the past twenty-five years Professor Ludwig von Mises, now of New York University, and formerly head of the School of Social Economics of Vienna, has been expounding the doctrine that communism or socialism or any state-planned economy must either fail in its "plan" or of necessity develop into a totalitarian dictatorship, thus arriving at a goal exactly opposite to that intended.

Professor Friedrich A. Hayek, a former pupil of Von Mises, has recently published *The Road to Serfdom*, which summarizes in popular form what both have been saying for twenty-five years. Italy, Germany and Russia have conclusively proved the soundness of this thesis. Marxian socialism fails as an alternate for totalitarianism or democracy, since communism, socialism or any planned economy inevitably becomes totalitarian.

We come back, then, to only two forms of government— either the state is to be the master or the state must be the servant of the people.

Von Mises [5] clearly designated the choice that must be made when he said:

In the history of the last two hundred years we can discern two distinctive ideological trends. There was first the trend toward freedom, the rights of man, and self-determination. This individualism resulted in the fall of autocratic go............., the establishment of democracy, the evolution of capitalism, technical improvements, and an unprecedented rise in standards of living. It substituted enlightenment for old superstitions, scientific methods of research for inveterate prejudices. It was an epoch of great artistic and literary achievements, the age of immortal musicians, painters, writers, and philosophers. And it brushed away slavery, serfdom, torture, inquisition, and other remnants of the dark ages.

In the second part of this period individualism gave way to another trend, the trend toward state omnipotence. Men now seem eager to vest all powers in government, i.e., in the apparatus of social compulsion and coercion. They aim at totalitarianism, that is, conditions in which all human affairs are managed by governments. They hail every step toward more government interference as progress toward a more perfect world; they are confident that the governments will transform the earth into a paradise. . . .

The most that can be expected for the immediate future is the separation of the world into two sections: a liberal, democratic, and capitalist West with about one quarter of the total world population, and a militarist and totalitarian East embracing the much greater part of the earth's surface and its population. Such a state of affairs will force upon the West policies of defense which will seriously hamper its efforts to make life more civilized and economic conditions more prosperous.

Then Von Mises adds:

Even this melancholy image may prove too optimistic. There are no signs that the peoples of the West are prepared to abandon their policies

[5] *Omnipotent government: The rise of the total state and total war,* by Ludwig von Mises. Yale Univ. Press. p. 8-10. 1944.

of statism. . . . The result will be a third war, more dreadful and more disastrous than its precursors.

We must make our choice. We must either completely re-establish our democratic system in America, or we must completely accept the totalitarian philosophy. There is no middle ground. Either system is workable if it remains true to its principles. Each has its own social, political and economic values—but they are complete opposites. The time to choose is now. We must adopt the Russian or the American way of life. If this be so, it is vital that we reappraise the Russian way, and redefine our own way of free enterprise under capitalism.

Russia is communistic, not capitalistic. Russia is not a democracy but an absolute dictatorship. In Russia there is no freedom of speech or freedom of the press. There is no bill of rights to protect the individual. That the constitution of Russia offers none of these rights and protections to her citizens was demonstrated by the great purges of a few years ago. In the concentration camps of Russia are great numbers of people guilty only of a desire for the freedoms our constitution guarantees to every one of us. There is no question but that in Russia the state is the absolute master.

What of communism's promise of a high standard of living for all the Russian people? The Russian planned economy has been in full effect for over twenty-five years in the Soviet Union. It is the ultimate in a planned economy and has undoubtedly given the people more security and greater unity than they had under the old monarchy of the Czars. Yet W. L. White in his book Report on the Russians, written after his recent visit to Russia with Eric Johnston, states that the average standard of living in Russia is much lower than was that of our unemployed on WPA during the great depression. True, an immense part of the productivity of the Soviet economy had to be devoted to defense as the dark cloud of World War II loomed on the horizon. Nevertheless, the fact remains that the planned economy of Russia has never shown evidence of its ability to raise the people's standard of living to a level even distantly approaching our own.

Now let us examine our capitalistic system. What is capitalism? There is a practical definition of capitalism which I think all of us in this country ought to thoroughly understand. Capitalism means production and service for *profit*. The profit motive has been the driving force behind every one of our great enterprises and achievements in mass production and mass service. All of us, as free citizens, can seek our own opportunities for profits with which we support ourselves, our families and our institutions.

Our automobiles are the best and the least expensive. They are made so in order that everyone connected with their production and sale can make money. Nobody under the capitalistic system can make for long anything that the public does not want. If he does, the public will not buy, there will be no profit and the enterprise will fail. Similarly, our government, as long as it remains truly democratic, cannot for long maintain policies the public does not want. If it does, it will lose the support of the people. The people are the masters because they control the purse strings economically and the votes politically. By benefiting and serving the public under capitalism we in America —all of us—are enjoying the highest standard of living in the world.

For years, however, we have allowed monkey wrenches to be thrown into the capitalistic system. Then, instead of removing the monkey wrenches when the machine slowed down, we tried to repair it with socialistic spare parts—parts which were never intended for and which did not fit our American machine. In the last decade so many of these spare parts had been added that our machine had become almost a planned economy model. Total war forced us to further change and our economic automobile became a military, totalitarian jeep. With the coming of peace a basic problem will confront us. Shall we complete the conversion to a planned economy or shall we reconvert to the American model?

No one can predict the future. But it is my guess that the American people, having had some first-hand experience with the compulsions of a planned economy here at home, and having had a chance to see the concentration camps abroad which are the inevitable end result of a planned economy, will not choose the Russian system for America. But, if we in America determine to go on with democracy and capitalism, can two systems of government continue to exist in the world?

For years Lenin, Trotsky and other Communists maintained that the Russian system could not long exist alongside capitalistic systems. They believed their survival depended upon undermining other countries. On the other hand we have believed that democracy and capitalism can exist parallel with other systems provided neither insists upon trying to dominate the world.

Is there then no way to avoid the ultimate clash of these two opposite ideologies of the totalitarian East and the democratic West? I believe there is a way. Let us say frankly to our friends in Russia:

> We have fought together in spite of our different systems of government and economics. Together we have been victorious over a common enemy. Our spheres of influence have been determined by the realities of war. The world needs peace. Let's declare a truce on further efforts to spread our conflicting ideologies. Let us permit each of these systems to develop to the fullest, unimpeded by interference from the other.

If such a course is followed, comparison of both systems would naturally be made. Such comparison would spur us in America to prove that our system brings our people more in physical comforts and in freedom. It would give the advocates of communism the same incentive to prove their point. In this way, there could develop a friendly competition.

I think the Russians would accept the implied challenge, because they believe in their system—just as we believe in ours. And, furthermore, I believe that both of us will want our systems judged by a comparison of results and not by a competition of promises such as we have largely lived by during the last decade. By results, I mean what the people have in physical comforts, what they produce per person and what freedoms they enjoy.

Now such a realistic attitude would give us in America a common goal. The conflict of ideologies that has bedevilled us for fifteen years would be behind us. We would be stimulated to make the capitalistic private enterprise economy of the marketplace produce results. We would make sure that the best brains of America are called upon to attain our objective and maintain the principles of the American way of life. If we really go to work to remove the socialistic monkey wrenches and the planned economy gadgets from the American capitalistic machine, to streamline it and modernize it, I will guarantee superiority over anything that a socialistic, planned economy dictatorship can produce.

There is no time here to even outline what needs to be done if we are to be successful in mastering all of the problems that lie ahead. But just to get ready for the race, certain things will be required after we defeat Japan.

1. We must decide that our government is going to be the servant and not the master of the people.
2. We must discontinue government controls and planned economy devices as rapidly as practicable.
3. We must create an atmosphere that will reestablish and stimulate the economy of the marketplace.
4. We must reeducate our people in the principles fought for in the American Revolution.
5. We must enlist every citizen in this effort to maintain our system so that it will continue to increase the standard of living of all our people.

Now you will say: This is all very exciting and interesting, but what can I, just graduating from college, do about it? You can do more than you think if your belief in the capitalistic system is a conviction, not just a casual acceptance. And you can *make* it a conviction, because you have developed your powers of discernment—the ability to discriminate between historic facts and demogogic fallacies. It is from a complete understanding of these facts that you can draw the courage to step out into the world with full confidence in your own destiny in a system which offers you practically unlimited opportunity to make the most of yourself.

As you meet obstacles, and there will be many of them, you can obtain full dividends from your education by using your knowledge and your ability to reason. You can overcome your obstacles by your own personal efforts and not seek to avoid them by surrendering your freedom and individuality for the tinseled security offered by bureaucracy and totalitarianism. Furthermore, you can and must become a compelling force to bring to others the same clear understanding and willingness to fight for this system of free initiative in which you have chosen to build your career.

"But," you may say, "how can I, one little person, affect the destiny of more than 130,000,000 Americans?" Let me give you my answer by telling you of an incident that took place out in Los Angeles about a year ago. In an effort to bring home the vital importance of individual effort in winning the greatest war in history, the United States Army staged a gigantic war show in the Olympic Stadium. More than 120,000 workers, from shipyards and airplane factories, filled the great stadium. I am told that the sight of one hundred and twenty thousand men and women, under the high-powered arc-lights, was breath taking.

But the culmination of this evening came when a wounded Marine sergeant stood up to speak. He said he supposed that it was a little difficult for each person who made some small airplane part or a spring for a machine gun to understand how their small effort was important in such a nation-wide and gigantic undertaking.

Then he said he'd show them. He asked that all the lights be put out. When the huge stadium was in total darkness, he struck a match and held up the tiny flame, which was hardly visible from the opposite end of the great arena.

"This single match doesn't give much light," he said, "compared to one of those powerful searchlights. But now when I give the signal, I'm going to ask every person here to strike a match. And if any of you haven't a match, borrow one from your neighbor."

There was a moment of rustling around in this darkened stadium. Then the wounded sergeant gave the signal. From all over the place tiny flames appeared and everyone held a lighted match aloft.

Suddenly the stadium was suffused with a stronger illumination, a clearer light, than the searchlights had produced. In it were to be seen plainly the uplifted faces of one hundred and twenty thousand people, each one of whom was inspired as he realized his tiny flame was contributing to a mutual effort that resulted in an almost supernatural brilliance.

PRICE CONTROL AND INFLATION [6]

CHESTER BOWLES [7]

Mr. Chester Bowles, then Director of the Office of Economic Stabilization, gave this address at the annual convention of the National Farmers Union, at Topeka, Kansas, on March 6, 1946.

From November 1935 to July 1946, Mr. Bowles directed the nation's fight against inflation, at times it seemed almost single handed. Groups that accepted wartime controls, quickly denounced them as peacetime shackles. Bowles' strategy was to abandon controls slowly and only when production overtook the tremendous demand.

Following Leon Henderson, Prentiss Brown, and Lou Maxon, each in succession in charge of OPA, Bowles simplified procedures of that office, organized industrial advisory committees, and set up information services for Congressmen. Applying his experience as newspaper man and advertising agency director, he used the art of persuasion to Congressmen, industrialists, labor, farmers, and the general public. He repeatedly addressed Congressional committees, various civic groups, radio listeners. He literally talked day after day, and night after night. He was sometimes soft spoken, always clear cut, concise, comprehensible, courageous, strong of voice, dominating as a platform personality; sometimes he was aggressive, hard boiled.

Although his battle against inflation was a losing one, he no doubt generated among his national audience a sufficient amount of "psychological resistance" to retard the irresistible sweep toward inflation in 1946. A considerable amount of his power was to be attributed to his leadership as a speaker.

Mr. Bowles preferred to write a complete speech for release, but delivered the talk from a topical outline. Usually his material for radio and conventions was fully written. Often, for example, before luncheon groups he extemporized without much memorization and with few "speaker's notes."

I am delighted to be here tonight with my friends in the Farmers Union. There is no group in America among our farmers, our workers, or our businessmen, who had a more enviable record of public service during the war period. There is no group in America which has more enlightened leadership.

[6] Text is from the *Congressional Record* (daily edition). 92:A 129-92, No. 41, March 8, 1946.

[7] For biographical note see Appendix.

There is no group in America which has more to contribute in our struggle to achieve a future of peace, prosperity and plenty.

To say that we have been going through a crisis during the last few months is something of an understatement. There has been widespread dissension among us. There has been bitterness and disillusionment. We have found ourselves pulling in different directions with every group blaming everyone else for the difficulties which inevitably confront us as we reconvert from war to peace.

If we stop to think about it, I believe we will agree that this situation was scarcely unexpected. For more than four years we had been concentrating all our efforts on an all-out war in all parts of the world. The problems of our economic reconversion from war to peace have been clear to everyone. The problem of reconverting our thinking, our loyalties, and our prejudices, although just as difficult, has been far less appreciated. It has not been easy overnight to adjust ourselves to the ways of peace. It will take time for all of us to realize fully that only by pulling together and working together can we achieve the kind of future which all of us seek.

Today those among us who are inclined to be pessimistic will find plenty to worry about. There is the problem of our relationship to Russia, a relationship which for the good of all the world must be worked out on a reasonable and friendly basis. There is the problem of industrial strife and the tendency of many of our people to pit group against group for their own selfish interests. There is the grave danger of inflation, a danger which is greater today than at any period since Pearl Harbor.

But the outlook is not all gray. There is also a great deal to give us confidence in our future. During the war we have learned for the first time the real potentialities of American production on our farms and in our factories. Labor and management have learned what the farmers always knew—that only through unlimited production can great wealth be achieved. We have learned that no group among us can profit at the expense of the other.

Finally, during the war period, I believe we have cut loose, once and for all, from the narrow isolationism of the past. Although we still have our American nationalists, our Gerald Smiths, our imperialists, the country as a whole has come to recognize that unless the world is at peace with increasing prosperity everywhere, there can be neither peace nor sustained prosperity here at home.

Exactly what are the greatest hurdles that lie today between our people and this longed-for future of prosperity and plenty? By far the greatest single danger is, I believe, the danger of inflation.

There is no group in America which understands the consequences of inflation better than our farmers. It was our farmers who suffered most in the boom and collapse following World War I. And no group was harder hit than our farmers when the Wall Street stock-market crash set off the depression of the early thirties.

What is the record on price control in this war period in comparison to the war of twenty-five years ago? What about production, profits, and income? Can inflation really be controlled?

During the First World War we had only moderate controls over prices and rents. As a result while production increased only slightly—on our farms the increase was only 5 per cent—prices and rents skyrocketed and eventually we were faced with a terrific collapse.

During this war prices and rents have been held more nearly in line, particularly during the last three years. During the war years, the cost of living has risen less than one third as much as during the World War I inflation that reached its peak in 1920. Since spring of 1943, the increase has been held to less than 4 per cent. And today industrial prices stand only about 4 per cent above where they were in May 1943. To those lobbyists who say that full production under price control is impossible, let me emphasize that it was in this same period that the records of production in our factories and on our farms have reached their greatest heights.

We have produced more in the price-control years than ever before in our history. More than that, each group has enjoyed greater prosperity. Our weekly earnings of factory workers have increased 86.2 per cent since 1939. Business profits before taxes were nearly five times as large in 1945 as before the war, and bankruptcies fell to the all-time low of 810—fewer than in any single month of the booming twenties. Our farmers as a whole are also better off than in any period in our history. The actual increase since 1939 in net operating income per farm is slightly over 300 per cent.

This, however, is a dangerously misleading figure because it fails to take account of the shockingly low incomes which our farmers had in the prewar years. An increase in income from $400 to $1,200 looks impressive to the statistician. But you and your family are only too well aware that $1,200 is still a long way from actual riches.

Since V-J Day various mistakes have been made in the handling of the economic stabilization program. In the first place, we moved far too rapidly in removing controls over industrial production. It was proper, of course, to scrap the great majority of these controls following the end of the war with Japan. But clearly more of them should have been maintained to assist us in our efforts to increase our supply of clothing and building materials and other essential products.

We were expecting also a considerable drop in city employment. Some experts estimated that there would be at least 5,000,000 workers walking the streets in search of jobs by January 1st. As a result of a drop in industrial wages, the experts expected a sharp decline in farm income.

Instead, employment has held up. Reconversion, although delayed by labor-management difficulties, is well ahead of schedule. The take-home pay of our factory worker, while less today than on V-J Day in spite of many increases in the hourly rates, has dropped far less than was expected.

As a result our national purchasing power has been maintained at a high level, and because the supply of goods is necessarily far below our actual needs, the pressure for higher prices and rents has been almost overpowering.

Two weeks ago a new economic stabilization program covering wages as well as prices and rents was developed to meet the new situation that confronted us. I was asked to leave my post at OPA to direct this over-all program and to see that inflation is kept under tight control.

Clearly the task will not be an easy one. The next ninety days will determine our success or failure. Between now and the first of June, one of the most fateful decisions in the peacetime history of our nation will be reached. In that brief period the forces of greed will finally overcome us and inflation will be a rapidly growing fact, or the strength of the people will be reasserted and the stabilization program will be strengthened and maintained.

The crisis is an immediate one because it is between now and June that Congress must choose between a continuation of the price and rent control legislation beyond June 30 until June 30, 1947, or a disastrous inflation. Congress has the choice of eliminating this act completely and letting prices and rents go skyhigh, or modifying and weakening the act so that it is useless as a means of protecting you against the inflationary pressures; or frankly and firmly granting us the necessary powers to continue to hold the line as we have held it since May 1943.

Between now and June, Congress must also determine whether we are to continue to use subsidies to maintain food prices at roughly their present levels, or whether these subsidies are to be eliminated with a resulting sharp and dangerous rise in the cost of living for tens of millions of our people.

Between now and June, Congress must decide whether the Office of Price Administration, the Office of Civilian Production, and the Wage Stabilization Board are to receive sufficient funds to carry out their enormous responsibilities, or whether reduced appropriations are to be used as a cellar-door method to sabotage our efforts to fight off inflation.

Finally in the immediate future Congress must decide whether we shall move vigorously ahead to build the homes which millions of veterans are looking forward to at reasonable prices, or whether we shall continue to fumble with the housing crisis in the name of reaction and narrow selfish interests.

The next few weeks represent the Guadalcanal, the Okinawa, and the Stalingrad in our fight to maintain a stabilized economy. To lose this fight will mean disaster. To win it will pave the way to a future of sustained prosperity for all of us.

Day after day, the battle lines are being drawn with increasing sharpness. On the one side we have all the millions of inarticulate little people who have made our country great in the past and on whom its future depends. On their side are many leaders among our farmers, among our factory workers, and among our businessmen.

Opposed to them are some of the most irresponsible, reckless, greedy organizations in America. Let there be no question about whom I am talking. I am talking about the lobbyists of the National Association of Manufacturers. I am talking about the heads of the National Retail Dry Goods Association, with all the phony propaganda with which they seek to cash in on the apparel shortage. I am talking about some of the real estate lobbies, and your old friend the packers' lobby, and the textile lobby. I am talking about the dairy lobby.

I am talking about those lobbyists who haunt the Washington hotels and the halls of Congress and the governmental agencies, endlessly scheming and plotting to trade the interests of the great majority of our people for the narrow short-range profit of the groups which they represent. And finally, I am talking about those speculators in the commodity markets and those speculators in Wall Street who time and again have played the American public for suckers in their promise of speculative profits from stocks and securities, and who today are again irresponsibly whooping it up for inflation.

These people do not represent business. They do not represent the majority of our manufacturers, or our retailers, or our landlords, or textile operators, or dairymen, or our investors. They represent only themselves. But let's not underestimate their skill, their perseverance, or their reserves. They are out to eliminate or wreck the only controls which stand between our people and inflation. We are on the eve of a crisis which cannot be exaggerated. Between now and early June, we shall determine whether we are to have stable prices and stable rents; whether our savings and insurance policies are to be protected; whether our bonds are to be worth the money which we paid for them; or whether we are to start down the primrose path toward another inflation which will surely bring disaster to our economy and sweep away the life savings of tens of millions of our people.

During the coming months we shall also go a long way toward deciding the strength of our American democracy, for if the lobbyists and pressure groups can win this fight against the people, then our democracy indeed will have suffered a dangerous defeat.

A great deal depends in the next few weeks on our farmers. Every effort has been made and every effort will be made to embitter our farmers against the working people of our cities. Over and over again our farmers will be told that industrial workers and businessmen have been "getting theirs," and that now its their turn to get even. This is a demagogic and dangerous appeal.

As you listen to this particular siren song remember that farm income has been maintained since V-J Day only because there has been only a relatively moderate drop—roughly 5 per cent—in the total income of our city workers. Part of this has been due to the unexpected continuation of overtime work and part to the increases in wages that have already gone into effect. As the normal work-week becomes the rule, it will, of course, take increases in the hourly wage rate of many more of our factory workers to make up for the loss in take-home pay if we are to maintain demand for farm products and the income of our 6,000,000 farm families.

Most farmers dislike subsidies. Naturally, they would prefer the same amount of income as a result of a higher price. For this reason many farmers have told me, "I am highly in favor of price control. I want to see the price of farm machinery held down—farm fencing—building materials—apparel and housefurnishings. I am solidly behind you on that score. But I simply cannot go along with you on subsidies."

That is a natural viewpoint for farmers to take. But it has one basic fallacy, and that is the fact that without subsidies on food the stabilization of our economy is completely impossible. If subsidies were to be removed on July 1st when our present authorization runs out, food prices would promptly move upward 8 per cent.

Milk would increase at retail two cents a quart. Meat by from three to five cents a pound. Cheese by fourteen cents a pound. Butter by twelve cents. Bread by one cent. Most canned fruits and vegetables by one cent a can. This would be a severe blow to millions of families living in the cities on narrow incomes. It would bring about widespread demands for wage increases and very probably the collapse of our wage stabilization program. And let's not forget that would not add a single penny to the income of our farmers.

On the contrary, as wages moved higher, manufacturing costs would again move upward, and so would the prices of things you buy in the store. The increase in the cost of the products and services you buy would leave our farmers considerably worse off than they are today. This would lead to further demands all around and an increasing inflationary spiral which could have only one final disastrous result.

Let there be no mistake about it. Whether we like it or not, subsidies and effective price control are indivisible. Without one we cannot have the other. That is why I say that the attitude of our farmers will decide the success or failure of our efforts to control inflation. If our farmers will close their ears to the propaganda of some of their own leaders and to the voice of the National Manufacturers Association and other groups which have subtly tried to drive a wedge between them and the other working groups; if our farmers will lend us their support and backing along with all the tens of millions of people in our cities, then there can be only one result between now and June, and that is a resounding people's victory over the forces of inflation.

Clearly, this victory over inflation is essential if we are to achieve the kind of future toward which every thinking person is hoping and praying. It is essential if we are to maintain the high purchasing power on which the prosperity of all of us depends. Throughout the war and particularly since V-J Day our farmers have learned the extent to which their own incomes are dependent on the purchasing power of our city people. The most effective over-all program for farm prosperity is a program that brings prosperity to all of our people and keeps all our millions of workers employed at good wages.

In the period which lies ahead, however, we must take additional steps designed specifically to help the 6,000,000 families who live on our farms. We must continue to push vigorously ahead with our program of rural electrification. We must move ahead in the field of crop insurance so that the farmers may have the same protection that businesmen and industrial workers have long enjoyed against mishaps beyond their control. We must develop long-range programs on all basic feeds to give us stability of supply and price. We must develop a program for the South which will raise the income of southern farmers as well as southern workers, a program which will take specific notice of the problem of cotton, the need for diversification of farming, and increased farm mechanization. We must move ahead vigorously in providing grants for rural schools, roads, housing, and health projects.

There will be opposition to many of the programs which are developed in the long-range interest of the farmer. But the farmer's fight for a more prosperous future is a fight which belongs to all of our people. The 25,000,000 men, women, and children on our American farms represent our greatest undeveloped market. Intelligent businessmen and city workers realize this. They know that until our farmers receive their just share of our national income that there can be no broad sustained prosperity for the rest of us.

Together—businessmen, farmers, and workers—we can and must move ahead to greater and greater heights of achievement. Working together as we worked together to win this greatest of all wars, we cannot fail.

Today the whole world is looking toward America. What we do or fail to do in providing additional food for Europe, India, China, and other areas faced with malnutrition and starvation will mean life or death to tens of millions of people in the immediate future. What we do or fail to do here at home in our fight against inflation, in our efforts to develop a sustained full-production, full-employment economy will have repercussions for good or for evil in every corner of the globe for generations to come.

Will we move ahead under a vigorous democracy to greater and greater heights of production? Will we move ahead to higher incomes for all of us, toward the elimination of slums, disease, ignorance, and ill health? Or shall we embark on an inflationary joy ride to disaster, with the spectacle of some strange new American fascism arising out of the bitterness and the disillusionment which will surely result? What will our American answer be to this gravest of all questions which ever faced our nation during peacetime?

Will it be the answer of the NAM which has fought on the wrong side of every public question for the last thirty years? Will it be the answer of the pressure groups, the answer of organized greed?

Or will it be the voice of the everyday people of America, clear, strong, determined, confident—with their heads held high, and their eyes firmly fixed upon a future that for generations to come means the difference between hope and despair not only for 140,000,000 Americans but for all the people everywhere throughout the world?

PRICE CONTROL VETO [8]

ROBERT A. TAFT [9]

Senator Robert Taft, of Ohio, delivered this talk over the National Broadcasting Network, on July 1, 1946. The speech was a direct reply to President Truman, who in a message to Congress on June 29, 1946, and in a broadcast to the nation on the same date had given his reasons for vetoing the Office of Price Administration legislation extending that agency for another year.

The President had objected especially to the Taft amendment to that law, which amendment would have given farmers and manufacturers opportunity to charge higher prices through a formula based on the rise of prices since 1941. Truman pronounced the formula a "bonanza" and a spur to inflation.

On June 30, Sunday night, over the radio, Taft charged that the President's rejection speech was a "personal attack" and that the President had "chosen to plunge the economy of this country into chaos." On the next evening, also over a national network, Taft, in the address here printed, continued his rebuttal.

The student, with the Truman messages before him, will note especially the modes of Taft's refutation, including the citation of counter-evidence and argument.

Taft, in this talk, avoided rhetorical embellishments; he relied for persuasion mainly on his facts. The Ohio Senator was generally recognized as the Republican leader in the Senate at this time. He was heavily scored for his "conservatism." In the thick of many a debate, he impressed by his energy, his rapid, somewhat aggressive delivery, and by his wealth of information. He was a thorough student of intricate Senate problems, and often dominated by his superior grasp of issues and of the relevant facts.[10]

Last night I pointed out that the President was trying to make a political issue out of the OPA by a personal attack on me, because I introduced one of the amendments to the bill which he disapproves. I pointed out that the bill was passed by a Democratic Congress and its signature urged by the Demo-

[8] By permission of Senator Taft. Text was furnished by the Senator.

[9] For biographical note see Appendix.

[10] For further comment on Senator Taft, see *Representative American Speeches: 1938-1939*, p. 119, ff.

cratic leaders in Congress. I pointed out that the President's veto has brought chaos to American business, already discouraged and confused.

Tonight I wish to discuss the whole price control question on which Congress has been working for five months before reaching the conclusions set forth in the bill vetoed by the President. Price control was enacted in 1942 as a war measure. It was made necessary by the tremendous deficit of the Federal Government. It was impossible to avoid serious inflation when the Federal Government was spending fifty billion dollars a year more than it took in through taxes. Price control can do something, and in my opinion it was necessary. I helped draft the bill and supported the various extension resolutions.

Price control was reasonably effective during the war. The general increase in the cost of living from January 1, 1941 until V-J Day was about 33 per cent if we disregard black market prices. Wage control was not so successful. Average hourly wage rates of factory workers went up about 62 per cent, and farm and mine labor went up correspondingly. Since there was no increase in the productivity of workers, this means that labor costs of employers increased by 60 per cent. This fact did not affect most of the larger companies with war business. A few companies were put out of business but they could only be re-garded as casualties of the war.

But when the war came to an end the situation grew rapidly worse. Just after V-J Day, the President removed all semblance of wage controls. Then he encouraged and approved the demand for a further 20 per cent increase in hourly wage rates. This may well have been deserved in some industries, but it has set a pattern which extends to all kinds of wage costs. The President and the OPA encouraged the extraordinary theory that wages could be increased without increasing prices; in other words, all workers were to get something for nothing, a nice theory for politicians but a difficult thing to bring about in this world. Of course, it promptly became evident that the President was wrong. Price increases had to be granted to obtain any produc-tion at all. He had to grant five dollars a ton increase in steel, which increased the cost of materials for many other manufacturers who also had the increased labor cost. The ultimate result is shown clearly by the coal settlement. The President granted the United Mine Workers an equivalent of 23 cents an hour increase, and the government then promptly raised the price of coal by 40½ cents a ton for bituminous and 91 cents a ton for anthracite, which increases the cost of living of every family and the cost of manufacture for every other product. And this is the man who preaches about stabilization and the danger of inflation! The big labor unions and the big companies got what they wanted, but the little business man waits around on the OPA doorstep for weeks while his increased costs eat up his working capital and destroy his business. Since March first, over five hundred different increases have been granted, many of them, however, too little and too late. Since wages constitute 70 per cent of the national income and of the cost of most products, the President's claim was always ridiculous.

As a matter of fact, price control is impossible once wage control is completely abandoned. For a while you can hold prices down to the increased costs and prevent speculative rises. Even if we now continue OPA for a year, I doubt very much if we can avoid a complete breakdown before January 1, 1947. I think we should continue OPA simply to prevent the speculative rises, but we might as well recognize that it is coming to an end and that in the meantime costs must be reflected in prices.

There is already plenty of evidence that OPA has completely broken down in many fields. Before June 15th, although slaughter of cattle was up to normal, only 20 per cent of the meat moved in legitimate channels. The other 80 per cent was all black market and OPA did nothing about it. Probably nothing could be done. Every legitimate lumber yard is empty and yet lots of lumber is being carried around on trucks and sold at black market prices. There is no butter and little bread and cheese in the market today. Farmers are selling their dairy herds and getting rid of their poultry. Night before last the President said the price of automobiles under the bill he vetoed would have gone up $250. Yet almost anyone can buy an automobile in the black market by paying a $400 premium. The general effect is that legitimate dealers in many fields are being put out of business while black market racketeers flourish.

That is an example of the administration of the OPA which takes the position that its powers must be continued without the slightest change, and that Congress must in no way try to improve the situation by introducing some practical sense into the theories of the brain trusters who dictated the policy.

The OPA has been primarily concerned with regulating profit instead of prices. The administrator required many products to be sold at a loss or at cost and, of course, there is no production of those products. They have been interested in controlling profits instead of controlling prices. They have fixed the price so low that only the largest manufacturers could operate, and forced every small manufacturer to come down on bended knees and ask for special prices for his own output. The reason that there have been no white shirts, no standard garments, no butter, no cheese, is that they could not be made at the ceiling prices.

I receive almost constant complaints against the Enforcement Division of OPA. Small grocers and other retailers have been dragged before Price Panels and forced to pay illegal fines on the threat of more serious prosecution. At the same time racketeers have run riot with little interference. Prosecutions have been filed often for purposes of publicity against reputable concerns for technical violations, and then been dropped or settled with no publicity at all. Applicants for relief in Washington have had to wait for weeks and months before final action.

As a result of this breakdown and confusion there are many members of Congress who sincerely believe that OPA should be completely abolished at once. Admitting that there ought to be some price control in theory, they say that no price control at all is better than the mess we have. My purpose throughout the Committee hearings has been to continue OPA, but force some reforms in their practices to eliminate the worst features that exist today. I think this met with general approval from Congress, except those who wanted to abolish OPA altogether. Senator Barkley himself introduced an amendment, with OPA approval, I think, providing that price control should be liquidated as rapidly as possible, product by product, and OPA abolished on July 1, 1947. The only question is how fast this should be done. There is no difference of principle. Only one of timing. The Senate adopted an amendment providing for the immediate decontrol of meat, dairy products and poultry. It seemed to me that there was no solution for the present scandal in the meat situation except to take off controls. I think the price of meat would actually be lower than it is today in the black market, and there would be meat to buy. But when this amendment was dropped in Conference, I urged the adoption of the bill leaving this meat decontrol to the discretion of the Secretary of Agriculture. It was not an easy job to get the Senate to agree to the bill without specific decontrol of meat, dairy products and poultry.

The President says that the Taft amendment will bring about inflation. As a matter of fact, inflation has already been brought about by his own policy of abandoning wage control. His reference to the Wage Stabilization Board is ridiculous, because the control of wages by that Board is a farce. Any employer can pay whatever wages he wishes to pay. If the Wage Stabilization Board does not approve the wages, the employer is not given credit for the increase in his costs, but if he is an important employer and the union is an important union, particularly a CIO union which is on strike, any increase is promptly approved. It is ridiculous for the President to claim credit for preventing inflation when he has abandoned all wage control. It is equally ridiculous for him to talk about preventing inflation when he has recommended every possible project for government spending and we look forward during the next twelve months to a deficit of about $6 billion.

The President spent most of his message in attacking the Taft amendment, but his attack was utterly unfair. All that the Taft amendment provides is that producers, including farmers and manufacturers, shall be allowed to charge prices which reflect the increased cost of labor and material which they now have to pay. This is done by permitting them to charge for each major product a price equal to their 1941 prices plus the average increase in the cost of labor, materials, et cetera, since 1941. After all, this is peacetime again. Why shouldn't the producer be placed in the same position he was in before the war? There is no question of a freeze any more, because the OPA itself has put over five hundred price increases into effect since March 1st. All we want to prevent during the next six months are the speculative rises in price over and above the increase in costs. The danger I am concerned about is taking the roof off, as the President does by his veto. But how can anyone hope to get production if we don't allow the producers to charge enough for their products to pay for the increased cost of labor and material? Even the President admits in his message that this principle has a "superficial" reasonableness. There is nothing superficial about it except to the master minds among the New Deal economists at the OPA.

As a matter of fact, there is nothing new in the principle. The original Price Control Act expressly provided that the Administrator should start with the prices prevailing between October 1st and October 15, 1941, and should make adjustments for general increases in costs of production, distribution, and transportation, among other factors. The language was pretty general, and the OPA never paid any attention to it. Then, in 1945, we passed a law which expressly provided that "modification shall be made in maximum prices established for any agricultural commodity and for commodities processed or manufactured from any agricultural commodity, and that means nearly all food and clothing in any case where, by reason of increased labor or other costs incurred since January 1, 1941, the maximum prices so established will not reflect such increased costs." As usual the OPA didn't pay much attention to Congress, but they did use almost exactly the formula of the Taft amendment in pricing canned vegetables in 1944 and 1945. Futhermore, the so-called Bankhead amendment for several years has compelled them to follow more or less the same formula as to all cotton textiles.

In many fields, however, the OPA has by express regulation, forced manufacturers to sell some products at cost or at a loss, because some members of the industry were making profits on other products. Of course, nobody makes the things which have to be sold at a loss. This is the reason for the shortage of butter, of many standard types of clothing, of building materials and many other articles. The President's figures on possible increases are wild guesses and for the most part dead wrong. I was called by the Association of Washing Machine Manufacturers who said that the President's estimate of one-third more for washing machines was a gross exaggeration, that the manufacturers hoped there would be no price increase at all, even if price ceilings were removed entirely. Any steel increase would be less than half that stated by the President. You can judge from this how accurate his other figures are. Any increase in manufactured goods brought about by the Taft amendment would be of minor importance compared with the importance of actually being able to buy them.

Furthermore, the President deliberately misrepresented the effect of my amendment when he said six times that price increases would result "immediately" or "right away." Under the amendment no increase can occur until the Industry Advisory Committee has presented complete figures to prove its case. This would take from 30 to 60 days. Then the Price Administrator is given 60 days in which to examine the figures and fix the amount of the increase. The burden of proof is on the industry. If the Administrator refuses to admit any increases, there is an appeal to the Emergency Court of Appeals, which would take several months more. Long before that, I hope we would be well on the way to the end of all price control. I hope the Administrator would act more promptly, but there is nothing immediate about it. Whereas the President's veto removed all controls of every kind at midnight last night.

It is significant that the President admits that the Taft amendment would have no direct effect on food or rents. But his veto ends food and rent control altogether. He argues that because other prices would go up, food and rents would be bound to rise. I admit that ultimately there would be some effect if other prices rise, but the effect would be about one tenth of the effect on food and rents of the wage increases stimulated by the President. Long before there is any substantial effect on food and rents from the Taft amendment, price control will have come to an end. But the ultimate and unavoidable breakdown of price control will result directly from the President's policy, not from act of Congress—certainly not from the minor requirement that manufacturers be allowed to reflect their increased costs in prices.

One of the President's arguments against the Taft amendment is that the margin between costs and prices was unduly wide in 1941. There is no evidence that this is true. The Bureau of Labor Statistics shows that the cost of living had increased 10 per cent from the 1939 average to October 1941. Straight-time hourly earnings had increased over 17 per cent during the same period, so there is really no evidence that there was any wide margin in October 1941. I picked out the date because it is the date fixed by the original Price Control Act as the base period from which the Price Administrator has always been required to begin. True, he has not paid much more attention to that than to any other part of the law. If he would prefer 1940, that would be just as satisfactory.

I might say here that the Committee has had no help whatever from Mr. Bowles or Mr. Porter at any time. They denounced every effort to improve the administration of OPA as a crippling amendment. They fought every proposal made. They denounced Congress in the press and over the radio. They were unwilling to abandon one iota of their power, or modify in any way the policy by which they tried to make businessmen absorb the increased costs of wages and materials. I have no special pride in the form of the Taft amendment. I only insist that if we are going to get production, we must permit the price of each product to reflect the increased costs of wages and materials.

The President argues that there is now a greater volume of business, and, therefore, businessmen should accept a lower margin over cost. Of course this argument is wholly fallacious. Perhaps some industries as a whole have a larger volume. Others do not. Perhaps the big companies have a larger volume, but there may be many smaller concerns, particularly people just starting in business, who do not have a larger volume. We have to fix prices, not for the larger companies, but at a level which will encourage small business to continue in business, and which will encourage new men to go into business.

Why on earth in peacetime should we try to hold business margins down below where they were before the war? If men could survive in a competitive industry then, they ought to be able to do so now. This bill restores price control as it was originally planned. Incidentally, the price of many products will be held below the maximum price by competition and this will be an increasing force as production increases. The Taft amendment guarantees no man a profit.

It is claimed that OPA will have a difficult time to enforce the formula of the amendment. Anyone who has studied the kind of formulas the OPA has used, anyone who reads their complicated price regulations, will realize that nothing could be more complicated than the existing theoretical abstractions of the present brain trusts in OPA.

The amendment leaves the final determination of cost to OPA and puts the burden of proof on the Industry Committee. If it isn't met, there is no increase. Furthermore, the application of the formula can only be demanded by the Industry Advisory Committee. It will, therefore, be possible in most cases for the Price Administrator to reach an agreement with the Industry Committee on some figures which approximates the increase in cost. In nine cases out of ten the Advisory Committee would be willing to compromise to secure prompt action.

As a matter of fact, the objection to the Taft amendment is a smoke screen. The President was determined to veto the bill to please the PAC, and if it had not been my amendment it would have been another amendment. He objects to the decontrol formula requiring products to be decontrolled when the supply equals the demand, the simple formula laid down by Congress. We tried in vain to get Mr. Porter to say that he would decontrol petroleum though the supplies are backing up today because they are greater than peacetime demand. It is evident that neither Mr. Porter or the President intends any decontrol at all. The President objects to the stopping of subsidies on April 1, 1947. He objects to any formula which takes away from him the power to fix prices as he pleases. Those are his real objections to the bill.

In short, in the Act passed by Congress, the President received complete power to prevent speculation and speculative increases in price and all increases in rents. We merely reaffirm more vigorously the original principles of the Price Control Act. Yet, he has chosen to plunge the economy of this country into chaos. In such a controversial field where feelings already run high, we cannot hope that the Senate will act without debate, and it should not do so, because the issues to be settled are vital to the welfare of the country. I hope price control will be continued, and I should vote to reenact the bill he has vetoed; but I am afraid the bill which the President will get the next time, if he gets any, may go further towards decontrol than the one he has vetoed. In the meantime there are no price controls. No businessman knows what he should do or what price he should charge. I hope that everyone will exercise the reasonable restraint which Americans always exhibit in a crisis.

The President had a choice between a reasonable transition from price control back to the free enterprise system on the one hand, and the ending of all OPA powers by veto. He chose to take all the chances of chaos, followed by speculative rises in price. He chose this course having been warned by his own Democratic leaders of the necessary result of his policy. He has repudiated their leadership and assumed to write a law for Congress, although the Constitution of the United States gives the Congress power to state the conditions on which price control shall be continued.

MANAGEMENT AND LABOR

SHOULD INDUSTRY GRANT LABOR'S DEMANDS? [1]

George V. Denny, Jr., Walter Reuther, and George P. Romney [2]

This debate was presented on Thursday evening, October 11, 1945, as one of the regular Town Hall programs and was held in the Town Hall, New York. It was broadcast over the network of the American Broadcasting Company. The moderator was George V. Denny, Jr., founder of America's Town Hall Meeting of the Air.

These programs have been given continuously since May 30, 1935. More than five million usually listen. The series has provided a striking demonstration of the working of American democracy. The supporters of the American principles of the free discussion of crucial national and international problems have observed with much satisfaction the success with which national leaders of varied opinions have expressed freely their points of views in this radio series. An important feature has been the question-and-answer period in which the audiences have participated.

Mr. Denny, in addition to his skill as moderator of these Town Hall debates and discussions, some of them turbulent, is an able platform lecturer. He has excellent vocal resonance, control of pitch, rate, and intensity, and good audience projection. His extempore skill has enabled him to make appropriate audience adaptations of material and language. [3]

Mr. Reuther, as director of the General Motors Department of the United Automobile Workers, "red-haired, pint-sized, pale," has been a powerful leader of unionists in their demands, strikes, and threats of strikes. He led the negotiations attending the strike of 1945-46 in that industry. Under his direction, that stoppage, beginning November 21, 1945, continued until March 13, 1946, one of the longest and costliest strikes in the history of the United States. The wages were increased 18½ cents per hour. Reuther's followers hailed him as a highly successful leader of their cause. At the annual meeting of the United Auto-

[1] Reprinted from *Bulletin of America's Town Hall Meeting of the Air*, Vol. 11: No. 24, October 11, 1945. By permission of the speakers, by special arrangement with the Town Hall, Inc., and through the courtesy of the American Broadcasting Company.

[2] For biographical sketches see Appendix.

[3] See *Representative American Speeches: 1937-1938*, p. 52; *1938-1939*, p. 138; *1939-1940*, p. 233; *1940-1941*, p. 209.

mobile Workers, in March 1946, he was elected president. His ability to grapple with his opponents both through pamphlets and on the platform, together with his aggressive enunciation of policies within the councils of his union, stamps him as one of the outstanding speakers for labor.

Mr. Romney was educated at the University of Utah and at George Washington University. He travelled in Europe as a speaker for the Latter Day Saints, became a salesman for the Aluminum Company of America, and after 1939 was associated with the Automobile Manufacturers Association, first as Detroit manager and later as general manager. During the war he was also managing director of the Automobile Council for War Production. Like Mr. Reuther, he has been in constant demand as a speaker. On the platform, he is alive, quick in his responses, clear in articulation and persuasive through his voice and personality. On March 29, 1945, he appeared on America's Town Hall Meeting of the Air program, on the topic, "Why strikes in wartime?"

The material of the debate here printed is "dated," but the argumentative techniques, the analogies, analysis, refutation methods, furnish profitable study. Behind the specific issue of this management-labor controversy lie basic questions that, as new conditions arise, will continue to challenge the American public.[4]

MODERATOR DENNY: Good evening, neighbors. Have you got a dollar in your pocket? Well, of course, you have. Take it out and have a look at it, will you? You worked hard for that dollar, didn't you? I just want you to realize that everything we say here tonight has to do with the value of that dollar in terms of the things you want to buy, and your prospects for getting more or less of these dollars. In short, this discussion concerns you very much, indeed.

Our topic is "Should industry grant labor's demands for a 30 per cent wage increase?"' Walter Reuther says, "Yes." George Romney says, "No."

Mr. Reuther, vice president of the United Automobile Workers Union, CIO, is spearheading this movement in his union, and has stated the demands of his union in an open letter to Mr. Charles E. Wilson, president of General Motors, in which he states, "Our demand is made with the knowledge that it will not necessitate any price increases." And this, of course, is our main interest as members of the public.

Last week, Mr. Wilson replied to Mr. Reuther on this point, "Your demands are definitely inflationary and your union is re-

4 The limits of this volume prevent the reprinting of the "Questions, Please" from the audience, following the debate.

sponsible for trying to start an inflationary spiral of increasing wages, costs, and prices."

Mr. Reuther and his associates maintain that industry, in general, and the automobile industry, in particular, can make the wage increase out of profits, without raising the prices of cars. He arrives at the figure 30 per cent, as this represents the drop in the take-home pay anticipated by the reduction of the wartime 48-hour week to the normal 40-hour week.

Mr. Wilson disputes this claim on the basis of his analysis of the facts and concludes his letter to Mr. Reuther with the statement, "We reject your unreasonable demands."

There's one point, however, on which both Mr. Reuther and Mr. Wilson agree. That is, that this is more than an ordinary collective bargaining quarrel. It's a national problem. We are, therefore, fortunate in having with us this evening representatives of both sides of this important controversy who are competent to discuss the question specifically and in national terms.

Mr. Reuther, as vice president of his union, assigned especially to General Motors, has been in the forefront in negotiations which have attracted national attention for several years.

Mr. George Romney is general manager of the Automobile Manufacturers Association, and is, therefore, in a position to present the views of industry on this question.

Now we hear the side of the affirmative presented by Walter Reuther. Mr. Reuther.

MR. REUTHER: The basic issue before us tonight is one which transcends the interest of labor and management. It affects the welfare of Americans in every walk of life. A realistic and equitable solution to the problem of wages, prices, and profits is an economic "must" if we are to win the peace.

To debate this issue in America's Town Meeting of the Air is in the best American tradition. In the same tradition, our union has proposed to the General Motors Corporation that our wage demand for a 30 per cent increase be discussed in public negotiations. Unfortunately, the corporation has refused such public negotiations.

General Motors has stated that the question of wages, prices, and profits is not the public's business. We believe that it is. We shall continue to urge the Corporation to agree to public negotiations. When both parties put all their cards on the table, the public can then judge who is acting in the public interest.

Our 30 per cent demand is not a wage demand in the ordinary sense. We are fighting to restore the purchasing power of workers whose take-home pay has already been cut 30 per cent or more.

The challenge this country faces in peace is how are we to put purchasing power into the hands of the people so they can consume in abundance the things we know how to produce.

Our fight for greater purchasing power requires that prices must not be increased. To get increased wages out of higher prices is robbing Peter to pay Paul.

We have told General Motors that the facts prove that they can pay us 30 per cent higher wages without increasing prices one cent. It is on the basis of these facts that we make our demand.

Production is not our problem. Our problem in this country is consumption. In 1929, we got into trouble because we had a 12-cylinder Cadillac production economy, with a Model-T distribution system. In cities, millions of workers went hungry while farmers lost their farms.

We didn't have overproduction. People simply didn't have the money to buy the things they needed. The old Model-T distribution system just couldn't keep up with the Cadillac production machine.

Now we have a B-29 production machine backed up by all the potential power of atomic research. If we got into trouble in '29 because the old Model-T wouldn't keep up with the Cadillac, it is just A-B-C economics to know that we are heading for more serious trouble unless we develop a B-29 distribution system to keep up with our B-29 production machine.

Judge Vinson, now Secretary of the Treasury, recently said, "The American people are in the pleasant predicament of having to learn to live 50 per cent better than they ever lived before." That is pleasant, all right, but it is not a predicament. All we have to do is to use common sense and get our distribution know-how in balance with our production know-how. During the war, Uncle Sam, the ninety billion dollar customer, kept the wheels of industry going. His place must now be filled by putting purchasing power into the pockets of farmers, workers, white-collared, and professional groups. If private industry is to survive in America, it must provide that purchasing power through higher wages.

In 1918, we won the war on the battlefield abroad, but we lost the peace on the economic front at home. It can happen again, unless we demonstrate the courage and the unity of purpose in peace as in war.

The challenge of peace demands that we have an economy of full employment, full production, and full consumption. Our fighting men must not again come home to sell apples on our street corners.

The question of higher wages is a question of fact. Name-calling will not solve our problem. It cannot be settled by full page propaganda ads, by General Motors and other corporations. It must be settled on the basis of sound, economic facts.

Here are a few of those facts: The total profits of U. S. corporations in 1944 were 25 billion dollars, or five and one-half times their average prewar profits. The tremendous profits made during the war prove that wages can be raised without increasing prices, when maximum production is maintained.

In 1940, we had high profits in industry; '43 was even better. If we had taken only the increase in profits from 1940 to 1943, and had given it to the workers in the form of a wage increase, every U. S. industrial worker could have had a 30 per cent wage increase without increasing prices. Think of it—30 per cent wage increase—no increase in prices, and a high-time 1940 profit for American industry.

Mr. Romney knows that in 1941, the last year of automotive production, General Motors made a profit of $510,000,000 before taxes. He also knows that between 1935 and 1941 General Motors earned, after taxes, mind you, a total return of 124 per cent on the stockholder's investment.

I am certain that millions of farmers and small businessmen would be pleased to realize a return of 124 per cent on their investment in a period of seven years.

Conservative business journals are already predicting the highest profits in history for 1946. The key to these higher profits is greater volume.

Here is an example of what increased production did for General Motors between 1935 and 1941. Wages went up 37 per cent, prices up only 16 per cent, but profits jumped 84 per cent. Why? This was because production increased 21 per cent.

Greater volume is the answer to our problem of raising wages without increasing prices. A 21 per cent increase in production enabled General Motors to increase wages more than twice as much as prices and still make 84 per cent greater profits.

In 1941, GM produced two and a half million cars, and yet for every dollar they paid out in wages, they made more than a dollar in profits. Profits in 1941 were high enough to have given every GM worker a 30 per cent wage increase without increasing the cost of the car one penny, and still the corporation would have made $235,000,000 in profits—all this, mind you, because of 21 per cent increase in volume.

Now, here's the payoff. General Motors has stated publicly that they expect their volume of production to increase 50 per cent over 1941. The tremendous economies and reduced unit cost of production which will flow from this 50 per cent increase in volume, will enable GM to grant our 30 per cent increase, maintain '42 prices, and still make a substantial profit.

We know that this larger purchasing power we are talking about must represent a larger volume of goods and services. We aren't kidding ourselves. We want wages to buy things. We want to buy the things all the rest of you make and we want you to buy the cars we make.

Another important factor enabling industry to raise wages without increasing prices is the tremendous increase of labor productivity because of improved technology.

Here are two examples taken from GM's own report: "At Buick, a newly designed electric welding machine makes it possible to speed up welding of crankshaft balances from three to thirty-six per hour." Another example: "New multiple drill performs fourteen lapping operations previously done by a single machine."

These examples multiplied a thousandfold, give you an idea of the march of the machine. Time will not permit to go into all the details on the ability of the auto industry to give us a 30 per cent increase without raising prices. But you are entitled to all the facts, because it affects your welfare. That is why we say that General Motors should agree to public negotiations. We want the press and the radio there so that they can get the facts and pass them on to you.

It is understandable that the public is alarmed at growing reports of labor unrest. But the answer to labor-management relations cannot be found in screaming headlines and hysterical editorials.

This problem must be solved by removing the basic causes of unrest. American labor won the battle for production in war. It wants to do the same in peace.

Management must learn that human engineering is just as important as production engineering. Working conferences of labor and management should be called immediately in every basic industry to discuss a realistic wage program including industry-wide wage agreements based upon equal pay for equal work, and a guaranteed annual wage.

These conferences would need to develop a new concept of wages, suited to the age in which we live. Wages that are fixed arbitrarily, either by management or by labor, will not work. Wages must flow from our true productive potential and must reflect our ever increasing ability to create wealth.

In August, 1940, we proposed the conversion of the auto industry to war production. These gentlemen who now say we can't raise wages without increasing prices said then that we could not convert the auto industry to war production.

We did convert the auto industry to war production because we had a war to win. We can raise wages without increasing prices because we've got a peace to win. (Applause.)

MODERATOR DENNY: Thank you, Walter Reuther. Now for the viewpoint of industry we hear from the extremely able general manager of the Automobile Manufacturer's Association, Mr. George Romney. Mr. Romney. (Applause.)

MR. ROMNEY: I thought our subject tonight was "should industry grant labor's 30 per cent wage demands?" But apparently that just means General Motors.

I'm here because this demand should be settled on the basis of public interest. Now, yesterday Detroit won the baseball World Series. However, the gravest and most momentous series of all times which started for America on December 7, 1941, is not over. Whether we will win or lose has not been determined. We lost the one that ended in 1918 because after winning the first two contests we failed to win the last two.

To win the world series of which I am speaking a team must win four straight: First, the race of conversion and war production; second, the battle of military supremacy. For the second time we have won these two struggles. We must still win the third of reconversion and transition to a peacetime economy, and the fourth and decisive battle of higher living standard for all peoples and permanent world peace.

Fantastic as it would be in a baseball series, it is nevertheless true in our infinitely graver world series that key players on our team have made demands in the form of a ultimatum that they say must be met or they will stop play at the end of the fifth inning of the third contest.

Their demands are an immediate 30 per cent increase, or else. This is being demanded for all players on all teams in the industrial league independently of their merits or of the gate receipts.

Listen to these cost of living, wage, profit, and productivity facts. First, is the demand of Walter Reuther's union justified by increased living cost?

A majority of a special committee appointed by President Roosevelt reported in February of this year that living cost during the war had increased about 30 per cent. This cost of living study was made because unions insisted that a 45 per cent increase had occurred. Do you think a committee appointed by President Roosevelt would have differed with labor unless compelled to do so by the facts?

The public members of the National War Labor Board say that during the war average straight-time hourly wage rate, which they considered most comparable to the cost of living, increased 36.7 per cent. In addition, due to longer hours, take-home pay at these rates increased about 51 per cent. Where overtime has been completely eliminated, wage rates are still close to the average straight-time hourly wage rates which increased 36 per cent.

This means that the demand for 30 per cent increase, due to the elimination of overtime, is a demand that wages be increased greatly in excess of the 30 per cent increase in the cost of living.

Now, is this demand of Walter Reuther's union justified by increased productivity?

Listen! Because there was no car production, the usual technological advance, which normally increases productivity 2 to 3 per cent a year, was stopped. The job of our industry was to apply its previously developed mass production methods to the output of guns, tanks, and planes and both methods cited by Mr. Reuther were prewar methods applied to war production.

Each year until the 30's automobile companies produced cars more efficiently and more cheaply. Prices were reduced and wages increased. In other words, productivity increased.

However, since the middle 30's, the rate of increase in productivity has declined and prices have increased. This alarming situation developed before the war. It resulted primarily from shortsighted auto union policies which, according to the Senate testimony of its own president in 1940, had decreased the industry's productivity between 5 and 10 per cent.

Last spring, five years later, union, government, and industry witnesses told the Senate Mead Committee that automotive production efficiency on war work was from 15 to 50 per cent below the production efficiency that prevailed in peacetime.

In other words, productivity in the automotive industry declined during the war. It did not increase above peacetime levels.

What are the prospects for the future? A few vehicle and parts companies have resumed their peacetime production. What has their experience been in terms of productivity?

An automobile company sustained a four-day strike when it refused paint-spray men 20 minutes relief time an hour instead of 15 minutes, because they were doing less than two-thirds as much work as before the war.

In a parts plant where 385 pieces were made each day before the war, the company had a strike over union demands to reduce production below 350 pieces per day.

A foundry in Cleveland is using 25 per cent more men than before the war to get prewar production.

A tool company's new methods and equipment were supposed to raise productivity almost 50 per cent, but nothwithstanding these improvements efficiency is 15 per cent lower than before.

A truck company out West states its productivity is 25 per cent below prewar levels.

The story is the same whether you talk to production men in Detroit, Chicago, Milwaukee, Cleveland, or eastern cities. Company size makes no difference. Employers with 100,000 workers and those with only two dozen men give the same answers.

Under these circumstances, how can a 30 per cent wage increase be granted in anticipation of greater productivity?

It is Walter Reuther's position that the 30 per cent wage demand can be met without charging the public more for automobiles.

Listen to these facts—all broken down to a man-hour basis so that everyone can understand them:

The average basic hourly wage rate in the automobile industry is about $1.15 an hour. The 30 per cent increase would be 35 cents an hour. In the biggest wartime production year, 1944, car companies paid taxes of 25 cents for each man-hour worked and about nine cents to stockholders, making a total of 34 cents. But these funds have been spent.

All other wartime earnings were earmarked for reconversion and expansion. If the total amount of these funds for 1942, 1943, and 1944 were still available, which of course they are not, they would only amount to 25 cents per hour for a twelve-month period.

At the present time, every automobile company is losing money and is willing to continue to do so until production has reached volume proportions. The 35-cent wage increase in our industry simply cannot be paid out of current profits. There aren't any.

Perhaps Mr. Reuther wishes to divert into wages money to be used to maintain and add to the tools of production. If so, he is betraying his own members. A farmer can feed his hogs his seed corn and the goose that lays the golden egg can be eaten, but then there will be no more corn and no more golden eggs.

This wage demand attacks the public interest. Farmers, professional workers, white collar workers, and foreign buyers constitute 70 per cent of the industry's customers. If this wage demand were granted, every American, as a customer, would have to pay it through higher prices.

Former warworkers cannot secure wage increases at the expense of other customers without disastrous results. This wage demand is inflationary. Americans have a potential inflationary spending power of 160 billion dollars. After World War I, it was an inflationary boom followed by a deflationary depression that lost that world series.

Under present conditions, improper wage policies could touch off an inflation that would make the last one look like child's play.

Automobile companies have always paid increasingly higher wages to match the increasing productivity of workers and will continue to do so as productivity increases.

But wages must be based on productivity. If 52 hours' pay for 40 hours' work would increase car sales, automobile companies would do it. If that's prosperity, why not 52 hours' pay for 10 hours' work. Then we could all get rich. But obviously we would all starve. It is equally obvious that only by constantly producing more can we get more.

Economics is like a beautiful song or a good story. If the singer is a little off key, or the storyteller gets the order of things mixed up, it spoils everything. Walter Reuther is famous for hatching plans. As usual, his latest—how to raise wages without raising prices—just get things a little mixed up. The automotive story is how to raise wages and reduce prices. The key argument of his plan is that to get production we must first increase purchasing power. Now, I can understand the dilemma about whether the hen or the egg came first, but I can't understand any doubt about whether production or purchasing power comes first. Every American knows that our pioneers in any part of the country, first had to produce before they could exchange or buy.

It is production that makes purchasing power not the other way around. Yes, and in the western desert areas where my people made the désert blossom as the rose, it was work—hard but satisfying—that wrought the transformation. This principle has not changed.

Americans must decide whether they want more idle time and job loafing, or are willing to work more efficiently and longer hours to achieve a rapidly increasing standard of living. If some are paid excess wages for work not performed, others are going to do without goods and services.

The irony of this situation is that unions are deliberately sabotaging their own future. The American consumer cannot be kicked around. Most people don't have to buy new cars, and at excessive prices, they won't. That would mean that Mr. Reuther's men would be out of a job.

Whether they like it or not, labor and management are on the same team and to win, they must please the All-American customer. As Walter Reuther said, according to the newspapers, his union does have the power to destroy industry but in doing so it would also destroy itself.

MODERATOR DENNY: Thank you, George Romney. It seems that management and labor are both fortunate in having such confident spokesmen. Now, will you two confident spokesmen come up here around the microphone and continue this discussion. I expect Walter Reuther has something to say on what George Romney just said. Mr. Reuther.

MR. REUTHER: Mr. Denny, you know I have heard Mr. Romney talk so much about baseball games here that I am very happy the Detroit Tigers won because if they had lost, it would have been because of our wage demand.

MR. DENNY: Well, he couldn't have been for the Cubs, Walter.

MR. REUTHER: I'd like to get this discussion down out of a realm of higher statistics and talk about people. After all, this war was fought to make a better place for just ordinary people to live in—give them security and a chance for their kids to grow up.

I'd like to talk about two people who work for General Motors. The first person is a veteran. His name is Oliver Ostrom. He works at the Oldsmobile plant in the city of Lansing. He's a veteran of this war—five and a half years in the armed services. He has a wife and two children. Before V-J Day he made $1.14 per hour and because he worked long hours his take home was $59.28.

After V-J Day because of cut-backs, his hours were reduced to 40 hours and he was downgraded to a $1.05 an hour job. He now gets $42.00 a week. If he gets the 30 per cent wage increase we're asking for, his wages would be increased to $1.36½ per hour. In 40 hours he would get $54. If you'd take out the 20 per cent social security, his insurance and all that, he would take home approximately $40.

Now get this, Mr. Wilson of General Motors and Mr. Romney speaking for the auto industry say, our demands are unreasonable. And yet, Mr. C. E. Wilson, the President of General Motors, who tells this veteran his demand is unreasonable, get more in ten minutes than this fellow would get in a whole week if he got a 30 per cent wage increase. Mr. Wilson makes more in eight hours—because he gets more than $200 an hour—than tens of thousands of automobile workers make in a whole year. Now who's unreasonable?

MR. ROMNEY: Well I think Hank Greenberg, going back to baseball, also gets a great deal more than a lot of other people. I'd like to take all these figures that Walter Reuther has cited here about GM and so on, but I'm not here for the purpose of negotiating their wage demand.

However, contrary to what Walter Reuther has said, GM has stated this demand is a public issue and, furthermore, they have insisted in the past that these wage negotiations, when they reached the point where they are to be decided by public authorities sitting in, must be held on a public basis.

Now let me just take the one figure that Walter Reuther cited in the course of his discussion to show you how mixed up he gets on these figures. I don't think he can really understand

a balance sheet and the figures that are put out. Now you take—
[*Confusion*]

MR. DENNY: Just a minute, I've got to attend to a gentleman over here. There's only one rule here at Town Hall—one person speaks at a time. Now if you have to speak, there's a door out there. Just be courteous to the gentleman on the platform. Will you please? Thank you.

MR. ROMNEY: Mr. Reuther said that in 1941, GM made over $1 profit for every $1 paid out in wages. Now the facts are that in order to arrive at that figure, he included the taxes paid by GM on all of its income. He also included the profit from corporations in which General Motors has stock holdings, such as North American Aviation and Bendix and their foreign countries. Then he divided the profits from all sources by the factory workers alone in the General Motors Corporation alone.

Now the facts are that, after you deduct taxes from that figure, it represents less than a fourth of the figure cited by Mr. Reuther. After all, we don't consider the sales tax paid when we go to Macy's as a part of the profit of Macy's. We know that the United States Government is using corporations and businesses to collect taxes and that's the case in this connection.

I think that if you consider the increase in wages that has occurred in the automobile industry—and they have increased there tremendously—that the automotive industry has brought about a productive system that has enabled it to pay the highest wages in industry. That is an accomplishment that indicates the extent to which the automotive industry is interested in the welfare of its workers.

MR. DENNY: Thank you. Now Mr. Reuther. Let's make it short this time.

MR. REUTHER: Mr. Denny, why should we argue about arithmetic? We think our figures are correct. Mr. Romney says his figures are correct. Why should we argue about it. Let's have a public hearing. We'll lay our figures on the table. Let General Motors bring in their books and open up their books. Let's find out what it costs to make an automobile, and how much profit there is in this business and then we'll see this arithmetic. I'd like to ask Mr. Romney whether he would recommend to the auto industry that they have such hearings and that the corporations open up their books for public scrutiny. Let's see what the arithmetic is in these books.

MR. ROMNEY: The automobile companies all make available facts on their profits, on their wages, on their productions. They make many more facts available with respect to their activities than the UAW does with respect to what it does with union dues.

UNITED MINE WORKERS DEMANDS [5]

JOHN L. LEWIS [5]

Mr. John L. Lewis, president of the United Mine Workers of America, gave this talk at the opening session of the National Joint Wage Conference of the bituminous coal industry at the Shoreham Hotel, Washington, D. C., on March 12, 1946.

On March 1st Mr. Lewis had filed a thirty-day strike notice. From the start of these negotiations, Mr. Lewis refused to discuss wages, even though these were a crucial issue. His chief demand was that the operators pay a "royalty," ten cents a ton, to a Union Security and Welfare Fund. A secondary issue was the union's demand for better safety regulations. Such was his strategy in the March 12th address. His tone was comparatively mild. The speech was even hailed as "conciliatory." At one point when Lewis recited the record of killed and injured in the coal mines, both miners and operators arose in a silent prayer of tribute.

Sixty days of intermittent negotiation followed Lewis' speech. He was the fiery orator and debater. On March 19th, throwing aside completely his restraint, he declared to the operators:

"By the record, the management and stockholders of the bituminous coal industry in a period of fourteen years have, through mismanagement, cupidity, stupidity and wanton neglect made dead 28,000 mine workers.

"By the record, in the same period the same management and stockholders have, for the same reasons, violently mangled, crushed and shattered the bodies of 1,400,000 mine workers.

"By the record, the industry does not bury its dead or bind up the shattered bones and the mangled flesh of its victims in any adequate, humane or modern sense.

"By the record, the management and the stockholders of the bituminous coal industry indulge in systematic and widespread financial exploitations of the families of the dead and practice commercial extortion upon the yet living victims of its industrial violence.

"By the record, the industry extorts annually from the pay envelope of the mine workers sixty millions of dollars for pseudo, hypothetical and substandard medical service, hospitalization and insurance of an actual value of less than one third of the aforesaid $60,000,000.

"We challenge on the record, refutation point by point. We demand abatement of this slaughter. We demand cessation of the accompanying extortion."

[5] Text from *United Mine Workers Journal*, v. 57:6ff., March 15, 1946. By permission of Mr. Lewis.
[6] For biographical note see Appendix.

On March 31, as the old contract expired, the miners "stayed home." For ten days negotiations continued until Lewis broke off further talk. Said he in a closing speech, "We trust that time, as it shrinks your purse, may modify your niggardly and antisocial propensities."

The country quickly felt the effect of the coal shortage. Great industrial areas subsided into lifelessness. The operations of steel, automobile, and railroads were badly crippled. On May 10th, a twelve-day truce began when the operators had agreed to make any subsequent contract retroactive. Later in the month the President seized the coal mines. Finally, after the railroad strike was settled, the bituminous miners and management resolved their differences.

Lewis got what he wanted in wage increases and an employer-subsidized welfare fund—administered, however, by both groups rather than exclusively by the miners. Thus did John L. Lewis emerge as the most colorful, aggressive, and successful of the union leaders. No small part of his dominating leadership lay in his power of debate and oratory.[7]

We meet again. We assemble after the conclusion of a great World War to negotiate, if possible, a new peacetime contract. The joint instrument which now governs the bituminous coal industry is an instrument negotiated during the travail of war. It was negotiated under the pressure of a demand for coal as the energy source of our civilization from all the peoples of the civilized world. It was negotiated at a time when, of all those countries, only the United States and its mining industry, its manpower, and its investitures in the coal industry were capable of producing a surplusage over domestic requirements and extending the usages of those millions of tons of coal to the people in such sore need in other countries.

Naturally, an instrument negotiated under those conditions needs modification and amendment when hostilities cease and peace comes. In every major sense the war is over. It is true there is yet armed conflict in some countries. It is true that internal revolution is developing in others. It is true that famine stalks the earth, and it is true after the war as well as during the war, only this great country of ours, this country of private enterprise and personal liberty on the part of its citizens, with freedom of contract as a part of our philosophy and the political structure of our government, can continue to have a surplus of

[7] For further comment on John L. Lewis as a speaker, see *Representative American Speeches: 1940-1941*, p. 113 ff.

this vital commodity that energizes the wheels of industry and the economy of the world.

So there devolves upon this conference a great responsibility. That is not a new responsibility, because many of us have appreciated through the years the importance of the coal industry and the importance of the service rendered by the coal miners of America, not only now to our own country, but to other struggling peoples. The coal industry has done a job during the war. That goes for the coal operators. That goes for the coal miners. None of our citizenship has rendered any greater service. Without the necessity of utilizing vast sums of money derived from taxation and taken from the public purse the coal industry, with its manpower deleted by hundreds of thousands of men, with restrictions placed upon it through the inadequacy of supplies, with the interruptions of production that came from causes for which the industry was not to blame, the coal industry supplied the nation and moved this excess tonnage to other countries. That feat and that accomplishment, unparalleled in economic history of this or any other country, has gone unsung. No medals have been handed out to the men in the coal industry, either for working or for dying—and many have died.

The coal miners have been little rewarded. They received no increase in wages as applied to their basic hourly rate since 1941. They were permitted to work more time, which they gladly did do. They were permitted to have pay for travel time which hitherto had been denied them, and the fact that they were permitted to work more days and more hours and receive pay for something they had been doing without pay was considered by many people of this country a great favor to coal miners.

I suppose that it is always true that the average man who wants to work more days or more hours in time of great demand can always increase the total amount of his weekly or monthly wages if he is strong enough and healthy enough and has time enough to work more hours and more days. The mine workers do not consider that opportunity much of a favor. The mine workers voluntarily lengthened their work day by one hour; they voluntarily lengthened their work week by one day, so that during the war and now in peacetime they are working underground nine hours per day, six days per week. Those are longer hours than exist in any other American industry of magnitude or importance. Those are longer hours than exist in the mining industry of any other country in the world, even in those countries where forced labor exists and where chattel slavery has returned and where prisoners of war are forced to work in the coal mines.

I wonder if that fact and those considerations will have any weight either upon employers in the industry or on the public at large in causing them to now give some consideration to a modification of this agreement, so that coal miners in America may be accorded the same treatment, the same privilege and the same opportunity here under our flag that is given to any other citizen. I would call it most unkind for any thoughtful person to disparage their motives before they had opportunity to present their suggestions, make known their objectives, and portray the character of the service which they render. We would like the opportunity to do that in this conference before judgment is rendered by the operators of the industry and before judgment is rendered by the American people. Surely a sense of fair play which animates the mind of every American should cause him to desire now, of all times, to give to the mine worker of this country his day in court and an opportunity to be accorded a just position in the internal economy of our great land.

During this war, production surpassed all records hitherto known. All credit to management, to our engineers, to our technicians in the industry, but give some credit to those hundreds of thousands of men who daily entered those mines and, as their strength permitted and as their health withstood the vicissitudes of the industry and the conditions under which they lived, gave day by day all they had to sustain our armed forces and to uphold our flag, come what may.

On February 1st, according to the records of the Department of the Interior, there was on hand a total of 46,313,000 tons of bituminous coal in storage above ground, most of it delivered to destination points of consumption. On the basis of consumption at that time that was an average of 28 days' supply, which was on

February 1st far above the average prewar amount of storage coal.

Production since January 1st has been well above an average of 12,000,000 tons per week—some weeks 12,500,000 tons, some weeks 12,600,000 tons, with one or two weeks falling below that figure. And yet the average exceeds the amount I mentioned. More than 2,000,000 tons for every working day; more than a quarter of a million tons for every productive hour; more than 4,000 tons for every productive minute. In one minute, as I speak here this afternoon, the production of bituminous coal in the United States will be approximately four and one-half thousand tons. There has never been such a production record achieved in industrial history.

Contrast that record with the production in the United Kingdom of Great Britain, which for decades past, next to our own country, has been the ranking producer of coal of all character. The average weekly production in Great Britain for January 1946, was 3,287,700 tons. To do that they used the services of 686,000 men. With 686,000 men they only produced in one week as much as we produce in American in one and one-half days with 400,000 men. Is that an accomplishment? I ask you. And yet that achievement goes unsung in the public press and in the councils of the operators, if you please, and in the sub-divisions of government it is totally unknown. They never heard of it, and some of them would not understand it if they heard it.

To achieve that production we killed in the coal mines outright an average of 1,981 men a year. We crushed and injured in a year an average of 66,968. We scrapped with silicosis, miners' asthma, chronic rheumatism, arthritis, blindness and scores of other occupational ailments additional thousands per year who do not even have the chance to be recorded and enrolled in these figures which I read to you. Coal is being produced at a rate hitherto deemed impossible, but at what a price in human agony, in human sorrow, in shortened lives, in the privation of opportunity on the part of countless human beings, victims of the unjust and the improper conditions under which they serve, who now come to this conference, through their representatives, and ask for fair treatment.

In addition to this production for home requirements we have been shipping abroad to the continent of Europe, independent of our Canadian and other exports of production, an average of 1,400,000 tons a month to allay the necessities that exist in stricken Europe. And that coal must continue to go, for the need is very great, and, next to the requirement for food, coal is an essential necessity among men and women in our time and in this day who expect to live and who hope that their children will also live.

But during the past year we have been working under an existing wartime agreement. We haven't been happy about it, because we do not think our contribution has been recognized either by the industry or by the public to the degree that should exist. We could have asked for a reopening of our agreement under its contractual clauses many months ago when the governmental policy changed. We could have joined the hue and cry at that time and added our weight to it, and perhaps our efforts would have been noticed had we chosen to do so. But, as a matter of sound, constructive policy the United Mine Workers chose not to exercise that right, and in so doing deprived their membership of advantages that might have accrued to them for many months, so that there would be no possible disturbance of coal production, so that confusion and cavil would not exist in the councils of the industry at a time when it might have seriously impeded the production of coal for our population and the countries abroad. So we waited to take this question up in the orderly way, after the winter is gone and after an adequate supply is above ground, after Europe has had its coal, and we come now to this conference asking for consideration, asking for tolerance, asking for recognition of the necessity of fair treatment for the men who make it possible for the stockholders of these coal companies to continue to draw their dividends and receive a return on their investment.

After all, it becomes a pertinent question some day, when does a stockholder begin to make his contribution to the maintenance of a stable economy? Does the stockholder have any responsibilities other than always drawing his dividends for reinvestment or other purposes, or is he, too, charged under the moral law of civilization with having some responsibility for his brother? Frankly, the United Mine Workers of America have been disturbed during the past year by the seeming lack of appreciation, even in the councils of our industry, on the part of the coal operators of the character of the service that is being rendered by their employes whom we have the honor to represent. The ink was hardly dry on the last contract before the coal operators got together and wrote what they called an interpretation of the contract and circularized it throughout the country to their constituent coal companies. That unilateral interpretation became the contract by the coal companies who received that document from the National Coal Association, and those ex parte and unilateral interpretations did much to impair the confidence of the mine workers in the coal operators. . . .

The conference should note that the mine workers propose the creation of a health and safety fund for mine workers. May I say that throughout the years since coal mining began in the United States a huge toll of life has been snuffed out annually as a result of inadequate safety provisions, lack of thorough mine inspection and proper ventilating facilities.

Wilful negligence in the enforcement even of inadequate safety laws in many states has repeatedly resulted in major disasters. The records available, dating from the year 1839 to 1945, reveal a total killed of 108,691. The foregoing figure is incomplete. Several of the leading coal producing states kept no record of the fatalities until 1900 or later.

The number killed from all causes annually, 1906 to 1945, averaged 1,981, which means that for every working day five men are killed outright; that on every second working day six men are killed outright and carried home from the mines, dead.

The average yearly number injured, 1930 to 1944, which is a fourteen-year period, is 66,968.

Permanent total, permanent partial and temporary disabilities, for the period 1930 to 1944, 1,004,524—more than twice the number of men employed in the industry. Statistically, every man was injured during that period twice, and he took his own statistical chances whether his injury was one that enabled him to return to work in a few days or a few weeks, or whether he was crippled for life and permanently incapacitated, with his back broken or his eyes shot out or his limbs gone. I submit that there is no industry in the world that paid that price in blood and bone and human flesh, in the lives of men and the tears of women, as our own bituminous coal industry.

Despite all efforts to achieve compensation legislation commensurate with the injuries and permanent disabilities, as well as outright death, today's payments are totally inadequate. There is not a single coal mining state that provides compensation payments adequate to maintain a widowed family or fairly compensate the injured.

Compensation laws are elective in 13 coal states and in the territory of Alaska, which in 1944 produced 456,778,000 tons, or approximately three fourths of the total national output. The 12 mining states in which compensation is compulsory produced 162,767,000 tons in 1944.

Ineffective compensation laws have aided in the perpetuation of the so-called company doctor system, a scourge foisted upon mine workers representing well over half the total annual production of coal. An investigation by the United Mine Workers covering 800 coal mines showed that this system prevails throughout Alabama, Kentucky, Tennessee, West Virginia and Virginia, all of which have elective compensation laws, as well as in certain districts of Pennsylvania and Ohio. Just recently the legislature of Kentucky, after the horror of the Straight Creek explosion, has now passed a compulsory act. Medical service under this system is mediocre and inadequate.

A company doctor does much more than treat the sick and injured. He acts as company representative in compensation cases. He is the company agent in insurance claims. He determines the physical fitness of job applicants.

The company selects a doctor of its own choosing. Although his salary is paid out of deductions from the miners' wages, the doctor works for the company, not the employes. A doctor thus selected testifies against workers in compensation cases where the company disputes the extent of an employe's injuries. He does the company's bidding in passing upon the physical fitness of job applicants.

In many cases doctors are hired with the distinct understanding that they will treat compensation cases free of charge. This set-up pays double dividends to the company:

1. It transfers to the miners, who pay the doctor's salary, the duty imposed upon the company by the Workmen's Compensation Law of paying for medical treatment of injured workers.

2. It enables the company to show low cost medical maintenance, thereby entitling it to a cut in its compensation rate.

During a slack season, when company income drops, it is not uncommon for the company doctor to recommend that a slightly injured employe be placed on insurance, paid for by the employe through the check-off, rather than on compensation, thus cutting down the company's compensation costs.

The group insurance prevails in the same states, including certain areas of Pennsylvania, as the company doctor system. This "protection" is also bought out of the miners' pocket, although the insurance contract is made with the coal company and the company has the supreme word in determining a claimant's eligibility. Insurance rates for coal miners are exorbitant.

Insurance companies admittedly increase their base rates for coal miners due to the nature and hazards of the industry. For non-occupational health and accident insurance they add on the average a flat 40 per cent to the base rates.

Under what is known as an experience rating system of adjusting cost of insurance premiums, earned rebates are paid to the coal company contracting for the insurance. But, although insurance companies maintain that as a general rule covered miners are given their share of the rebate, insurance companies have no jurisdiction to enforce division of the rebated funds among covered miners and they receive no report on the disposition of such rebate.

The mine workers' investigation disclosed further that in most districts miners participate in group hospitalization plans, but that the hospitals entering into these agreements are, for the most part, virtually inaccessible owing to their distance from the mine, ranging up to 160 miles; that they are understaffed; lacking in modern equipment and ambulance service. For the poor service provided them and their dependents by hospitalization insurance, miners pay an average of $1.95 monthly.

The overwhelming majority of local unions in the Southern districts maintain burial funds, supported through monthly wage deductions. The burial check-off averages $1.29 per month per miner.

In addition to what he pays into the burial fund and for hospitalization, the miner pays an average of $1.94 per month for medical service, and $2.56 for accident insurance. None of these fees, however, entitles him to dental care. In most instances he also must pay an additional fee for certain vaccines, special medicines, treatments such as X-ray and radium, house calls beyond prescribed limits. Delivery of his child costs him from $10 to $50, ambulance service from $10 to $30.

Base expenses for medical treatment, etc., average $7.74 per month. The extras bring the total average check-off per month up to an estimated $10.68 to $12.68.

The mine workers will want to present to this conference amplification of that statement showing the conditions as they exist in detail throughout the mining sections and showing that this system of medical attention is infamous from many standpoints, that it is a harsh, systematic, sordid, brutal exploitation of the mine worker, that he is the unhappy victim of this condition, and that his prayers to prolong his life and preserve the health of his family go unanswered because of his inability as an individual to rise above the grafting circumstances foisted upon him by this terrible scheme of exploitation, maintained through the years at a cost which is staggering.

The mine workers are asking an increase of wages and the lowering of their working hours. We say in our proposals that this question is a negotiable one, as are all other questions submitted by the mine workers. We expect them to stand or fall upon their merits, and if they will not stand an examination through the white light of cold logic they will fall. By the same token, if they withstand that test on examination by this joint conference, we hope and trust that you will grant them. That, however, is merely a hope.

Various statements have been made by the operators antecedent to this conference and anticipating this conference as to the cost of the coal and their reluctance to take any step that would increase that cost or lay the industry open to the ravages of competitive fuels. The industry is not suffering from the ravages of competitive fuels. It has not suffered from those ravages since before the World War. To read some of the statements of the operators you would believe that in 1944, when the country produced 620,000,000 tons of bituminous coal, millions of tons were displaced by competition of substitute fuels, yet that 620,-000,000 tons represented the greatest production in all history, the highest production ever attained by the industry, which was in World War I, being 585,000,000 tons.

The coal industry has a job to do as far as domestic consumption in this country is concerned. The industry has got to make its product available under conditions where greater convenience will accrue from its uses. But that is a constant, every day obligation and matter of consideration for the coal industry. When the industry becomes sufficiently hard pressed it will do it. As long as it is not imperative it probably won't be done. That is a constant task and is no question to be raised at this time as an argument as to why the mine worker should not have a reduction in his working hours and an increase in his wages.

On the question of price, public statements of the operators, renewed from time to time in advance of this conference, have been misleading to the public. I am quoting the labor cost, weighted, of bituminous coal produced during 1945 in the Appalachian area, with Illinois and Indiana added, based on cost figures reported by the operators to OPA for the second and third quarters and November 1945. The tonnage figures are from the Department of Interior production reports. This study covers 485,000,000 tons of production, and the labor cost which I will quote includes wages paid to mine management, clerical and supervisory forces, which average from 8 cents to 15 cents per ton. On that 485,000,000 tons, which is 84½ per cent of the annual production of bituminous coal, the labor cost per ton, loaded like it is with every conceivable item, including management, clerical and supervisory forces, is $1.79 decimal. In that cost is computed all the excess costs due from the long work day and the long work week in the form of time and a half for extra hours each day, time and a half for the sixth day and double time for Sunday. With the elimination of this overtime from the industry it now becomes possible, because the statistical condition of the industry will permit it as of April 1st, that there will be a vast saving in labor costs which will sharply reduce this average cost of $1.79 and will materially help in providing for a higher wage standard for the American coal miner.

The problem is not as difficult as some would believe or as the public is being asked to believe. In addition to that, the shorter hours and the shorter work week will bring a higher degree of efficiency and additional lowered unit costs as the expenditure of the strength of the men in the industry is compressed into a shorter period during the week.

A coal miner, upon the limited diet he has had during the war and now, with respect to many items of food, can only generate so much energy in a week. If you cause him to expend that energy over a period of six days he will still only expend so much energy. If you reduce his work week and reduce his daily hours he will expend that energy in an increased tempo of performance, a higher degree of skill, a more natural nervous reaction, and his efficiency will be increased and costs will be lowered. That is one reason why, in the history of the American mining industry, as the hours of labor were decreased from the ancient 12, 11, 10, 9 and 8 to the basic hours as we had them before the war, every decrease in hours resulted in a higher productivity of the men, a lowered unit cost, and added to the prosperity of the industry. Those things are elemental and known to everyone associated in the mining industry.

Of course there is a point as you go down in limiting the hours where the factor of diminishing returns will intervene, but we have not yet reached that point in our industry. Our industry needs these readjustments. Our men are tired and exhausted. both physically and in a nervous sense, from the long hours and the long weeks, and the nervous strain incident to a long war. Our young men were taken out of the mines and went into the armed forces, 140,000 of them. Many others of our men were absorbed into higher paying industries before our own industry could get around to the task of adjusting its wage structure and its working hours and its earnings opportunities. Our ranks are decreased, and the men are weary and they want relief, they want more food.

The record of Europe and other countries is that production increases as the food value available to the mine workers increases. It takes strong meat to keep a coal miner going, or his bodily vigor becomes impaired and his health is menaced, and we must care for him.

We have nearly 35,000 men in the industry now who are too old to continue working in this hazardous occupation. They want to retire and have their social security payments. Many of them came back into the mines when the war came on, in order to render what service they could in an attempt to replace the loss of some of the younger men. But they won't be in the industry long, they are going to leave, and the wastage of the industry is very great, and I say to the coal mining industry of this country we had better begin to treat our coal miners in this country better, or we will awaken some day to the same fact that England has awakened to, that she does not have enough coal miners to keep the wheels of civilization turning in the United Kingdom.

The problems of England affecting its economic structure have little to do with the problem of achieving our questions here in the mining industry. The facts that confront them basically, however, are interesting from a comparative standpoint. England is threatened with an inferior position henceforth in the world commerce because of her stupid management of her coal industry and because of her barbaric treatment of her coal miners. The availability of coal and adequate supply and the cost of coal in England is a factor that runs now into the entire internal economy of Great Britain, and upon that factor will depend whether or not she can resume her place in the world commerce which she held for centuries and which is now gone.

The number of men employed in the British mines in 1938 was 782,000; in 1942 it was 709,000; in 1945, 686,000.

Production in January was 3,287,000 tons. In 1938 the weekly production was 4,365,000 tons, which is a shrinkage of production both in manpower and the productivity of man. Production in Great Britain has been falling per man per day employed since May of 1943. The highest peak production achieved in Great Britain during the war period was 2,100 pounds per day per man employed. Production per man per day now is less than one ton, and the cost of coal at the pithead is more than three times the average cost of coal at our pithead, and the cost of coal at destination is more than three times the cost of our coal at destination.

While the wages of the British miner are fixed by law at a minimum of five pounds, equal to $19.75 when it was negotiated, but less now, because they compute the English pound sterling at about $3.80—the average earnings of all the men in the British industry, which includes the earnings of the hewers, or the producing miners, as we call them, is just six pounds per week, and at $4 to the pound or less, it is $24. Well, hundreds of thousands of the men make only the statutory minimum for the week. Absenteeism reaches as high as 19 per cent. The British, with their Labor Government, are resorting to forced labor to man their mines. Some 40,000 of these so-called Hopkins-Bevin boys have been forced into the mines, first, under the elective system, and second, under the arbitrary system of allotment. For a long time they offered their soldiers as they were drafted the option of going to the mines or going to the war, and the war was then in activity on the continent. They got no men that way—one, perhaps, two, maybe three out of a draft of five hundred or a thousand. So then they began to order them to the mines and they built great dormitories for them, but they haven't produced any coal. There has been a wastage of 50 per cent of them.

The breakdown from psychoneurotic diseases has been just as high in the British mines among these boys as it was in the Army. Their hazard in the coal mine was greater than the hazard on the battlefield, so thousands of cases of insanity and mental impairment are the result. The physical infirmities of these boys from the congested working settlements of Great Britain assigned to the mines made them incapable of withstanding the rigors of coal mining, and thousands of them have become physically incapacitated, while the absenteeism among the remainder amounts to 50 per cent. Now they are conducting a great campaign in England to attract into the mines what they call juvenile labor. Boys to the age of fourteen are being offered inducements to go into the mines. These are boys who are sons of miners in mining communities who do not want to go into the mines, because they do not want to starve and they do not want to die, but the British Government is giving them a four weeks' course of explanation and understanding and training and allurement, and the British Government now is undertaking the training of mothers to train their boys to go into the mines, and when the poor little chaps get there they are incapable of producing or adding to the production of coal for Empire consideration.

Well, you may say, what has that to do with America? Nothing, if you don't want to give it any consideration. I merely point out that the preservation of a well-trained, competent, able, rugged, powerful working force in our mining industry, which is to safeguard the future economy of the United States in peace and in war is essentially treating the coal miners right—right. It is not only an act of humanity, it is a business proposition. There isn't anyone else who can do the work that the mine workers do. If they don't do it, who will? Oh, I suppose the government could assign a half million government clerks to go into the coal mines and put these fellows out, but if the government ever does that it ought to arrange that each government clerk carry his own coffin with him, because it is dangerous enough for men who know something about it and have lived their lives in it, and God knows, an inexperienced man would be butchered there in a short time.

I think it is a matter of sound business policy. I think it is good economics. I think it is making a contribution toward the stability of the republic and the safety of future generations in this country, to pay our coal miners and to treat our coal miners in a manner that will retain their self-respect and protect their lives, preserve their health, and permit them to render this increasingly valuable service, so important that it affects the destiny and the future of our republic and the American people.

We ask your indulgence in this joint conference while these questions are being considered, and we hope that you will not resort to arbitrary conclusions and hasty press statements, nation-wide advertising, and the employment of a horde of press agents in the Shoreham Hotel to turn out this propaganda to pervert the understanding of the people on problems so vitally essential to you and to me and to every citizen. We ask these considerations on merit. If our position has no merit, we will expect nothing. If it does, we will expect something.

THE RAILROAD STRIKE EMERGENCY [8]

HARRY S TRUMAN [9]

President Harry Truman broadcast this address over the national radio systems, from the White House, on Friday evening, May 24, 1946, at eight o'clock, Eastern Standard Time.

His message was one of the most dramatic ultimatums to be proclaimed by any recent American president.

The railroads had been on strike for twenty-four hours. Declared the President, "If sufficient workers to operate the trains have not returned by 4 P. M. tomorrow, as head of your government I have no alternative but to operate the trains by using every means within my power. I shall call upon the Army to assist the Office of Defense Transportation in operating the trains, and I shall ask our armed forces to furnish protection to every man who heeds the call of his country in this hour of need."

The Presiden's tones were decisive. His voice vibrated with unrestrained indignation. Striking was his condemnation of Presidents Whitney and Johnson. Gone was the perfunctory, almost amateurish vocalization of his previous public utterances. Here was audience-speaker rapport, in spite of the radio barriers. Here was genuine eloquence, born not of words, but of compelling ideas. For the moment, the President was powerful in speech-making as well as in executive leadership.

On May 17, after the processes of direct negotiation, beginning in July 1945, mediation, arbitration, and Presidential intervention to appoint a fact-finding board to make recommendations had all failed, the government seized the railroads. The Brotherhood of Railway Trainmen, A. F. Whitney, President, and the Brotherhood of Locomotive Engineers, Alvanley Johnston, President, some 293,000, rejected the board's recommendation of some sixteen cents an hour increase. The other eighteen railway unions, some 1,470,000, had accepted. The trainmen and engineers proposed a five-day delay for further negotiation. On May 23rd the President offered a compromise settlement. One day later, the unions again turned down the proposal and set the strike in motion.

Immediately, the nation was paralyzed. The 348 major rail lines stopped. Freight shipments generally ceased. Steel mills, denied fuel, began to shut down. Food shortages swiftly threatened every sizable city. The Capitol was flooded with telegrams demanding action.

[8] Text furnished by Charles G. Ross, Secretary to President Truman.

[9] For biographical note see Appendix.

In this crisis, the President took to the radio, and on the next day appeared before Congress. He interrupted his message to the lawmakers, to announce that the strikers had capitulated and were returning to work.

My Fellow Countrymen, I come before the American people tonight at a time of great crisis. The crisis of Pearl Harbor was the result of action by a foreign enemy. The crisis tonight is caused by a group of men within our own country who place their private interests above the welfare of the nation.

As Americans you have the right to look to the President for leadership in this grave emergency. I have accepted the responsibility, as I have accepted it in other emergencies.

Every citizen of this country has the right to know what has brought about this crisis. It is my desire to report to you what has already taken place and the action that I intend to take.

Negotiations between the unions and the railroad operators started in accordance with the Railway Labor Act. Twenty unions were involved. Eighteen of these unions agreed to arbitrate the wage question, and an award was made. Alvanley Johnston, president of the Brotherhood of Locomotive Engineers, and A. F. Whitney, president of the Brotherhood of Railway Trainmen, refused to arbitrate the matter for their unions and instead took a strike vote. An emergency board heard the case of these two unions and recommended the same wage increase awarded to the other 18 unions. Mr. Johnston and Mr. Whitney, however, rejected the emergency board's recommendation in its entirety.

I began conferring with Mr. Whitney and Mr. Johnston as far back as February 21, 1946, in order that every effort should be made to avert a rail strike. When it became evident that the parties themselves were unable to agree, I submitted a compromise proposition to all the parties involved.

Negotiations were made considerably more difficult by the attitude of Mr. Whitney and Mr. Johnston in refusing my request that they meet with the operators and the other 18 unions in a joint conference in the office of the President of the United States. They agreed to meet with the operators but not in the presence of the representatives of the other unions. Accordingly, three separate conferences had to be held in the White House.

The unions had been awarded an increase of 16 cents per hour and certain changes in rules by the arbitration and emergency boards. I recommended that they accept the 16-cent increase awarded by the boards, plus 2½ cents in lieu of rule changes. These rule changes had been considered by the emergency board, which recommended that most of them be negotiated by the parties.

After consideration this compromise was accepted by the operators and by 18 of the unions. These 18 unions were co-operative. They placed the interests of their country first. The compromise was rejected by the locomotive engineers and the trainmen.

This offer of an increase of 18½ cents per hour was eminently fair. It would have resulted in actually increasing the take-home pay of the union members above the greatest take-home pay which they enjoyed during the war. In addition, these two unions are among the highest paid unions in the country. It is also important that the suggested increase of 18½ cents was within the wage stabilization formula—and this formula must be maintained.

Instead of accepting this offer as did 18 of the unions and the operators, Mr. Johnston and Mr. Whitney chose to reject it and to call a strike of their unions. I assume that these two men know the terrible havoc their decision has caused and the even more extreme suffering that will result in the future. It is inconceivable that the rank and file of these two unions realize the terrifying situation created by the action of these two men.

The effects of the rail tie-up were felt immediately by industry. Lack of fuel, raw materials and shipping is bringing about the shutdown of hundreds of factories. Lack of transportation faciliites will bring chaos to food distribution.

Farmers cannot move food to markets. All of you will see your food supplies dwindle, your health and safety endangered, your streets darkened, your transportation facilities broken down.

The housing program is being given a severe setback by the interruption of shipment of materials.

Utilities must begin conservation of fuel immediately.

Returning veterans will not be able to get home.

Millions of workers will be thrown out of their jobs.

The added inflationary pressure caused by the drop in production cannot be measured.

While the situation in our country is extremely acute, the condition in Europe is tragic. Most of our friends today in liberated Europe are receiving less than one third of the average American consumption of food. We have promised to help the starving masses of Asia and Europe, and we have been helping them. We have been exerting our utmost efforts and it is necessary for us to increase our shipments. At this minute 100,000 tons of grain are being held up by the strike of these two unions. UNRRA has 12 ships scheduled to leave from our ports with grain. Those ships cannot sail because the strike of these two unions is keeping the food from reaching the ports. If these ships are held up any longer it means that the bread supply of 45 million people will be cut off within one week.

These people are living from hand to mouth. They depend upon weekly shipments from us to meet their minimum daily needs. This grain held up in this country by the strike of these few men means the difference between life and death to hundreds of thousands of persons. This is stark, tragic truth. If the operation of our railroads is not resumed at once thousands of persons, both here and abroad, will starve. During these past weeks I have told Mr. Johnston and Mr. Whitney of the tragedy that would result from a strike. They have refused to heed my warning. I doubt whether the rank and file of their unions have been told these facts. I am telling them now so that each one of them can face his conscience and consider the spectre of starvation and death that will result from the course which Mr. Whitney and Mr. Johnston are following.

I do not speak tonight of the situation in the coal mines of the nation, for the men are now at work and negotiations for settlement are now taking place between the government and the unions.

I am a friend of labor. You men of labor who are familiar with my record in the United States Senate know that I have been a consistent advocate of the rights of labor and of the improvement of labor's position. I have opposed and will continue to oppose unfair restrictions upon the activities of labor organizations and upon the right of employees to organize and bargain collectively. It has been the basic philosophy of my political career to advocate those measures that result in the greatest good for the greatest number of our people. I shall always be a friend of labor.

But in any conflict that arises between one particular group, no matter who they may be, and the country as a whole, the welfare of the country must come first. It is inconceivable that in our democracy any two men should be placed in a position where they can completely stifle our economy and ultimately destroy our country. The government is challenged as seldom before in our history. It must meet the challenge or confess its impotence.

I would regret deeply if the act of the two leaders of these unions should create such a wave of ill will and a desire for vengence that there should result ill-advised restrictive legislation that would cause labor to lose those gains which it has rightfully made during the years.

As President of the United States, I am the representative of 140 million people and I cannot stand idly by while they are being caused to suffer by reason of the action of these two men.

This is no contest between labor and management. This is a contest between a small group of men and their government. The railroads are now being operated by your government and the strike of these men is a strike against their government. The fact is that the action of this small group of men has resulted in millions of other workers losing their wages. The factories of our country are far behind in filling their orders. Our workers have good jobs at high wages but they cannot earn these wages because of the willful attitude of these few men. I cannot believe that any right of any worker in our country needs such a strike for its protection. I believe that it constitutes a fundamental attack upon the rights of society and upon the welfare of our country. It is time for plain speaking. This strike with which we are now confronted touches not only the welfare of a class but vitally concerns the well-being and the very life of all our people.

The railroads must resume operation. In view of the extraordinary emergency which exists, as President of the United

States, I call upon the men who are now out on strike to return to their jobs and to operate our railroads. To each man now out on strike I say that the duty to your country goes beyond any desire for personal gain.

If sufficient workers to operate the trains have not returned by 4 P.M. tomorrow, as head of your government I have no alternative but to operate the trains by using every means within my power. I shall call upon the Army to assist the Office of Defense Transportation in operating the trains and I shall ask our armed forces to furnish protection to every man who heeds the call of his country in this hour of need.

This emergency is so acute and the issue is so vital that I have requested the Congress to be in session tomorrow at 4 P.M. and I shall appear before a joint session of the Congress to deliver a message on this subject.

NATONAL ATTITUDES AND IDEALS

RESPONSE AT A RECEPTION [1]

Francis Cardinal Spellman [2]

His Eminence, Francis Cardinal Spellman, Archbishop of New York, gave this address on the occasion of a reception in his honor at the Metropolitan Opera House, New York City, on March 5, 1946. The Cardinal had landed that day at La Guardia airfield, on Long Island, on his return from his investiture as Cardinal, at Rome.

The consistory and ceremonies of investiture, beginning on February 16th, at the Vatican, were of especial interest to the 24 million Roman Catholics of the United States and of the American public in general. Thirty-two archbishops, representing nineteen countries, were honored with the Cardinalate rank. For the first time in six centuries the Italian members of the College of Cardinals were outnumbered. Four, including Archbishop Spellman, were from the United States.

Archbishop Spellman was widely heralded, even before this high honor, as the number one representative of the Catholic church in this country. Pope Pius XII, formerly Eugenio Cardinal Pacelli, was a close friend. Repeatedly this American priest had served the Pope in important assignments of the church. Pius had elevated this relatively obscure young New England bishop to the Archbishopric of St. Patrick's cathedral of New York. During the War, as Military Vicar of the Armed Forces of the United States, he had visited every important battlefront where American forces were represented, had ministered to the wounded and dying, and had given many an inspiring message to his military audiences.

The welcome to New York and the reception at the Opera House were a tribute to the personal as well as official leadership of this comparatively young Cardinal. Large crowds cheered him on his fifteen-mile trip from the airfield to St. Patrick's Cathedral, for the formal ecclesiastical ceremonies. Mayor O'Dwyer, Governor Thomas E. Dewey, and Postmaster General Robert E. Hannegan, representing President Truman, paid eloquent tribute to His Eminence at the evening reception.

Cardinal Spellman is an excellent speaker. His discourses are invariably well constructed, based upon a close analysis and philosophical interpretation of events and national attitudes. Without abandoning logical elements, he invests his talks with emotional-imaginative appeals,

---

[1] By permission of his Eminence, Francis Cardinal Spellman. Text furnished through the courtesy of His Eminence.

[2] For biographical note see Appendix.

couched in language that at times approaches the poetic. His delivery is that of an easy, mature speaker, with vocal ease, clearness of enunciation, variety of emphasis, and conversational directness. His sincerity, geniality and other personal traits underlie his appeal as a speaker.

The Archbishop prepares carefully his formal addresses. "However, his position is such that his presence is required at many formal functions, and at many of these he is called upon to speak, or he may feel that the occasion is such that he should address the gathering. On all these latter occasions, he speaks extemporaneously." [3] The address here reprinted was given extemporaneously.[4]

A few hours ago I returned home to America, to my own people of the City and Archdiocese I so deeply love. Truly I had not left you, for wherever I go—you are in my thoughts and prayers, and thus you were with me in Rome and there shared with me the honor conferred upon me by our beloved Holy Father. Even briefly to glimpse Christ's holy Vicar is an inspiration exalting and compelling. What then can I say of the emotions of my heart, the sentiments of soul, the exhilaration of mind, the flaming of will, as I found myself honored by intimate association with him, who so calmly, so courageously and so perfectly portrays in all things the presence of Christ in our midst! I can simply say that I shall pray ever to be true to that cherished relationship.

I would not even be remotely worthy of this honor were it not that I am aware that its greatest glory lies in its opportunity for service. This I have said before, and again I say, that in these days of chaos and crises while mankind is still engulfed in war-heated hatreds and bigotries, honors can be weighed, measured and considered only in terms of opportunity to serve. And service to the utmost and to the end I shall give. To serve my brother and share with him all honors bestowed upon me, all burdens imposed upon him, is the foundation of my faith and love for my fellowman.

A priest, is Christ's envoy on earth that he may, in humility, beseech God's grace and mercy for his people and himself and the plea of the Holy Father to us is that we lead our people to

[3] Letter to the editor of this volume from the Secretary to the Archbishop, April 3, 1941.

[4] For further comment on Cardinal Spellman as a speaker, see "The One Road to Peace," *Representative American Speeches: 1940-1941*, p. 187-95.

pastures of eternal truth, feed them with the food of Divine Grace and direct them with the example of our lives. These words sounded a vibrant challenge and a wise-hearted warning as he cautioned: "the honor is great but your responsibility is greater." Knowing that many have God upon their lips but little in their hearts, I shall ever pray as the Good Shepherd of you, my flock, with your help and prayers for me, and mine for you, that we may fear nothing and flee nothing except sin, that together we may live in simple obedience and love, that we may desire only that which is of Christ, and thus live and fulfill our Faith.

Yes, the honor is great, but its responsibility greater—and any who in vanity think otherwise must be the scorn of wise men and the slaves of their own folly. But one honor there is, out-ranking all others—the honor of sacrificing oneself unto danger or death for the good of God or country. That is the honor I hold most precious in my heart—that is the honor you, my bish-ops, priests and people, must share with me, as you share the honor bestowed upon me—on us—in Rome; that is the honor with its command imposed upon me with the dignity of the Cardinalate when our Holy Father repeated those momentous words: ". . . by this you are to understand that you must show yourself fearless, even to shedding your blood in making our Holy Faith respected, in securing peace for Christian people. . ."

In humility, devotion and gratitude, from every corner of the world we came, to the home of the living God, the citadel of the treasure of truth, to receive this honor and command. Differ-ences of language, custom or climate did not separate us. No matter which soil we called our own, one common bond we had: our faith, our religion, our God. For our faith, yours and mine, is built upon the Rock, and neither the waves of war, the treacher-ies of our times, nor enemies who never sleep—no man, no thing, can its holiness decay—for its holiness lies in Christ. Faith alone can survive and surmount the ruthless, mutinous passions of pre-tenders to peace who presume the power to define and impose it. Peace is the work of justice and justice cannot yield her ripe fruit of wisdom while freedom is still shackled by the conceits of men, confused and fumbling, oft'times selfish and small, thus barring peoples and nations from the mutual understanding upon which true peace must be based.

Peace cannot rise in this atomic age of discord and decay where nations, divided against themselves, are prey to leaders' lust-born sins of bigotry, hate and greed, which, like the swellings of the sea, engulf, overpower and destroy them! In a world where men make mockery of the meaning and majesty of faith, the Church, grounded in God, stands as the symbol of truth, eternal, changeless and divine, secure in the strength of her unity. Yet perverse, stubborn men, though fearful of each morrow, will not awaken to the simple, ageless truth that peace can be found in God alone. For only when God lives within the depths of each man's heart will the cruel grow merciful and just, the bigot turn his fierce, foul hates to tolerance and love, the lustful shed his pride and greed, and each shall be friend to all, the foe of none, and humbly live God's plan. Then only will the grandeur of God's peace penetrate the world!

Hunger-ridden peoples throughout this wailing world know not peace—they are but fodder to feed the fires of new conflicts —for they who deliberately cultivate wars know that the core of war is rooted in hunger. Our "Young Dead Soldiers" bequeath-ing to us their deaths, plead: "We leave you our deaths, give them, we pray, their meaning." [5] And *their* meaning is rooted in love of God and country. The cause for which they fiercely fought, suffered, bled and died was neither new nor novel—the defense of the belief "that all men are created equal, that they are endowed by God with unalienable rights—life, liberty and the pursuit of happiness." Our American sons have always been victorious as again and again they have been called upon to sacri-fice themselves in war to preserve our liberties and bring freedom to imperiled peoples of the earth—to make the world itself free. Dare we besmirch our birthright even before our soldier-dead come home to lie within the soil on which they spent their youth, their dreams, their blood, their lives to guard and save? Guilty of their betrayal we shall be, if, still in the wake of war, we do not learn to lean upon our God, follow Him in the Christly ways of life and in His power and ours stop the ungodly gusts of greeds that sweep like scythes across a nation's face—and leave it broken, bloody, bereft of all things human and humane.

[5] Newspapers credit Archibald MacLeish's poem "The Young Dead Soldiers."

"We leave you our deaths, give them their meaning," cry a million faithful, fighters whose dauntless, selfless service bought for us, our victory. From the ramparts of their heavenly homes they beseech us build of the old, a new and warless world: a world where enemies be friends and each respects God's image in his brother. And I once more profess, that every human being is my brother, and, in the prayerful hope that everywhere men may be free I pledge myself anew to defend the God-given rights for which our sons have died. I pledge myself anew to love God and to serve Him only, striving ever to emulate Christ's Vicar on earth, unsparingly to spend myself for the spiritual and temporal welfare of you, my people. And to you, my people, I make the plea adopt the motto—"Follow God," for in Him and with Him even in defeat and death is victory and life!

THE WAR ISN'T OVER AT HOME [6]

BEN KUROKI [7]

Ben Kuroki, son of a Japanese seed potato farmer at Hershey, Nebraska, gave this speech at the first session of the New York *Herald Tribune* Forum, held in the Grand Ballroom of the Waldorf-Astoria, New York City, on October 27, 28, and 29, 1945. It was the fourteenth annual Forum on Current Problems. The theme was "Responsibility of Victory." Mrs. Ogden Reid presided at each of the four sessions. Schools, colleges, civic organizations, and various other groups throughout the nation were invited to send delegates. The ballroom, seating some 2,000, was filled at each session. Several sessions were broadcast. The speakers represented a wide variety of points of view and of occupations. Included were leaders of governments, military commanders, scientists, cabinet members, business men, and writers. Foreign representatives also participated.

The theme of the first session was "Responsibility in the Pacific." The contributors included Captain Harold Stassen, General Jonathan Wainwright, Major General Claire Chennault, General George C. Marshall.

Mr. Kuroki had joined the Army Air forces on the day following Pearl Harbor. Combatting racial prejudice, he was finally permitted to complete his air training as a gunner and became part of the crew of a B-24. He flew thirty heavy missions in the European zone, including the famous raid on the Ploesti oil fields, and twenty-eight more against Japanese home islands, as gunner on a B-29. He was twice awarded the Distinguished Flying Cross, the first Japanese-American to receive that medal.

Sergeant Kuroki, after his return from the European theatre, first addressed the Hershey High School. Later he talked before the Commonwealth Club of San Francisco, on February 4, 1944. Although Kuroki was relatively inexperienced, he received a ten-minute standing ovation at the end. At that time, the Japanese-American situation was tense on the West Coast.

Fresh from the Far Eastern operations, he gave the address printed below. As he states, "Since the Army hadn't paid me for two months, I arrived at the Waldorf Astoria practically penniless. I had just returned from overseas and felt embarrassed. Mrs. Ogden Reid told me I

[6] By permission of and through the courtesy of Sergeant Ben Kuroki. Text furnished by Mr. Kuroki.

[7] For biographical note see Appendix.

was to deliver my speech the next evening (about which date I had been in the dark). I really got nervous then." [8]

Later, the Sergeant appeared on America's Town Meeting of the Air, on November 22, 1945. It was his first experience in the give-and-take audience-speaker exchange. Many other speaking engagements followed. As a speaker, he has invariably scored. His speaking aim, he declares, is "constantly to keep up this fight against racial intolerance."

The address printed below has been widely used for school declamations.

The town I came from is called Hershey, Nebraska. It's near the Platte River, between Cozad and Ogallala, about twelve miles down the road from North Platte. We've got a farm there—my father and mother and my brother George and I. We raise sugar beets and seed potatoes. Dirt farming isn't a very easy life, but it suits us fine.

I never traveled much. I'd go down to North Platte for feed, or go fishing up in the mountains over in Colorado or down to Chicago to see my sister. I figured some day I'd get to New York, but I didn't plan on visiting Tokyo. Japan is the land of my ancestors, but I never had any desire to go there. And yet, one morning like a lot of other American boys, I started out down the road from my house and I was headed for Tokyo. And like a lot of other American boys, I got there the hard way.

The day after Pearl Harbor my kid brother and I piled in the Chevrolet and drove 150 miles down to Grand Island and enlisted. I remember, after we were sworn in and before we got our uniforms, we were on a train headed for camp. There were some people on the train and they stared at me and said, "What's that Jap doing in the Army?" They said it good and loud, so I'd hear. It just knocked me off my feet. After coming from a town where I knew everybody, I suddenly realized that no matter where I was born or what was in my heart, to these people I was an alien. All the way to camp people kept looking at me, staring at me. I'll never forget that train ride.

I went into the air force and applied for flying. Somehow my papers got lost; they always seemed to be lost, or held up somewhere, or going through channels. When I finally got overseas it was as a clerk with the 93d Bomb Group. It was quite an outfit—the newspapers called it Ted Timberlake's Flying Circus.

Those were the early days in England and things weren't going so good. Liberators were getting knocked off like flies, and there was a shortage of gunners. I remember one day in England, I picked up a magazine and read about an organization called the Native Sons and Daughters of the Golden West. They had a plan to isolate all Japanese-Americans down in the swampland somewhere. I kind of blew my stack when I read the article. I volunteered for gunner. I had five days of training, and then the outfit pulled out for Africa.

I flew my first bombing mission over Bizerte. Our tail gunner got it on that mission and I moved back to the tail turret and that's where I stayed. We tagged some rough missions those days—Naples, Wiener-Neustedt, Rome. We had a saying, "On the way to the target, you're flying for Uncle Sam. On the way back, you're flying for yourself."

My twenty-fourth mission was to Rumania, to a place called Ploesti. It was the first low-level raid on that target. It was murder. Two out of nine planes in my squadron came back.

I finished my tour of missions and our outfit was set to go home, but I volunteered to stick around and fly five more. My kid brother still wasn't overseas and so I figured I'd just check off five missions for him.

The last mission was Muenster, where flak ripped open my turret, the plexiglass cut my face, and the blast ripped off my oxygen mask. A gunner named O'Connel from Superior, Wisconsin, got a mask and held it to my face and everything came out okay.

Then I came back to the States, back to Nebraska. I felt like a kid on Christmas morning. Everybody looked at my ribbons and shook my hand. It was wonderful to know that people appreciated what I'd done and respected me for it.

When I reported back to the Army in California, they asked me to go on a radio program. That was still pretty early, when returned veterans were something special. I really felt like a big wheel. I invited some of my buddies to see the show, and they all sat there in the front row. And then an hour before we were to start, word came through that I couldn't go on. They didn't object to my being a tail gunner. They didn't mind my having two D.F.C.'s. But it seemed I was a Japanese-American and that made it a controversial issue.

In California I met a boy I'd flown with in Europe, Ed Bates, a kind of rough-and-tumble kid. He'd had his fingers frozen off on a mission. It didn't seem to bother him. Nothing bothered Bates, except his brother. His brother had just been killed in the Pacific. He went half crazy when he heard the news. Bates wanted another tour in the Pacific, but they wouldn't let him go on account of his hand. Maybe that was when I first got the idea I wasn't through with this war. And when I got to Denver, that cinched it. I started to get into a taxicab with somebody, and he said he wouldn't ride with "no lousy Jap." I was wearing my wings and all my ribbons, but it didn't matter. I almost cried, I was so mad.

After that, it was Tokyo or bust. I wanted to fly in a B-29 and for about three months I listened to people tell me, no, it was impossible; there were regulations against it. But I also ran into some people who were willing to go to bat for me—Dr. Deutsch, vice president of the University of California; Chester Rowell, of "The San Francisco Chronicle," and Ray Lyman Wilbur, of Stanford University—a lot of people all over the country who believed my record earned me the right to be trusted. A Congressman from Nebraska, a former commander of the American Legion from Wisconsin, the head of the War Relocation Authority—they all put up a holler, and the next thing I knew I was training for B-29s. It gave me a little courage to meet people everywhere who didn't judge a man by his grandfather's nationality or the color of his skin.

It was just before I left for the Pacific I heard about Gorden Jergeson. I guess he was the closest friend I ever had. Back in Hershey we had played together since we were kids. We were on the basketball team. In high school he was president of the class and I was vice president. I got a pass and went to see his folks. We sat there and his mother remembered how we used to go duck hunting and I'd come by at three in the morning and honk the horn and wake everybody up. Gorden was killed in the Solomon Islands. That was another reason for going to Tokyo.

We flew out of an airfield on Tinian in the Marianas. The name of our bomber was "Honorable Sad-Saki." I flew twenty-eight missions in the Pacific, over Kobe and Osaka and finally Tokyo. I even had a crack at my mother's home town—Yokohama.

When the boys in my outfit found out I'd flown a tour over Europe they figured I had holes in my head for volunteering again. I used to kid around and tell them that communications were all cut off from Japan and that this was the only way I could visit my Uncle Nagasaki. I never talked much about my real reason for being over there.

Not only did I go to war to fight the Fascist ideas of Germany and Japan, but also to fight against a very few Americans who fail to understand the principles of freedom and equality upon which this country was founded.

I'm no authority; I'm not an expert or a big wheel. I don't know anything that any boy from Nebraska couldn't tell you. But I know this: I fought with a lot of men in this war, all kinds—a Polish gunner, a Jewish engineer, a German bombardier and even a full-blooded Dakota Indian. I saw men wounded, and whatever land their grandfathers came from, their blood was always the same color. And whatever church they went to, the screams of pain sounded just about the same.

I've had fifty-eight bombing missions now, and I'm still tired enough so my hands shake, and plenty of nights I don't sleep so good. I'd like to go home to Nebraska and forget the war, and just lie under a tree somewhere and take it easy. It's hard to realize that the war is not over for me. Not for a lot of us, Jewish-Americans, Italian-Americans, Negro-Americans, Japanese-Americans. While there is still hatred and prejudice, our fight goes on. Back in Nebraska on our farm, when I planted a seed, I knew that after a while I'd get a crop. That's the way it was with a lot of us in this war: we went to plant the seeds to bring in a crop of decency and peace for our families and our children.

Back in high school in Nebraska, one of the things they taught me was that America is a land where it isn't race or religion that makes free men. That's why I went to Tokyo. I went to fight for my country, where freedom isn't color, but a way of life, and all men are created equal until they prove otherwise. That's an old idea we have in Hershey, Nebraska, just down the highway from Cozad, which is near North Platte.

WHAT TO DO WITH LIFE TODAY [9]

JOSEPH FORT NEWTON [10]

Dr. Joseph Fort Newton gave this address at a combined Honors Convocation and baccalaureate service at the Field House of the State University of Iowa, on Sunday, June 2, 1946.

Some three hundred honor students received special awards and prizes. Part of the program included a service in commemoration of Iowa students who had lost their lives in World War II. Four hundred of those present were in the graduating class.

Dr. Newton is widely known as churchman, writer, and speaker. His autobiography, *River of Years*, was chosen as the book of the month by the religious book club. Before audiences he is dynamic, fluent, conversational, but highly eloquent. He is a master of pause. His pronunciation and enunciation bear slight traces of his cosmopolitan, especially English, associations; he was for several years pastor of the City Temple, London. The Iowa address was delivered extemporaneously and without notes. His audience regarded the sermon as appropriate in thought and language and highly effective in presentation.

President Virgil Hancher of the State University in introducing the speaker, said:

"We are privileged to welcome to the campus tonight a friend who is bound to us by many ties of mind and heart. When I was a student here, I recall having heard him preach before University audiences many times. At that time he was also a member of the faculty of the University, lecturing on his particular specialty. He was a near neighbor, living in Cedar Rapids and commuting to Iowa City frequently, so that he was well known to the members of the faculty and student body.

"Years later, in Washington, I happened to see a list of distinguished preachers who were to come to that city in the autumn of 1926, and I saw the name of Joseph Fort Newton, Rector of the Memorial Church of St. Paul in Overbrook, Pennsylvania. The name, it seemed to me, could not be duplicated twice in a generation, and I went hopefully, and was rewarded by hearing again this great preacher.

"He has had an extraordinary career. He started his ministry in the state of Texas. He has held pastorates in Illinois, Cedar Rapids, Iowa, in the City Temple in London, in the Church of Divine Paternity in New York, and in recent years, in churches in and about the city of Philadelphia. He has written many books. He is an authority on the

---

[9] Text was taken by transcription and approved by Dr. Newton, and is here included through the courtesy of the author.

[10] For biographical note see Appendix.

life of Lincoln. He is a preacher sought for throughout the length and breadth of the United States, and at the special request of the British Government, went to England during the war to interpret to the English people the points of view of the Americans, and to speak to the American troops then stationed there.

"We are most fortunate in having this distinguished preacher with us tonight, and I wish to assure him of the heartiest welcome imaginable as I present him to you now. I sincerely hope that he will return to us many times again. He will speak to us on the subject, "What to do with life today." I have the great pleasure of presenting to you the Reverend Joseph Fort Newton."

It is a very great happiness indeed to return to the University of Iowa, if only for a brief time, and I can assure you that I feel utterly at home in this atmosphere and environment in which I lived and which I learned to love years ago.

My text this evening tells us what one of the greatest men that ever lived did with his life in the age in which he lived—a stormy age, when the Roman Empire was beginning to crumble and to reel to its fall. The words of St. Paul: "For me to live is Christ." [Philippians 1:21] In those few words he sums up the secret of his great life, a life so great that it has projected his vision and his personality through two thousand years. A frail little man he was, tormented by some mysterious malady, the nature of which we do not know. But he had an intrepid faith and courage, and in spite of malignant enemies and all sorts of obstacles, he patrolled the Roman Empire and kindled little centers of Christian life. He it was who carried the flag of Christian faith from Asia into Europe. He did a great labor, having turned over, surrendered, his life to One greater than himself.

What can you do? What are you to do with life today in this stupendous age in which we have the honor to live? After all, life is all that we have. If we cannot find meaning in its mystery, if we cannot make music of its discords, there is nothing else for us. It is soon over, and done, and gone, and we have either lived or not lived, or partly lived. There it is, your life, in your hands, to be, within limits, what you decide. If dreams were on sale, what would you buy? What kind of a life do you want to live today? A self-centered, self-seeking life, using the world as a kind of automat for self-service? Or a self-spending life which adds something to the worth and beauty of the world in which you live?

In static times, institutions make men, they are struck off a common pattern, but in dynamic times, men make, unmake, and remake institutions. And we are living, as you will agree, in a dynamic era. Many times the world has been torn to pieces and put together in a different pattern. But never has our humanity suffered a disaster on so gigantic a scale involving even the remotest tribe. In our days, before our eyes, at the sacrifice of our sons and daughters, the world has been blown to bits and we are trying to pick up the pieces of civilization built up since the fall of the Roman Empire, and put them together in some sort of design.

It is a great time in which to be alive. Lewis Mumford did not greatly exaggerate when he said that a thousand years of history swept between 1930 and 1940. If he had made the dates 1914 and 1946, he would not have exaggerated at all. So amazing, so confounding and baffling, so swift, so utterly radical have been the changes, wrought round about us and, more than we realize, within us! What to do with life today? All that an animal needs is something to live on—food, drink, and some sort of shelter. Man needs these things too. But he cannot live by bread alone. He cannot live without bread. He cannot build greatness of soul upon hunger, squalor, and poverty.

In many parts of the earth, the physical conditions of the spiritual life do not exist. All semblance of civilization has died, for many parts of our earth. Stark starvation stalks the earth. Man must have not only something to live on, he must have something to live for—some ideal, some idea, some purpose. If there is no reason in life, there may be no reason for it. The quest of the ages has been for what human aspiration and divine revelation give us as an interpretation of what life means, and to what high issues it can attain.

Many great men and women who have taken life with hardship, have handled it and grappled with it, and have shaped it toward duty and power, show what can be done with it.

There are really only four things that a man can do with his life. The first is, he can run away from it, or try to, as men have been doing since the days of the prophet Jonah. The story of Jonah is one of the tiny, great books of the Bible. It has two truths, first, the superstition of escape, and second, the pathos of how God looks at a great city. Yes, the superstition of escape! Jonah ran west when he was told to go east, but he was brought back and made to do the thing he was sent to do. Peer Gynt in the Ibsen drama would never face a difficulty. He would always go around it. And always, he ran into more difficulty on the other side, as we always do—inevitably—because a duty dodged, a demand evaded, is like a debt unpaid. We must come back at last and pay it, with the interest compounded by our cowardice. It's futile to try to run away from life, because the world is round, and if you keep going, you come back to where you started.

Or a second way of dealing with life is to run along with it, run with the herd; to hunt with the pack; to accept the current thought, or stupidity; to do a thing because everybody's doing it —which may be exactly the reason why we should not do it, if we have any principle, or any standard, or any stamina. But how many there are who just coast through life, and do not climb; who are drifters and not drivers? They get nowhere, and leave no trace behind them. They are like pieces of dead wood floating down stream. Nobody knows that they have ever lived.

In a vivid little story, some years ago, called "Angry Dust", one man asked the question, "What is the devil?" and before anybody could reply, he answered his own question. "The devil," he said, "is not a huge monster with horns and a harpoon tail, and a wicked glitter in his eye. No, the devil is just taking the line of least resistance. It is inertia. It is doing nothing." Well, surely, that is a partial description of the spirit of evil. But in our day we have seen the spirit of evil become aggressive, vindictive, malignant, cunning, utterly ruthless and unscrupulous and organized, in an effort to drag the human race down to a subhuman level, in the name of the foulest tyranny that ever tried to crawl across the earth. And yet, in a sense, the man in the story was right. Inertia of the multitudes breaks the heart of every leader of mankind. Yes, you can run along with life.

Or there's a third and better way. You can take hold of life firmly, with some plan, with some purpose, some faith and discipline—and run it to good account. In the book of the "Wisdom of Solomon," one of the apocryphal books, although this wisdom is certainly not apocryphal, we hear these words: "The desire for discipline is the beginning of wisdom." You are here, or have been here, to acquire certain disciplines and techniques in this University; you have won honors because, instead of killing time, you filled it. You used it. You turned time into life, into certain skills, and certain achievements of which you have a right to be proud.

Think of the diligent way in which Lincoln disciplined himself; in the use of words, for example. He was not a born orator, he was a made orator. He studied the meaning, the music, the color, the weight, and the worth of words. Through long years he practiced. He amputated adjectives, until at last he spoke with a stripped and clipt simplicity which enabled him to put more flesh on the skeleton of an idea and use fewer words in doing it than any man who has spoken in America. That's discipline. Even chance, Pasteur tells us, prefers a prepared mind. And how much more does truth!

Montague, the English novelist, told one time when he was at Oxford how, with a group of friends, he went to hear Benjamin Jowett preach. They wanted to be able to say that they had heard that famous scholar preach. The service was held in old St. Mary's Church, that exquisite Gothic structure, so haunting in its memories and associations. Well, the service moved with a quiet, decorous rhythm. The sermon began, and went along for awhile in the same rhythm. Then suddenly the preacher said, "I have seen it set down in tables that the average length of life of a man of 21 is 36 years. He may hope for a little more, he may fear for a little less, but roughly speaking, it is 36 years—that is 13,000 days." And this bit of precision from the pulpit, so utterly unexpected, made those young men sit up, and their minds were open for what followed. And this is what followed: "He is a shabby sort of fellow who wastes any part of those 13,000 days; a gentleman is the man who refuses to take out of life more than he puts into it." When the service ended, those boys went back to their same "diggs," as living quarters in Oxford are called, and did some figuring. They estimated that they would spend one third of those 13,000 days in sleep, and one third in making a living—and that left one third, 4,333 days in which to make whatever contribution they expected to make to the welfare of mankind. They decided they could not waste any time. They had to use every bit of it, and it was not an accident that almost every man in that group became distinguished in one field or another. This is what I mean by taking hold of life, and doing something with it.

Or better still, to return for a moment to St. Paul, we can put our lives into hands of One greater than ourselves and let Him run it. That's what St. Paul did. Years ago, more years that I like to remember, I heard Dwight Moody use a sentence that influenced hundreds of thousands of men and women—it stayed in my mind. I can never forget it. I can still see him when he spoke it, with his stocky form, and his long Prince Albert coat, with his beard turning from brown to gray, and his beautiful dark eyes; talking like a business man, stating a proposition when he said, "Let God have your life. He can do more with it than you can." It was not a pietistic remark but plain common sense. And he was an example of it in his own life.

It is the dedicated life, the life that is utterly given away to something greater than itself, asking no reward, that is happy. Now, to do anything with life, there are four things which I ought and need to name.

One is, we must have a faith that is fit to live by, a faith that satisfies the mind, and sanctifies the heart. That is, a relation in terms of belief and of action to the universe in which we live which makes our life intelligible, gives it a calm and purposeful meaning.

In the City Temple at London we had a literary society to which we invited famous men and women from all over the United Kingdom to lecture. Bernard Shaw came every year, and H. G. Wells, and among others, the late Dr. Osler gave a lecture on Walt Whitman, one of the most brilliant I have ever heard, or hope to hear. He took for his text a saying of Whitman in the preface of his first edition of poems in 1855, these words: "Faith is the antiseptic of the soul." A disinfectant of fear, foreboding, defeat or dismay! It makes us victors over life, and not victims of it.

Then we must have a philosophy of life. I do not mean a philosophy in a technical sense, as when we speak of the philosophy of Plato or Immanuel Kant. I mean philosophy in the sense of a life-wisdom. A friend of mine in Philadelphia had been having a bad, bad time, one blow falling upon him after another, one shadow after another. But he has met it with such poise, such patience, such dignity. And I asked him, "My friend, how do you do it?" He said, "I have a philosophy of life that stands me in good stead." Now the whole philosophy of life, in a sense of life-wisdom, can be summed up in six words. Two of them we owe to Greece, two of them to Rome, and two to Judea: "Know thyself. Control thyself, Give thyself." Or putting it a different way, I like to say that we must give ourselves, we must forgive others, and we must live with thanksgiving.

Also, we must have a self fit to live with, because we have to live with ourselves whether we like it or not, and if we cannot live with ourselves with peace, we cannot live with anybody else without friction. I am the confidant, I am sure, of more matrimonial miseries than any man in the United States, and every one of them can be traced to self-centeredness. Either one of both of the parties can't live with themselves, much less with anybody else, and such marriages inevitably go on the rocks.

And finally, we must have a work fit to live for. Great causes make great men and women. Had it not been for the slavery issue injected anew into American life, nobody, perhaps, would ever have heard of Lincoln. That cause, as Edmund Spencer would put it, "drew out the lines of life, from living knowledge hid." The world is full of great causes and aching needs that cry out for help. We are here to make a living, yes, to pull our weights in the boat. But we are also here to make a life, and we can do that only by giving it away. Such is the call of our highest devotion. Our country, our home, science, and the church —one or more of a thousand things, we can dedicate our lives to, and make them memorable.

What to do with life today? Hope much, fear not at all. Do your best, be your best, seek and find the best in others. If you have trouble, bear it. If you meet danger, dare it. If you find happiness, share it. Trust the great God, in whose hands we stand, and may God bless us, every one.

EDUCATION

CIVIL COURAGE [1]

JAMES B. CONANT [2]

President James Conant, of Harvard, gave this address in the Memorial Church, at Harvard, at the opening of the fall term, on September 25, 1945. This service was a memorial one for Harvard's war dead and a commemoration of the war's end. It was the first time that he addressed the students in that Church since his Valedictory Service on January 10, 1943.[3]

During those three years, he had been active in Washington as leader in the development and application of scientific materials to War uses. He was, for example, representative of the Office of Scientific Research and Development in the production of the Atomic bomb.

His appeal for civil courage should be analyzed against the background of events of September, 1945. The atomic bomb had fallen; Japan had surrendered; this nation was rapidly demobilizing, both economically and psychologically. The inevitable disillusionment and lowered national morale, accompanying economic and social reconversion, were already apparent.

President Conant has continually impressed audiences with the clarity of his statements, the dignity and originality of his prose, the depth of his philosophical insight into American life and patterns of thinking, his grasp of educational trends, and his overtones of inspiration, free from triteness or sentimentality.

The last time I had the privilege of speaking in this Memorial Church was at the Valedictory Service on January 10, 1943. Less than three years have passed; thirty-three months, to be more exact. Long months, we can all agree; unhappy months for those at home anxiously awaiting news; harrassing and exhausting months for those engaged in combat duty overseas. Today we open a new college term—the first in the postwar era. We

[1] By permission of President Conant. Text supplied through the courtesy of the author.

[2] For biographical note see Appendix.

[3] For that address, see *Representative American Speeches: 1942-1943*, p. 257 ff. For further comment on President Conant as speaker, see also *Representative American Speeches: 1939-1940*, p. 337 ff.

rejoice that the job is done. The Axis powers have been beaten to their knees; they have surrendered without condition. Here in the University we await with keen anticipation the return of large numbers of those who prematurely left us to enter the armed forces; we no less eagerly look forward to the enrollment of many veterans who for the first time will enter Harvard.

But even in the midst of constructive tasks of peace, we are little prone to joyful exultation. For in our minds are other thoughts: sad thoughts, as we contemplate the sorrowing families in every city and town—the permanent reflection of more than a million casualties; solemn thoughts, as we consider the difficult domestic problems, the product of an industrial civilization; grave thoughts, as we weigh the international responsibilities of the United States now so powerful as a military nation.

I have used the adjectives "solemn" and "grave" deliberately, and equally deliberately rejected the words "frightening" and "terrifying." I have done so although such adjectives have very often been coupled with the word "responsibility" in the last few weeks. For it is the burden of my very brief remarks this morning that all ideas of terror and fright must be outlawed if we are to take the next step forward along the road of freedom. And let us never forget that the possibility of taking that precious step— the fact that the road of freedom now lies open before us—we owe to the skill, stamina, and courage of our fighting men.

To my mind, there have been too many public manifestations of panic and alarm in the press and on the air in the last six weeks. Fear is too common a human failing for us to need invoke it as an aid to any cause however good. The great moments in human history are records of collective or individual courage; the leaders of a free people rightly rely on the courage of each and every citizen, not only in times of war but in the days of peace.

We are at the beginning of a period of psychological reconversion no less important than the readjustment of our economic life. The moral imperatives of the battlefield must be transformed into those of a free society which believes in the supreme significance of each individual man or woman. War and peace are, as regards methods, miles apart; but as regards objectives, this war for us, a free people, has been identical with the job that now lies ahead—keeping open the road of freedom. There was a danger, as I pointed out thirty-three months ago, that the winning of the war would engender such conditions in our minds that we would be unable to preserve liberty when victory had come. There are few signs that such is indeed the case. On the contrary, on all sides we see evidence that the nation recognizes fully the necessity for reorienting our sights. We know that the end no longer justifies the means. We know that the collective demands of a group—a ship's company, a regiment or a bombing crew—no longer have life or death hold over an individual. For military courage we must substitute civic courage.

How significant this latter transformation is may be illustrated by considering the case of our prostrate enemy, the Germany of Hitler. For just as a careful study of individual abnormalities provides clues to health, so an analysis of the disastrous course of nations may help us as a country to avoid dangers. The strange case of the history of the German nation from 1933 to 1945 should never cease to be a matter of study and reflection to those who value all that the Nazis despised and sought to destroy forever.

Questions like these keep recurring in our minds: How could the Nazi doctrines gain such ascendency among a highly literate and apparently well-educated people? How could that nation breed such rulers and such brutal gangsters and allow them to terrorize the population? One answer to such questions has been given by a learned German professor in a private letter I saw not long ago. The writers philosophizing on the triumph of the Nazi party (which he had done nothing to prevent) explained the situation in these words: "One reason is that the education of the German people was carried out not only in frequently excellent schools but also on the military drilling grounds. Consequence: high mental and intellectual development, great military bravery, yet at the same time lack of civil courage, as many including Bismarck have said before. Lack of civil courage fosters political mass psychosis."

These few sentences, I believe, represent an essentially correct diagnosis of one important element in the complex of diseases which proved fatal to the Germany of the Weimar Republic. But let us not be unduly complacent about the strength of our own immunity. The lack of civil courage in a people is no new or rare phenomenon; history records many examples of political mass psychosis. Our present highly industrialized and over-urbanized society provides a medium highly favorable for the development of this disease. It may well prove, therefore, that the strength of the civic courage of the American people will be the determining factor in the next two or three decades—determining not only in regard to our handling of domestic crises but in regard to war or peace.

The military courage of the younger generation of Americans has been written on the pages of history of the last three years. It is a record the nation will continue to read with pride. We, a free and peaceful people, suddenly plunged into a global war, not only turned out a stream of weapons (some new and very strange) contrary to the predictions of Hitler's well-informed advisers, but confounded the hopes and expectations of our enemies by enrolling, organizing and training in a miraculously short time the men to use these weapons. Of all that went contrary to the calculations of the military experts of Germany and Japan, however, the most amazing phenomenon from their mistaken point of view was the extraordinary fighting qualities of the Americans on every front and in every branch of service.

How long ago it seems that our now beaten enemies were saying that our soft American youth couldn't and wouldn't fight! Rereading what was said on the subject five years ago seems like reading the record of another age. But all that is past. The strategy of peace, not war, now must determine all our thoughts and actions; the tactics of civil affairs (including the relations between nations) now demand our study and attention. With these matters, all of us—those who stayed at home, returning veterans, the still younger generation—must now proceed to deal as boldly as we can.

Fear, panic, foolish short-sighted action—thus runs the well-known sequence of words describing the road of human folly. The reverse pattern—courage, bold examination, intelligent far-sighted action—is admittedly all too rare, but is always available as an alternative even for the sons of Adam. Listen for the emotional overtones in a group discussion. Whether they portray fear or proclaim courage will usually provide the key to the subsequent course of a bit of human drama. Cries of fire in a crowded theatre almost invariably set in train a series of actions as awful in their consequences as they are unnecessary in their origin; all of which is recognized later when the story is retold in the light of reason.

The educational implications of an emphasis on civil courage are similar to those which arise when one stresses such phrases as "the moral responsibility of the individual." Three hundred years ago a wise man said that "to be ignorant of what occurred before you were born is to be always a child." But the color of the glasses through which one views the past is influenced by and in turn influences our emotional attitudes toward different sets of values. To read history either with a sneer or conversely only after the black pages have been deleted, is the equivalent of drinking water from a poisoned well. To be sure, cold, unemotional, purely factual analysis of human history is difficult and a similar examination of contemporary events is impossible to achieve. Yet the easy attitudes of complete cynicism on the one hand or Pollyanna optimism on the other are equally disastrous; it is a narrow and perilous knife-edge that teacher and student alike must walk. Yet walk it we must, for in one way or another a large portion of the nonvocational education of a citizen must be concerned with a study and analysis of fairly recent occurrences involving human beings. The spirit in which such study is undertaken is, therefore, a matter of great significance for the future of the nation.

The battle is the pay-off for new weapons, as many scientists and engineers have come to realize in the course of their wartime education. Similarly, adult behavior is the only measure of education as regards an individual or a group. There can be only one verdict as to the overall effects of the education of German youth during the last hundred years. To the extent that we see in the downfall of that country a failure in education, we become aware of the responsibility of our schools, colleges, and agencies of adult education. Is it too much to place the task of developing a maximum degree of civil courage high on the list of priorities for our teachers, our writers and our public speakers? Is it too much to ask that in our discussions of education at all stages we never lose sight of the kind of behavior a free society must demand of its responsible citizens? Not if I read the past correctly; not if I discern at all accurately the true dimensions of those problems of the future now only dimly visible but which lie across our course in the years ahead.

NEW DIRECTIONS FOR HIGHER
LEARNING [4]

HAROLD F. HARDING [5]

Colonel H. F. Harding gave this address before the Phi Kappa Phi Association of Hawaii, at Honolulu, on May 25, 1945. At that time he was Chief of Staff, Headquarters, Replacement Training Command in the Pacific Ocean Areas.

In March 1946, after five years with the army, he returned to George Washington University, Washington, D. C. Here he was appointed Professor of Speech and Executive Officer of the George Washington University Department of Speech. He also accepted a Rockefeller Foundation Postwar Fellowship in the Humanities, for a year's research in rhetoric and public address.

Dr. Harding served as colonel in the Pacific theater of war from January 1942, until the end of 1945. While in service he received the Legion of Merit for his record as Chief of Staff. He organized, trained, and directed the staff which provided replacement support for operations against the Japanese. Previously he had been awarded the Bronze Star Medal for service as Assistant Chief of Staff as G-1, and later regimental commander in the Hawaiian Seacoast Artillery Command and as executive officer of the Harbor Defense Headquarters at Honolulu.

In preparing his speeches, Dr. Harding usually makes a somewhat detailed outline. For radio audiences, or before a learned society, as in the case of this Honolulu group, which expect to have the manuscript printed, he writes the address. Usually he does not read the speech from manuscript. He did so in this case with, however, interpolations to adjust the discourse to this particular audience.

This speaker suggests that the prospective speechmaker should reflect on a statement from John Morley's *Life of Gladstone*: [6] "The great political speech, which for that matter is a sort of drama, is not made up by passages for elegant extracts or anthologies, but by personality, movement, climax, spectacle, and the action of the time." [7]

In one of those brilliantly illuminating passages of *The Republic* Plato tells us that "The direction in which education starts

[4] Text furnished by the author. Permission for this reprinting through the courtesy of Dr. Harding.

[5] For biographical note see Appendix.

[6] Morley, John, *Life of Gladstone*, vol. 2, p. 589-90, Macmillan Co.

[7] For further comment on Professor Harding as a speaker, see *Representative American Speeches: 1943-1944*, p. 306 ff.

a man will determine his future life." This is the text I want to take to discuss with you tonight some "New Directions for Higher Learning."

We are now at the threshold of what can be the most influential educational era in history. There are literally millions of young men and women presently standing in search of the right direction for their future education. Likewise, those in charge of our institutions of higher learning are seeking the right approach and the right road and thus the right direction for the higher learning of their students. It is my purpose to examine with you this evening some of the needs of the postwar world as they relate to colleges and universities. This is indeed an ambitious undertaking and only one, such as I, who has been away from the academic world for four or five years would venture the attempt. But if I have been away from formal teaching during that time, I have been close to the men who will make up a large share of the college students for the next few years and, of course, like all old men, I do not hesitate to take up the problems of the younger generation.

Late in February of this year the Committee on Education of the House of Representatives published the report of its special advisory committee on the study of higher education. Some dozen college and university administrators, under the direction of Dr. Francis J. Brown, have submitted a document entitled the "Effect of Certain War Activities upon Colleges and Universities" that will have far reaching effects in our educational planning for years to come. I commend to you the detailed findings of the committee's survey.

I cannot possibly summarize the document for you now. I merely wish to quote what the president of one institution wrote regarding the future:

Our whole system of higher education in the United States is reaching far too few persons with a program that is too low in quality. Certainly all the land grant colleges need to intensify and broaden their work. I believe most sincerely that we stand in danger of losing democracy in this country simply because we do not have enough minds that have been equipped to think broadly, deeply, and clearly. Instead of having 4 per cent of our population college graduates, we should raise the percentage to at least 10 per cent as quickly as we can. The quality of education needs to be increased; this is true of purely technical train-ing in such fields as electronics, and it is also true of general education, which needs to supplement, and even guard against the dangers of sheer specialized training. It is quite clear that a good share of the states cannot, by themselves, do the kind of job that needs doing. The Federal Government must extend aid and raise the necessary funds by a system of taxation that is fair to all.[8]

Three important pieces of legislation were enacted during the last Congress which will soon give a tremendous impetus to edu-cation at all levels. I refer to Public Laws 16, 113, and 346. The first provides for the training and education of veterans with 10 per cent or more disability incurred while in the service. The second provides for the education of persons injured in "war industry or otherwise." The most important, Public Law No. 346, sets up the means for training and education for all veterans with discharge other than dishonorable who have a minimum of 90 days of active duty. Honorably discharged veterans under this law will be entitled to one year of education or training or to a refresher or retraining course, suitable to their needs or desires, at any institution of their choosing. It provides, further, that veterans may secure federal support for up to three years addi-tional education if they were 25 or under when drafted, and depending on their length of service and ability to show satis-factory progress as a student. If they were over 25 and their edu-cation was interrupted by induction into the Army, they may secure the same privileges. The law provides that the govern-ment will pay tuition and incidental costs up to $500 a year and subsistence of $50 a month to a single man or $75 a month to one with dependents while he is actually enrolled as a student.

Public Law No. 346 thus establishes the greatest educational grant in American history. Unless the institutions themselves have made adequate plans to adapt their programs to the needs of students without letting down academic standards, the law is likely to degenerate into an enormous wasteful system of student dole. The burden of proving the worthiness to accept the pro-visions of the law rests squarely upon higher institutions and those who administer them.

[8] House Report No. 214, 79th Congress, 1st Session, *Effect of Certain War Activities upon Colleges and Universities*, February 23, 1945, p. 38.

I want to turn now to the book "Education for Freedom" published last year by President Robert M. Hutchins of the University of Chicago. In his first chapter Mr. Hutchins gives us an insight into his appreciation of his Army service during World War I. He says, "The horrors of war are all that they are supposed to be. They are even worse; for the worst horror can never be written about or communicated. It is the frightful monotony and boredom which is the lot of the private with nothing to think about. Since my education had given me nothing to think about, I devoted myself, as the alternative to suicide, to the mastery of all the arts implied in the verb 'to soldier.' I learned to protract the performance of any task so that I would not be asked to do another. By the end of the war I could give the impression that I was busy digging a ditch without putting my pick into the ground all day. I have found this training very useful in my present capacity. But on the whole, aside from the physiological benefits conferred upon me by a regular, outdoor life, I write off my years in the Army as a complete blank." [9]

This testimony comes from a distinguished administrator who is now the leading exponent in our country of a doctrine which he chooses to call "Intellectualism." By that I believe he means that the main and indeed the sole purpose of higher education is to train the thinking faculty. Dr. Hutchins has been opposed by another vigorous administrator, Dr. William H. Cowley, former president of Hamilton College and more recently Professor of Higher Education at Stanford University. Dr. Cowley advocates "Holoism" and by that he means the art of educating the whole man, that is, not only his thinking capacity but his physical, emotional, moral, aesthetic and spiritual as well. He believes in teaching the art of living and growing among men. Much as I admire the high purpose of education which President Hutchins stands for, my years of Army experience and of teaching convince me that both for the student and for our country his purpose is narrowly short-sighted. President Lowell of Harvard deftly expressed the view I prefer some years ago in the very beginning of his inaugural address when he said: "Among his other wise sayings, Aristotle remarked that a man is by nature

[9] *Education for Freedom,* Louisiana State University Press, 1944, p. 5.

a social animal; and it is in order to develop his powers as a social being that American colleges exist."

Sooner or later everyone connected with teaching must make up his mind whether he is for "Intellectualism," or "Holoism." In the very near future we will be confronted with thousands of eager prospective students, former members of the armed forces, whose minds may or may not be complete blanks as a result of their military service. For my part and by observation of a good number of enlisted men and officers during the past five years, I doubt whether the average soldier leaves the Army with a mind completely blank as a result of his military service. Indeed, if the educational statesmen who are now planning the postwar curricula have failed to take into account the kind of material they are going to teach they are in for a series of genuinely rude awakenings.

The postwar student who has had vigorous training and served overseas and particularly in the combat areas is likely to be a pretty mature, informed, well-travelled, and articulate individual, possessed with some convictions about subjects like war and peace, educational theory and practice, and possibly what the country needs in the way of educational reform. In spite of Mr. Hutchins' experiences, the average soldier of this war has had some time to reflect on these and other topics. Fortunately, the Army has assisted him with an extensive Information-Education program. Every company-size unit conducts a weekly orientation school where world affairs and soldiers' problems are freely discussed. Then too, the ordinary soldier of this war has acquired some standards for comparison. He has seen what happens, for example, to the untrained man in battle. Of course, the advocates of "Intellectualism" will say that training in the military sense and higher education in the sense of Intellectualism are vastly different things. Nevertheless, I suggest that the process of learning to think and to reflect is not gained entirely from books or in academic halls. Our soldiers and sailors who were the high school boys of a few years ago have aged. They have gained new insights and new understandings that cannot be lightly regarded when they return to college campuses. I remind you that these insights were gained in desperately costly places like the Kasserine Pass, the Anzio beachhead, Tarawa, Kwajalein, Bastogne, Iwo Jima, and Okinawa.

In a humble way I come now to some of the needs for the postwar educational program. These I shall discuss under the headings of The Student, The Institution, and The Nation.

The war has given American education a great historic opportunity. We shall kick it out the window unless we redefine the purposes of our colleges and universities so soundly and so clearly that the nation will understand, approve, and zealously support them. For a century education has been the chief religion of the American people but today discontent and criticism abound. Catastrophe lies ahead unless we return to the fundamental purpose of educating our students, first as citizens and second as vocational specialists.[10]

For the student in the junior college, the four-year college, and in the graduate schools we need in addition to this restatement of purposes a vast improvement in the content and teaching methods of practically all subjects. The survey recently conducted by the American Council on Education and published in book form under the title *A Design for General Education* [11] is a notable contribution to the content of the curriculum. But it is meant for the junior college level. Similar surveys and recommendations are urgently needed for more advanced levels.

In the postwar world we must have recognition of the indispensable function of the teacher as opposed to the researcher. Unfortunately, college administrators in the past few decades have tended to regard the attainment of higher degrees as sufficient index of teaching ability. Nothing is farther from the truth. We must devise methods of improving teachers, liberalizing and encouraging superior teaching, and recognizing it above all by rewarding the teacher with proper rank and salary. There is no other way to attract and recruit the teachers who can really teach.

We must make it possible, too, in the coming generation for the superior and promising student to gain an education without the necessity of long hours of self-employment. President Conant

[10] W. H. Cowley, "Freedom and Discipline," *The Educational Record,* January 1944, p. 22.
[11] Washington, D.C., June 1944.

of Harvard emphasizes "that equality of educational opportunity is still far from an accomplished fact. This is true in spite of our magnificent state and municipally supported colleges and universities and in spite of our scholarships in privately controlled institutions. . . . Nevertheless, anyone who is familiar with the operation of our American educational system realizes that all too often accidents of geographical and parental fortune determine who goes to college and who does not. Every survey of our educational system has emphasized this fact." [12]

New York State has recently led the way and its Department of Education is proposing legislation to bring up-to-date a scholarship policy that has been untouched for 30 years. The scheme sets up a $16,000,000 scholarship fund which would make available to the top 10 per cent of the state's high school graduates $1,500 towards an education in New York State institutions. Other states can emulate this program and the Federal Government can well afford to consider the proposals of Dr. Conant and others for federal scholarships.

In addition to better curricula, better teachers and teaching methods, better means of recognizing the superior student and enabling him to go to college, we must raise standards and devise ways of making college and university degrees mere uniformly high. A great many small colleges and poorly equipped, so-called universities have been hard hit during this present war and many have had to close. I regard this as net benefit rather than loss for the country at large. Although I am not an advocate of federal control of education, I strongly believe that the establishment of federally sponsored examinations and boards of examiners for both undergraduate and graduate degrees may be the best means of improving our educational standards.

For American higher institutions many vital changes and reforms are indicated. Administrations and administrators everywhere are sorely in need of repair requiring both major overhaul and complete replacement. Those who regard teaching as an easy way of gaining a living need to be rooted out. Properly done, teaching is one of the world's hardest jobs. Those who are ill equipped, poorly trained, and without a liberal out-

[12] "Mobilizing American Youth," *The Atlantic Monthly*, January 1943, p. 50.

look should be painlessly or painfully, as the case may be, set aside. There never was a day in which the needs for good teachers and good teaching were so preeminently important as they are today. The poor college and university teacher will soon find himself before a group of students who not only know at first hand much more about the world than he does, but they have learned it the hard way. Therefore they will be more concerned in improving themselves than in wasting their time listening to dull lectures poorly prepared and delivered in the old way by old fuddy duddies.[13]

Teachers everywhere must learn that there is something besides the lecture method and written examinations to teaching. In addition to conferences, panel discussions, forums, committees, and seminars, it may be useful in the postwar world to let some of the students do some of the speaking themselves. There will be many who by virtue of experience and aptitude are superbly capable. Their opinions, experiences, judgments, and good sense must be recognized and utilized.

Again, there must be more cooperation among institutions of higher learning. The facilities of libraries, laboratories, and research foundations should be more freely made available to those capable of profitably using them. We have barely scratched the surface in exploring and using the wealth of our libraries and teaching facilities throughout the world. If learning is to be really liberalized, its teaching equipment should be more freely disposed to those who deserve it.

Institutions should be far more concerned with the physical health of their students. The Army and Navy have keenly impressed our young men with the importance of physical fitness. Those fortunate enough to return without wounds will not be content with old-fashioned progress of inter-collegiate athletics and inadequate intramural programs. It is not too much to suggest that every American college graduate of 1950 should by demonstration be a competent swimmer, at least a reasonably proficient player in a minor sport, and have developed a real interest and liking for games like tennis, badminton, handball, and golf which he can continue to play in after-college years.

[13] See the excellent article, "Higher Education Plans for the Future," by A. J. Brumbaugh in *The Educational Record*, April 1944, especially pages 106 and 107.

In addition, student personnel officers must make more adequate provisions for the mental health of students. A strong indictment of American colleges has been made on the grounds of "impersonalism." College administrators and college teachers must learn that institutions are primarily for students to secure learning and not for faculty members to secure tenure. In short, we must remember that the student as an individual requires the most careful kind of preparation, observation, guidance, and counselling.

What are the needs of the nation at large for a higher education? First and foremost there is need for adequate numbers —and there never can be too many—of well-trained men and women to take their places as educated citizens. As Milton said, "I call therefore a complete and generous education that which fits a man to perform justly, skilfully, and magnanimously all the offices both private and public of peace and war."

I believe one of our most vital needs at the close of this war is for some workable system of compulsory military education. The longer we delay such a program the greater is the danger of lapsing once more into a state of national soft-headedness.

I have just reread *The Moral Equivalent of War*, that penetrating essay by William James, written in February 1910. Here are a few sentences that should mean much to us today: "All these beliefs of mine put me squarely into the anti-militarist party. But I do not believe that peace either ought to be or will be permanent on this globe, unless the states pacifically organized preserve some of the old elements of army discipline. . . . Martial virtues must be the enduring cement; intrepidity, contempt of softness, surrender of private interest, obedience to command, must still remain the rock upon which states are built . . ."

Properly organized military training can do much to preserve our national character and guarantee our respect among nations. To me at least this need comes before all others in planning for the postwar education.

The leadership of our country in the next fifty years will depend upon the education and character training the young soldiers and sailors and those now graduating from high school receive in the next five to ten years. The nation has a huge investment in education. It cannot be too good. It can always be improved.

We need to have facilities for training specially selected young men and women abroad if international good will and understanding are to mean anything. We must provide the means for international education and travel. The world of 1950 to 2000 will be vastly more internationally minded than even the world of 1945. Knowledge of foreign languages, foreign cultures, foreign relations are elementary requirements for those who wish to attain to the higher legislative and executive positions. Our country needs men and women able to take their places with the educated leaders of other countries. We must make the necessary provisions for them to do so.

Our country needs also a body of men and women, carefully selected and with mature insight, who can continuously devote their time to planning for the needs of higher education. The War Department General Staff devotes its full time in the years of peace to plans for war. It makes detailed plans and tries to foresee all possible contingencies. Is it too much for us to demand a similar high level planning staff, permanently assigned to the task of developing higher education?

Such a staff may well undertake the problem of equalizing educational opportunity in our country. It could set up standards and recommend contents for educational curricula. It could encourage the science of measurement and mental testing. It could assist in the compilation of rosters of scientists and technically trained personnel. It could plan for international congresses of education. It could aid and encourage the arts of visual education and direct research in teaching aids and methods. It could coordinate the requests and recommendations of other government agencies that relate to education. Its members could, in short, play the parts of philosopher-kings for higher education and wisely rule on a long-term basis so as to improve educational standards throughout the land.

Not the least of the needs of higher education in these postwar years will be some organization for recording, preserving, interpreting and evaluating the World War of 1939 to 1945 or 1946. If we cannot benefit by the mistakes that led up to and caused this greatest holocaust of all times, we have wasted by millions the dearest commodity in the world—human life.

In the middle ages Latin was the language of educated men in all countries. Scholars in England and on the continent corresponded with and understood each other because they wrote and spoke a common tongue and had read essentially the same great books. To prevent another world war a generation hence I believe an international commission should compile and collate the materials for a history of this present war, documented by original texts, motion picture film, and the testimony of witnesses. Such a detailed factual history made available in various languages to the students of the coming generation should serve to provide some incentive to keep the peace we are now fighting for and paying for in blood and death. It seems essential to me that young people throughout the world should read the same facts on the cause of World War II, just as the scholars of the early Renaissance knew the same great books. It will not do to have a distinctly American version of this war, a Russian version, a Chinese version, or German, Italian, and Japanese versions. This present war was fostered and incited by propaganda, spoon fed to German youth, on the main events of World War I and the gross hardships of the Versailles Treaty. Unless some precautions are taken now by world-minded historians we can be certain that political leaders in the defeated countries will nourish another war on the frustrated hopes of this one.

The time has come for the individual student, the institution, and our country to plot courses and determine directions for higher education of tomorrow. Peace and good will throughout the world are the natural by-products of education. Vision, imagination, and intellectual capacity of high order are demanded to maintain the peace.

It is significant to me that the war against Germany was ended by the signing of the armistice in a schoolhouse in Reims, France, in L'Ecole Professionale. The signing of that memorable document on May 7th last in a classroom is symbolic of the place education has already begun to play in the new world order. Students, teachers, administrators, and the nation at large are now turning to the greatest task in the world—that of creating the understanding for a lasting peace. I remind you again that Plato said, "The direction in which education starts a man will determine his future life." In the same way the direction in which we now plan for education will determine the course of our nation and of the world for the rest of the twentieth century.

THE GREATEST LACK [14]

ROBERT J. BLAKELY [15]

Mr. Robert J. Blakely gave this speech before the combined convention of the American Association for Adult Education, the Department of Adult Education, the National Education Association, the National University Extension Association, the Educational Film Library Association, and the Adult Education Board of the American Library Association, at the Horace H. Rackham Memorial Building, Detroit, Michigan, on April 23, 1946.

Robert J. Masske, President of the Department of Adult Education, presided over the Second General Session at which Mr. Blakely spoke. Mr. Luther Evans, of the Library of Congress, gave the other address at the session.

This talk is original in conception and expression, provocative in its analysis of American attitudes and political conduct. The speaker had recently returned from more than two years' service in the Western Pacific including Okinawa, with the Third and later the Sixth Marine divisions.

Blakely is a seasoned speaker both by training and experience. As high school debater and extempore speaker, representing Onawa (Iowa) High School, he was winner in the State Final Contests of the Iowa High School Forensic League. At the University of Iowa he won repeated honors in intercollegiate debate and oratory; he met in debate Oxford University. In his later activities as editorial writer for the *Des Moines Register* and as administrative officer in the Office of War Information, he addressed many audiences, and frequently participated in discussion groups, including radio round tables.

His outstanding traits as a speaker are extempore ability, wide vocabulary, clear enunciation and articulation, vocal force, and sincerity. His addresses are based upon systematic investigation. Of his methods he reports that he makes most of his speeches from outline, either written or mentally framed. Occasionally he writes a speech beforehand. Then he prepares an outline in some detail and fills it in. "For the most effective speaking," he says, "I prepare an outline, enlarge it, then put the manuscript aside and talk from the outline." [16]

Perhaps I take too much for granted, but I assume that most of us agree that the world faces this dilemma: On the one hand,

---

[14] By permission of Mr. Blakely. Text supplied through the courtesy of the author.
[15] For biographical note see Appendix.
[16] Letter to the editor, May 16, 1946.

we must establish soon a world government which, unlike the United Nations, is based on individuals instead of on states and which is responsive to democratic control. Confederation never has worked. It seems unlikely that it will work in the United Nations. We haven't time for gradual development. Yet, on the other hand, we feel that the human race is not ready for federal democratic government. The first authority which must be delegated to a world government is control over all military forces and the first guarantee we must establish is the basic democratic rights. But these ends seem likely to be the last, not the first, to be achieved. We cannot conceive that the members of the United Nations could agree upon such a radical revision of the charter as is needed, or that, if they did, their proposals would be ratified. As Anne O'Hare McCormick has said: "The jangle you hear is not so much national anthems out of tune as clocks out of time. The primeval tom tom still beats while the atom bomb ticks. Russia is straddling the centuries, in victory more than ever pounding backward to Peter the Great and racing at the same time to overtake Henry Ford and Henry Kaiser before she has caught up with Thomas Jefferson. The clocks of Europe are turning back and the clocks of Asia are turning forward. And there are places where time stands still because the night does not lift and there is no tomorrow." I add—the clocks of America jangle; technologically we prepare for the day after tomorrow; socially we strive to regain the day before yesterday. In brief—we've got to have world government now; we can't get world government now.

Of course, this analysis may be wrong and things may work out in the blind illogic of history. But as vertebrates we haven't the right to count on this. So, what should we do?

We should give full support to the United Nations, and all measures which strengthen it and grow out of it.

We should press and prepare for the transformation of the United Nations into a federation.

We should enter sympathetically into the minds of other peoples. This means particularly appreciating the Russians' pride and fear and the need of such peoples as the Chinese to telescope into decades processes which took centuries in the West.

We should work to overhaul our domestic society toward political, economic and social democracy.

We should rethink the fundamental nature of democracy and be imaginative toward the potential varieties of form which it might take. If democracy can be embodied only in the cultural forms it has received in the West, then it is doomed to a brief and provincial life, because to most peoples of the world these forms are alien. Yet, though we must be hospitable toward the varieties of form which democracy may take, I do not see how we can escape the conviction that all must somehow embody the freedoms to think, investigate, communicate and disagree.

As I give this counsel I am aware of how inadequate it is and I am haunted by the fear of atomic war, not coming as it came before—through deliberate aggression with the hope of victory—but coming with the pushing of a button in terror. If you haven't read, "Pilot Lights of the Apocalypse" in the January *Fortune,* I urge you to do so.

The truth is that we are already well along in an atomic armaments race. And the tragedy is that the three great powers are quickening the race by jostling each other for advantages which will soon be obsolete. Russia is trying to gain security through the establishment of a ring of buffer states. Britain is trying to gain security through preserving her life-line of empire. The United States is trying to gain security through holding bases and building planes for destroying the war potential of any aggressor. But neither buffer states nor naval and air bases nor bombers and fighters will count for much in a war of radio-controlled rocket-propelled atomic-warhead missiles, perhaps revolving outside our atmosphere.

This race must be stopped before it goes much further. For stopping it I see only one hope—the establishment of something similar to the Atomic Development Authority recommended by the State Department—international ownership and operation of all mines and factories dealing with dangerous fissionable materials.

A small hope—and yet a hard one. The plan is concrete. If we can remove the fear of sudden attack, we shall have gained time. Perhaps with this time we shall establish world regulation over what may be ultimately the chief source of energy and thereby go far toward solving the problem of war itself.

The plan advocates action on the one plane which rises above the barriers of language, politics, economics and psychology—the plane of science.

In my judgment educators have no more important task than to explain the need for this kind of plan. Perhaps Russia will not accept it, in which case it will not work; but certainly it will fail if the people and the government of the United States do not advocate it in good faith. The spirit in which we offer it might determine whether or not it is accepted by other nations.

When we as laymen support this plan we do so because we see no alternative. But most of us aren't able to understand the technical factors behind the provisions of the report. Most of us haven't the training to evaluate, for example, the dependability of the denaturing process upon which the plan is based. And most of the few who could evaluate this and many other technical factors won't be given the chance to do so because of security regulations.

We shall be advocating for reasons we do not fully understand a kind of world government by scientists whose decisions we shall be unqualified to criticize and whose actions we shall not dare to try to control because of the fear of the consequence of their failure.

Is this sort of plan democratic? No. Is it communistic? No. It can not be subjected to the errors of either a democratic majority or an autocratic minority, and it cannot be used to serve a political or economic creed, else it will fail.

What is it then? Don't you recognize it? It is technocracy—the new theocracy of science.

We are fortunate that at this stage so many of our great scientific minds are also philosophic. They are our philosopher-kings. But it need not necessarily be so. Great scientists served the Nazis. Lesser scientists are frequently contemptuous of the layman. Scientists in America in the past have had a group history of almost singular withdrawal from public affairs. Two of the human reactions on the part of some of the scientists to their new position of power will be, I predict, corruption and ambition.

Eventually we must establish democratic control over our technocrats too by establishing a stronger humane tradition within science and a broader public knowledge of scientific methods. But at the moment, just as during the war we had to trust our military leaders, now we must take chances on our scientists.

How did we get into this situation, anyway?

Let's briefly consider the relationship between science and modern societies.

Probably the two most distinctive features of the modern world are the coming into importance of the wishes of the masses of people and the development of systematic science.

The social movement which we know as democratic-capitalism, which I shall call democracy, developed and used science first. For a time the social and physical movements coincided. They worked together horizontally for a wider extension of government and economy and vertically for a broadening of participation in and benefit from society.

But then they parted company. The scientific movement continued faster toward the same goals. The democratic movement stopped with the national state, the middle class, and the white race.

Frictions arose between the conflicting tendencies of the social and physical movements on all three fronts. Science demanded larger economic and social units; nationalism not only stopped consolidating people and resources into larger units but began to break up some units into smaller states. Science demanded broader purchasing power and greater production; middle-class capitalism failed to solve either inadequate purchasing power, unemployment or business cycles. Science does not recognize race as a significant factor in technology; racism helped create imperialism abroad and discrimination at home.

Partly in protest against the failures of the democratic system, the communist-statist system, which I shall call communism, was inaugurated. This system responded with considerable success to several challenges which the democratic system had failed to meet—nationalism, class distinction, racism and unemployment. It exalted science and participation by the masses of the people, but under strict control. It denied to the individual in society the freedom which it urged upon him in the laboratory. It made no provision for its leaders' being wrong or for its being intermediate in historical development.

The democratic states did not cooperate with each other, nor did they and the Communist state cooperate, nor did either system give help and guidance to the peoples who belonged to neither. Overhead clashed the swords of nationalism and technology, honing each other. Beneath boiled the tensions of race and class.

Out of this chaos rose fascism—triumphant in several states but dormant in every country and in every human heart. Fascism accepted science. It adopted the worst and rejected the best features of the two conflicting social systems. From democracy it took racism, nationalism and class distinction. From communism it took tyrannical control over thought and behavior.

The democratic states were dominant in the world and it was therefore necessary for fascism to beguile them. To the dispossessed it promised security; to the disaffected, revenge; to the ambitious, distinction; to the established, protection from communism.

So, almost too late and not until each nation had been attacked, the democratic nations and the Communist nation came into negative alliance against these perverted caricatures of themselves.

Some of us had high hopes in the war.

Because we hated it so, because we saw its long roots, because we wanted it to have meaning particularly for those classes which carry the heavier end of the cross, we hoped that the war would result in a removal of at least some of the conditions which produced it.

We should not be embarrassed even now to list those hopes.

We hoped that the fundamental community of concern for human welfare between democracy and communism would be made clear to the citizens of both.

We hoped that the groups in both communism and democracy which were denied equal partnership in society would out of sheer necessity be called upon to help fight the war and would thus be permanently promoted.

We hoped that out of this same necessity for help, the exploited in all lands would play a new role and win a new status.

These hopes have been fulfilled to only a small degree. The postwar world in essential structure and content is the prewar world—"only more so." Certain pacifists and isolationists, noting this, smugly say, "I told you so!" But as they showed us no alternative to fighting the war then they can claim no vindication now.

Some wars have precipitated fundamental changes, even among victor nations. Why did not this war do so—the greatest the most nearly total and global?

I suggest that one important reason is that China, Russia and Britain had to fight too hard and that the United States did not have to fight hard enough.

Russia, to specify, suffered and exerted so that much of her human and world spirit has been transmuted into nationalistic fear and pride.

The United States won the war on its fat, without getting into more than moderately good shape. We entered the war with none of the issues of twentieth century democracy settled—neither political control over economic power, nor the need for a service as opposed to a policeman state; nor the right of the citizens to economic and social democracy; nor collective bargaining; nor the equality of both sexes and all races. Yet even when we entered the war we were concluding the longest "reform" era in our national history and already we had begun to settle back into a period of "consolidation." We stepped into the war backward, warding off blows to the groin. We won the war without resolving our domestic disputes, without discovering our ultimate capacity or the reason we were fighting, and without any real sacrifice except by a relatively few individuals. Most of us, though we worked hard, lived more luxuriously than ever before.

I have asked myself whether the United States would have progressed further toward reform if we had suffered a longer, harder war. I have decided no—not unless the war had been fought on our own soil, in which case the world would have been mobilized against us and victory would have been improbable.

In one way—and perhaps only one—the war made a greater demand upon the American people than upon the people of any other major warring nation—that is, in imagination. We had to fight without seeing or even clearly conceiving possible the devastation of our own homes. To have suffered more casualties overseas would not by itself, I think, have forced us to the housecleaning to which the British people were forced.

During those days when, whether we realized it or not, America was losing the war—1942 and early 1943—an experiment which should be significant to this group was conducted in the Office of War Information. It was under the leadership of Lyman Bryson and several members of this audience played major roles in it. Throught an adult education program we tried to draw into the war those groups of our people who are denied full participation in our society.

We tried to explain the real issues of the war, particularly to the American Negroes and to foreign language minorities.

We tried to stimulate pro and con discussion of the war among all groups.

We tried to reach the minorities which are out of the main standardized cultural stream. We tried to do this through their music, customs and art.

This was the part of the Office of War Information upon which Congress focussed its criticism at the end of the first year.

The congressional critics were against discussion of controversial issues because they did not believe that the issues were controversial.

They feared our informing minority groups.

They regarded all ideological treatment of the war as subversive.

They were contemptuous of attempts to interpret the war culturally to those who could be reached in no other way.

In this program we got no support from the administration. Already it was far in the swingback of "compromise"—which meant making concessions to bribe the dominant groups to continue supporting the war.

Winston Churchill truly said once that as defeat retreated and victory advanced, the war became less "ideological." Another way of saying this is that as it became less necessary to remove the inefficiency of injustice, less was removed.

Well, we won the war. What did we win? Time—more precious than uranium—time to tackle the lethal problems which produced the war *if we would only make use of it.*

But—and here is the joke—in winning the war we shortened the time which we won.

History offers no parallel to the alignment of social systems and national power which we have at the conclusion of the war.

The world is divided into three parts—one system whose essence is the supremacy of the individual which revolves around the United States; another whose essence is the supremacy of the state whose mass is the Soviet Union; and a third part unformed a yet for which the first two are in competition.

The two systems are in competition not because their peoples or leaders want them to be, but because each is on trial.

They are on trial because for the first time in history the entire human race is on the march at the same time. Everywhere man has the awareness that he can influence his own fate by his own activity. Incrustations of custom, ignorance, superstition and authority which have held human beings obedient for so many centuries have been broken. Humans everywhere mean to try to use science to get above starvation and to use government to run their own affairs.

Of the two ways of doing this—the individualist and the statist—neither has worked ideally. The members of each system fear the other and in self-defense the leaders of each seek to extend military and political control over the contested areas. So the members of these areas, groping for a way to realize their aims, ask which way they should adopt and which system they should ally themselves with.

The central question at the moment is whether the individualist system and the statist system can cooperate, not only in their relations with each other, but also in their relations with the rest of the world.

Even though they cooperate, they will still be in competition, for their own peoples and the peoples of the rest of the world will be comparing them.

The competition between the two can take either a malignant or a beneficent form.

The malignant form, in which each seeks to dominate the rest of the world so as to gain an advantage over the other, can lead only to war with no hope of victory for either but instead with the danger of extinction to both.

The beneficent form of competition is one in which each side discovers more and more ground for trust and cooperation with the other while each competes peaceably in demonstrating the advantages of its system at home and in offering help to the disputed areas so as to attract them.

This second kind of competition—to attract instead of to dominate—would pay off in peace and security. But immediately it would cost more—in attention, in money, in goods. It would have to be expressed in such programs as scheduled independence, agrarian reforms, agricultural science, industrialization, improved medical care and sanitation. Most of the money and equipment for these world programs would have to come from the United States at first. The United States might even have to lend money to Russia itself to help direct competition into friendly channels and to help influence the development of Russia toward peaceful enterprise.

The demand upon the United States would not be simply external, either. As the heart of the individualist system and as the nation with the greatest pretense and prestige, we would have to improve the domestic workings of our system in many ways.

We must recognize that although the competition between the democratic and Communist systems need not be malignant, in the months since V-J Day it has tended to become so.

On the part of Russia we cannot ignore a series of moves which have provoked alarm from the other great powers and disillusioned the peoples of small states and colonial areas. I do not believe that the Russian leaders have plans for world conquest or revolution. But their behavior reveals them to be provincial, nationalistic, suspicious and clumsy. Neither during the war nor since victory have they let their people learn anything which they did not want them to know. This is explainable—but it is also ominous.

On our part internationally we are failing to meet the world famine through neglect of the necessary discipline upon ourselves. The loan to Britain is receiving so much blind prejudice the more ambitious but equally advisable loans are probably out of the question. And although our government is showing some skill in blocking the awkward moves of Russia, it is apparently offering no leadership in the positive solution of the situations which lead to conflict.

Domestically we are in an unlovely period. The lust for nylons when one out of every four persons in the world is starving; the organized attempt to kill or castrate the OPA during the period of highest production in our history on the argument that price control is hampering production—an attempt which may succeed because while each group wants prices controlled for other groups, no group is unqualifiedly for control of its own; the obstructing of an adequate housing program and of price ceilings on existing houses—these require a strong stomach and do not bode well.

With regard to the welcome given returned veterans. I am reminded of Pavlov's experiment. Some members of various groups, notably the clothing and housing industries, have developed a conditioned reflex so that at the sight of a discharge button their saliva begins to flow.

To one returning to the United States after some time in another part of the world and in an entirely different kind of life, two impressions are strong. Our domestic groups are struggling with each other for a stake far above mere money—for power—without standards to guide them or fear of consequence to restrain them. Second, the profit motive unqualified by any other motive seems without either limit or conscience.

Thus, looking at the two nations, I see little evidence that they are entering into that kind of competition which could be friendly and productive—competition for human welfare.

If we continue on the present road, I do not expect war between the democracies and communism for a number of years— not, let us say, until enough time has passed to make it an exceptionally good war. In the event of this war, it is fashionable to predict the extinction of the human race. Though I do not think that the devastation of an atomic war can easily be exaggerated, I do not expect that it would wipe out the whole race. But it may destroy the warring nations as significant societies.

And should it not? Can we, who have laid low Germany and Japan because they could not fill a peaceful function in the world—can we escape our own logic and morality? It may be that the responses of both the democratic and communistic societies are inadequate and that therefore they must pass as other civilizations have passed which had no creative answers for the recurrent challenge which confronted them.

But the human race, I am convinced, will survive to make another try. In crannies, in small nations, in colonies, in far-off corners of the globe there will be humans who are now despised who will have energy, ambition, awareness and hope—and relative innocence of our crimes and follies.

Their rise will probably be swift. In addition to the opportunities left them by the removal of those nations which oppressed or obstructed them, they will have two priceless heritages—knowledge of science, which is now as universal as the human race, and the example of our awful and unnecessary failure.

I used to consider talk like this a taking refuge in some future endeavor which I could not believe in if I could not believe in the endeavor of my own time. But I have been forced to look full in the face the probability that our civilization may fall. And I no longer regard a projection of hope to other peoples and later times as escapism. Instead I think it is a transcendent faith in the human race.

As a civilization matures its problems tend to change from external to internal, from physical to spiritual. Once the difficulty of migrating Americans was how to get up a mountain or across a river. Now it is how to get through a traffic jam or avoid a collision.

Man is just now coming into the young maturity of his knowledge of the physical world. Most of this has been learned in the past four hundred years. This knowledge changes his problem from how to get enough from nature in order to live into how to get along with himself well enough to live. Perhaps he has not had time enough to adjust his primeval personal and social habits to his new problem. Perhaps he needs to receive a few lessons.

The temptation is strong to identify our community and our time with all of humanity. My faith in the potentialities of our species make me hope that what may be failing is merely particular individuals, groups and ideas. Just as we have solved problems which had baffled other times, others after us will conquer those which defeated us.

And though this time we and our fellows may perish, let us ask what is really so different from other catastrophes about the one which threatens now. Most of mankind has always been in misery and want. Floods, wars, diseases, famine have taken hundreds of millions of lives at all periods of history and never more than in our own time. What is the essential difference then? Is it not merely that this time it is likely to happen to *us*?

We who have been so indifferent or philosophical to the universal waste of humanity suddenly become concerned when our own skins are threatened. I am reminded of Ensign Nicholas Rostov in *War and Peace,* who, meeting the realities of war for the first time, flees from the field incredulous, wondering, "Why are they trying to kill me, me whom everybody loves?"

I do not mean to underrate the importance of our own, and particularly not my own extinction. But when one is sufficiently doubtful about his own group then one looks more widely for immortality.

And this is not merely the consolations of philosophy. Our democratic faith teaches us that the ultimate victory of our cause is not limited to the present, or to the United States, or to the middle class, or to the white race, or even (can this be true?) to ourselves individually, but is committed to man himself.

However, this is no funeral oration. We've still got a chance and we should use that chance until it is gone and then we should not recognize that it is gone. So—a few words on playing that chance.

First, more than a mere mechanical or social invention is needed for our survival. We need a change in outlook and attitude,

This change, I am convinced, though spiritual in nature, must come mainly through secular education, formal and informal. I do not expect it to originate in organized churches. Protestantism is too divided and too insipid. Catholicism is too militant toward other sects, too deeply aligned with such movements as Franco's, and too deeply embroiled with the Soviet Union.

And several things keep me from depending on the rise of a new mass millenial religion as our only hope.

No religion today is universal enough to fit the bill. All the great religions have universal implications, but each is restrictive politically. What we need is a religion which is to all the high religions of our day—Christian, Buddhist, Mohammedan, Confucian and others and all their fractions—as Christianity was to the welter of sects in the ancient Roman world. I do not see that religion. We haven't time to wait.

Any religion which meets the modern crisis will have to provide for an acceptance of science. All previous mass religious movements have been anti-intellectual.

In the United States particularly things aren't bad enough to provide a seed bed for a millenial religious movement. The dominant American today is a modern Nicodemus. He comes to Christ at night lest he be seen. He leaves sadly because Christ can't meet his conditions. He has not two but two hundred coats. He not only doesn't want to give one hundred and ninety-nine away but he doesn't even want to sell until prices get better. He wants to have the beam in his own eye removed free because he is a fellow Lion and to charge an exhorbitant price for removing the mote in his neighbor's eye because it is precision work. He wants to load down a camel with needles—if they are scarce—and pass into the kingdom of heaven on palm leaves strewn by grateful customers and employees who honor him as a Christian, a boss and a patriot.

The historical fact is that vast religious movements teach a contempt for this world; our current problem arises from our being too much enamored of it, and too dubious of the next. New universal religions grow within the bodies of disintegrating civilizations and stand amid the ruins as the spiritual matrix for the civilizations which come after; we are interested primarily in keeping ours from disintegrating. We want all this and heaven too. Let us not think that we can have it.

Second, in my judgment, the motive on which many current thinkers are counting for salvation—fear of the atomic bomb— may be a reed to bend under us or break and pierce our hands.

In some situations Franklin Roosevelt's dictum that "We have nothing to fear but fear itself" is incorrect. With regard to the control of atomic energy, it is truer that the first thing we have to fear is not being afraid. In Des Moines the other evening, 5000 persons went to see Sharkey the Seal and 500 went to hear Dr. Urey. Certainly there is therapeutic power in fear. Witness the remarkable bill reported by the Senate committee on atomic energy. But fear can also paralyze or degrade, bringing to pass that which is dreaded.

Fear of a common enemy can unite peoples against that enemy, as we have experienced. But what happens when you are your own enemy? Unless it is intelligently guided, interpreted and supplemented, fear of atomic war will drive us not into each others' arms but into arms against each other.

Beyond changes in weapons and technology endures the fact that human beings do not come together merely to live together; they come together in order to work together. It is not necessary to love or even to know a person to work with him if you have something to do together. We Americans, for example, have never liked each other. Every great nation or empire has been a project in common. When it lost the dream of that project, it began to fall apart, regardless of loyalties, friendships or pride.

The human race today needs an enterprise which will give it cohesion stronger than differences or dislikes. It must be different from all other political enterprises in history because all others in one way or another have been directed against some human beings.

Feeling the oppressive weight of human wrong and misery and looking at the vast potentialities opened by social cooperation and science, we can see that the world does not lack in things to do. We lack the imaginative drive to do it.

As inadequate as our human kind may be in character or intelligence for the task ahead, I think the greatest lack is in imagination.

Man is adequate to his environment when his reactions equal the problems which he faces. The problems of the modern world appear so impersonal to the emotions and so complex and abstract to the mind that they do not stimulate men's reactions, which are conditioned by his background as an animal or primitive to respond only to vivid personal experience. Thus a man may be cold to the news that 20 million Chinese are starving to death because he is indignant over how skinny the milk man's horse is. The impersonal and the personal, the direct and the indirect, the individual and the social can be bridged and the fabulous energy of thought and feeling harnessed, but only by the most skillful teaching. This is the social equivalent of splitting the atom—the breaking of the field of selfish force which isolates the atomized individual and the release of incredible personal power.

We have already gone far in some ways. Aristotle wanted to limit the state to the number of persons who could know each other and to the area which a man could walk across in a single day. Once a state increases beyond this elementary unit, there is no psychological reason why it should not increase indefinitely provided that communications can be maintained. There is just as much abstraction and symbolism involved in having a state as large as the American union as there would be in a world state. It takes imagination of a kind in order to be nationalistic.

Individuals who are narrowly patriotic are like deep-sea divers. They are adjusted to the pressures of their environment— the divers to the weight of the water, the patriots are raised above the pressures, it isn't enough in either case merely to remove external equipment, such as the helmet or the national state. Internal adjustments have to be made also, else they will burst.

Judging from the American serviceman's behavior in foreign lands, I would say that two of the internal pressures which must be altered in our ascent to world government are our incuriousness toward other peoples and our contempt for that which is different from what we know. Since we consider what we have as incomparably the best, there is no real point in learning about anything else; and for that reason, that which is different is considered inferior.

In conclusion, I offer this group of professional adult educators three bits of advice.

First, you need allies. Spend much of your time trying to convert the leaders of groups—all groups, from unions and chambers of commerce to amalgamated philetalists—to regard their jobs as an opportunity and an obligation to teach. Everything can be taught from anything. I am in sympathy with the tendency in universities and colleges to make broader the common foundation of liberal education beneath the next generation of specialists and laymen, but that won't help the present adult generations much. If skillfully done, the essence of humane education can be imparted even in the teaching of technical specialties. I would like to see one tenth of the effort now devoted to medieval or eighteenth century methods of teaching invested in an exploration of how the humane qualities can be taught through subjects which have immediate practical application.

The responsibilities of decentralized educational groups are the greater because of the eclipse of the office of the president of the United States as the most powerful seat of education in the country. Through himself and the men whom he attracted to him, President Roosevelt dramatized the importance of general issues to an individual and of his role in meeting them. The problems were reduced to human proportions and the individual was exalted to heroic proportions. This is what all great democratic leaders do. This is what we must try to do. Previously local educators needed to prod or supplement or correct the President of the United States. Now we must try to substitute for the President of the United States.

Second, you should clarify as sharply as possible why you are doing what you are doing. Whom do you trust? What kind of a world do you want?

Behind adult education is a philosophy which is perennially radical, because it states that the average man is educable, that he has rights, that when educated he can be trusted to exercise those rights. But when you teach people to think, who can tell what they will think? No one, least of all those in power. That is what terrifies some people.

The philosophy behind adult education is the philosophy of the Declaration of Independence, which sets up infinite goals and exhorts man to seek them. When revolutions less limited in concept and faith have run their courses to become in turn the enemies of change, the democratic philosophy is as explosive as ever. As Caspar Rausch said before the firing squad, "When the things for which I die have lost their meaning, strive with your lives that they be overthrown!"

It was not possible to handle the information about the war without asking what kind of a war we were fighting. If it was a war against change, the problem of information was of one kind. If it was a war for freedom, the problem of information was different. Some said, we will simply give the facts. But out of a multitude of facts, which should be chosen? What emphasis should they receive? And what did they mean? To answer these questions was to become philosophical.

Similarly to teach about or to interpret the present state of "peacelessness" it is necessary to ask what kind of period we are in. How did it come about? What does it mean? How do we want it to end? And to ask these questions also is to become philosophical.

And in basic philosophy, I hold with Lincoln, this time concerning the entire world. "No men are more worthy to be trusted than those who toil up from poverty; none less inclined to take or touch aught which they have not honestly earned." I quote this because it is all too easy for persons dealing in adult education to regard the poor and ignorant as guinea pigs and to conclude that their real allies are those with whom they can dine and drink and discuss the latest books.

Last, we must be vastly more skillful than we are in presentation. We must learn how to put things simply and dramatically. We must learn how to touch the liver and the heart as well as the mind.

The first essential is sincerity. I still get furious when I think of the way some of the war programs were sold to the American people. Most horrible example—the war bond campaigns. The war was sold as a Cecil DeMille production, which was bound to have a happy ending if only one bought bonds because Hedy Lamarr has pretty legs and went to great sacrifice to come out to Des Moines and incidentally you must see her next movie. This method was logically extended to the pasting of bonds on Queenie, the strip tease artist, whom you could peel and at the same time give guns to the boys in the front lines. That was indeed the best of all possible worlds.

This sort of appeal involves a judgment of the character of the American people which I reject. I mention this because it illustrates that, although one must be attractive, one must be real. If you try to sell war or peace as though it were a tube of tooth paste, people will throw up the same sort of defense which they must necessarily develop toward tooth paste.

If people are given the truth and if they are asked to do what is right and what is their duty, they will respond. People have an incorruptible sense for both reality and duty once issues and appeals are made straight.

Being popular does not mean being false. It means the translation of symbols as mysterious as mathematics into terms which move the hearts and minds of us all, sophisticated or ingenuous.

Once this is done, once the connection is revealed, once the applicability is demonstrated, people can cope with complexities. We all live lives which would make Cicero a schizophrene in a week were he suddenly revived. Those of you who have worked with farmers in the AAA program, for example, know how competent ordinary people can be with intricate programs once they see their importance. There also is the example of how quickly and ably American housewives mastered the point rationing system. There apparently is no limit to the mass of intricacy which the average individual can surmount. Then he stands upon it as gracefully and apparently as incapable of further achievement as the cave man stood on his lower plain of social complexity.

Alfred North Whitehead says that previous to our century the time span of change was longer than the life of an individual but that now for the first time in history it is shorter than the life of an individual. Since he wrote this, the time span of change has shortened even more and perhaps is now less than a decade. But there might be an advantage in this. If the time span of change is longer than a human life, each generation can escape recognizing the need to change. If it is equal to the length of a human life, a generation can recognize the need but fear the result. But if the time span of change is merely a few years perhaps a generation can come to regard change as natural just as previous generations regarded stability as natural.

One part of me cries out that our civilization must not perish. Compared to the systems which we fought, we are on the side of life. Among ourselves, and dealing with that which we can understand or want to understand, we hate violence, love justice and honor truth.

But today we are not being compared to the Nazis or Samurai. We are being compared with what we need to be. And in this comparison our society is revealed to be leprously sick. Much of it is trivial, or shoddy or false. Individually we do not stand ready to give ourselves for the corporate good, either because we do not think it is necessary or because we are counting on enough "suckers" to do so that we won't have to. With regard to other peoples, we ask, "Am I my brother's keeper?" forgetting that the answer is, "Yes!" and that this question was first asked by a man who had just slain his brother. We are hypocritical or un-self-critical, because we hotly condemn in others that which we defend in ourselves. We are charitable or merciful or benevolent where we ought to be just. We are arrogant where we ought to be humble. We scorn our friends because they are individual and therefore different and courageous and therefore proud. We forgive our enemies because they are neat, clean and obsequious. We fear those who champion today the causes for which we stood in other centuries.

Today we are opposed by a much more formidable foe than the Nazis or the Japs—ourselves.

Much that is good within us may rally in time. But the time is short.

Short or not, we should be grateful for it. Some of us personally feel that we are living on borrowed time. Remembering the past decade, we should all feel that our civilization is living on borrowed time.

Since it was borrowed from those who bought it with their lives, let us use it well.

But win or lose, it is good to be free and to have a fight worth fighting. Let's live each day as though it were the first and the last—and we may be at least half right. And let's have fun. Since the atomic bomb is so efficient, it doesn't need any help from ulcers of the stomach.

We may win. Sometimes I think that we shall win.

THE ISSUES IN EDUCATION: 1946 [17]

ROBERT M. HUTCHINS

Chancellor Robert M. Hutchins of the University of Chicago gave this address before the American Council on Education, at the Stevens Hotel, Chicago, Illinois, on May 3, 1946. Several hundred prominent educators, many of them college presidents, attended the dinner in the Grand Ballroom, at which the speech was presented. President Donald Tressider of Stanford University presided. Alexander J. Stoddard of the American Council on Education also spoke.

Dr. Hutchins presented his thesis with his usual vocal and intellectual alertness. He expounded with latent or overt humor and with unmistakable clarity and concreteness his analysis of the problem confronting American education, his educational philosophy as applied to "education for all," to adult education, and especially to the liberal arts college. He referred to his favorite ideas of the reading of "great books," the qualifications and training of liberal arts teachers, and the curriculum that stresses the humanities and social studies. These Hutchins principles were familiar to many who had followed through the preceding fifteen years his many writings and speeches. His tenets and programs of educational action, nevertheless, were here stated with fresh vigor.[18]

Dr. Hutchins, as an undergraduate at Yale, was an outstanding debater, logical and persuasive. He has steadily matured as a platform leader. He has readiness of ideas and of language, abundance of personal and emotional proof, analytical and organizational power, and extempore ability. He is especially resourceful in adapting his ideas to various types of audiences, including radio listeners.

The great problems before us are, first, can we survive, and second, what kind of life are we going to lead if we do.

Our monopoly of the atomic bomb will end within three to five years. There is no defense against the bomb, and there never will be. It can be brought into this country in any num-

[17] By permission of Chancellor Robert M. Hutchins. Text furnished through the courtesy of Dr. Hutchins.

[18] For biographical note see Appendix.

[19] For further exposition of Dr. Hutchins' veiws on education and politics, cf. his addresses: "A Philosophy of Life." *Representative American Speeches: 1937-1938*, p. 184 ff; "Organization and Subject Matter of General Education," *Representative American Speeches: 1938-1939*, p. 199 ff.; "Shall We Do Whatever Is Necessary to Ensure a British Victory?" *Representative American Speeches: 1940-1941*, p. 33 ff; "The University in War and Peace," *Representative American Speeches: 1942-1943*, p. 235 ff.

ber of ways. If it is brought into this country in any way it will destroy all our cities, no matter what our superiority in military power, including atomic bombs, may be. The alternatives before us are no longer peace or war; they are peace or the death of civilization.

When other countries have atomic bombs, the isolated, impregnable position in which the United States has luxuriated will be lost forever. This country will be in the geographical, military, and psychological situation of Czechoslovakia before the war. We may survive, but we shall constantly be wondering how long we are going to. And one false step in foreign policy, a field in which heretofore aimless blundering has been a harmless pastime, may precipitate universal destruction.

If we do survive, our economic and our political systems will undergo terrific strain. Virgil Jordan exaggerates very little when he says, "We can now make anything out of anything or nothing, anywhere in the world, in any amount, almost without measurable cost." When atomic power is available, and it will be any minute, distance and the scarcity of fuel and raw materials will cease to influence the location of industries and communities. New industries and new communities can be created anywhere because the cost of transporting the sources of atomic energy is negligible. These developments will be accompanied by the rapid dissolution of old industries and old communities. The whole economy, which has rested on work and scarcity, may fall to pieces in the new era of leisure and abundance. We may yearn for the depressions and unemployment we have known as though they were the good old days.

If we survive, the leisure which the atomic age will bring may make peace more horrible than war. We face the dreadful prospect of hour after hour, even day after day, with nothing to do. After we have read all the comic books, traveled all the miles, seen all the movies, and drunk all the liquor we can stand, what shall we do then? All of us here are old enough to testify that all forms of recreation eventually lose their charm.

These changes in the economy will be matched by similar strains on our political system. The accelerated rate of technological change will make for great insecurity. Only a powerful central government, it will be supposed, can supply stability. The physical forces with which we are dealing are so tremendous that we shall be unwilling to intrust them to private persons. Nobody has suggested that atomic energy should not be a governmental monopoly. The only question has been which branch of the government should monopolize it. Moreover, the duties of citizenship, which we have been able to take very lightly, will now be so complicated and burdensome that many people will feel that they cannot carry them; they will leave government to the government. We may even hear that we need a leader. The principal problems of the government will be security and boredom. And so the world comes back again to bread and circuses.

What has all this to do with American education as we have known it? Very little. These problems are of the utmost seriousness and urgency. American education has been happily free from any sense of either. Apparently our people have wanted it so. I know that education is the American substitute for a national religion; but many countries have been able to reconcile financial support of a religious establishment with complete disregard of its principles. There has been no particular reason why American educators or the American people should regard education as serious or urgent. Our country was rich, secure, and powerful. It was a country which even the grossest immorality and stupidity could not ruin. The American people have therefore been at liberty to devote themselves wholeheartedly to getting ahead. And though it was clearly possible to get ahead very nicely without any education at all, a social prejudice was fortunately established that you could get ahead a little better if you went to school a little longer. The more expensive and famous the school the greater the advantage it conferred. It followed, of course, that what went on in the school was of little importance to anybody. What was important was not what went on in the school, but the fact that the pupils had been there.

In this atmosphere all of us in American education have grown up. To these purposes our institutions, for the most part unconsciously, have been dedicated. Now we face a new and totally different world, which has come upon us with incredible suddenness. We may not know what will hold this new world together; but we do know what will make it explode, and that is the pursuit of those policies and ideals which have characterized our country, and most others, in the past. Civilization can be saved only by a moral, intellectual, and spiritual revolution to match the scientific, technological, and economic revolution in which we are now living. If American education can contribute to a moral, intellectual, and spiritual revolution, then it offers a real hope of salvation to suffering humanity everywhere. If it cannot or will not contribute to this revolution, then it is irrelevant, and its fate is immaterial.

I believe in world government. I think we must have it, and have it soon. But the most ardent advocate of a world state will not claim that it can be maintained, or perhaps even achieved, without the moral, intellectual, and spiritual revolution to which I have referred. The prospects of World War III are only a little less attractive than those of a world civil war. For a world state to come into being a higher degree of world community must exist than we can see at present, and for it to be maintained a still higher degree must be reached. Community requires communication, communication requires understanding, and, if understanding is not to lead to hatred and fear, the ambitions of the peoples of the earth must be such as not to arouse hatred and fear.

A world state demands a world community, a world community demands a world revolution, moral, intellectual, and spiritual. World government is not a gadget, which in one easy motion will preserve mankind. It can live and last only as it institutionalizes the brotherhood of man.

You will say that the task before us is impossible, and I admit it looks so. We must try to arrive at our destination in not more than five years. We must educate all Americans, for who can tell which Americans will have the decisive voice in the formation of our policies? We must try by example to lead the rest of the world to educate itself; for, if education succeeded in changing the hearts of Americans, and the hearts of other peoples remained unchanged, we should merely have the satisfaction of being blown up with changed hearts rather than unchanged ones. I do not expect an American audience to have enough faith in the immortality of the soul to regard this as more than a dubious consolation.

You may feel that there is a certain disproportion between the means I have chosen and the end I have in view. You may suggest that I have myself pointed out that little in the record of American education indicates that it is interested in or qualified for leadership in a moral, intellectual, and spiritual revolution throughout the world.

My answer to all objections is the same: this revolution is necessary, and therefore possible. We do not know what heights men can achieve if they understand that it is necessary for them to reach them. We do not know what education can accomplish, because we have never tried it. We never had to. Now education is a serious and urgent business.

Consider the question of time. I decline to take advantage of the opportunity for recrimination on the subject of the Chicago bachelor's degree and content myself with asking whether anybody honestly believes that it is impossible to complete a program of liberal education in less than four years. Or is there anybody who can prove that Father Gannon of Fordham is wrong in saying that liberal education should and can be completed by the age of 18, that is, four years earlier than is normally the case? Under present conditions the burden of proof is on those who would pretend that we have time to waste.

Consider the question of education for all. One of the most amusing features of the educational situation is the outraged cries of educators at the spectacle of the hordes of people clamoring for education. It is as though the bench of bishops should adopt a resolution complaining because too many people wanted to go to church. Isn't this the opportunity we have been waiting for? Don't we believe in education? Don't we agree that in a democracy we must educate everybody or abandon universal suffrage?

If we understood, and could make our people understand, that education is the most serious and urgent business in the world, could we have any doubt that we could find the means to carry on the work? And as for the geographical scale on which education must now operate, we may remind ourselves that the problem before Unesco, the United Nations Educational, Scientific, and Cultural Organization, is not more difficult under modern conditions of transportation and communication than that which Horace Mann faced in Massachusetts a hundred years ago. The imaginative use of the instruments which technology has given us, for education rather than destruction, could give education a scope of which our ancestors could not dream.

Think of the chance we have now in adult education, and the responsibility, too. Work is the enemy of education, and we are entering an age in which there will be unprecedented leisure for all. Leisure and recreation are not the same. Leisure has nothing to do with idleness. Leisure is that portion of the individual's time which he devotes to his moral and intellectual development and to participation in the life of the community of which he is a part. The more leisure there is the better for civilization.

If we want to help save the world within the next few years, we must attend to the education of adults, for only they will have the influence within that period to affect the course of events. If we want to save adults in the atomic age from the suicidal tendencies which boredom eventually induces, if we want to build a world community, we must regard the continuing education of our people throughout life as our principal responsibility.

It can no longer be looked upon as a causal activity conducted by a university for the purpose of helping underpaid instructors gain a little extra income, and attended by third-rate bookkeepers who want to learn how to become second-rate bookkeepers.

Think of the time, thought, effort, and money we have wasted on vocational training. Its relevance to a moral, intellectual, and spiritual reformation is certainly remote. And its relevance to the task of earning a living, which was always open to question in view of the obvious superiority of training on the job, will reach the vanishing point in the atomic age. When we can make anything out of anything or nothing, anywhere, in any amount, almost without measurable cost, the fraction of our lives that will go into making things will be about the same as that which fortunate savages devote to picking their daily diet off the bread-fruit trees, and the training needed for the job will be about the same, too. The vocational education the world needs is education for the common vocation of citizenship. This is liberal education.

In the United States the phrase "college of liberal arts" conveys no meaning to the mind. Certainly it does not mean that here is an institution devoted to liberal education. It usually denotes an institution in which the liberal arts are not taught. The only other definition that would cover almost all, but probably not all, of the enterprises called colleges of liberal arts is that they are institutions which do not award the Ph.D. degree. The trouble with this definition is that it does not differentiate these colleges from kindergartens, elementary schools, and high schools. We do not know what these colleges could accomplish if they organized themselves to give a liberal education and then proceeded to give it, without regard to the demands of graduate schools, parents, football coaches, and academic vested interests.

Many colleges boast that they have a highly diversified curriculum, or indeed none at all, in order to develop the special aptitudes of their students. I have the impression that this kind of program results from the special interests of professors rather than the individual interests of students. Students can be interested in anything that is made important to them. A liberal college should have no difficulty, in the present world situation, in making liberal education important to the young people committed to its charge.

If the student-centered college is really a professor-centered college, its curriculum, if any, is unlikely to add up to a liberal education. The graduate schools which prospective professors must pass through to gain entrance to the faculty club are composed of narrow departmental specialists engaged in training narrow departmental specialists. Such narrow specialization is a necessary ingredient of the advancement of knowledge; it must be maintained for the purpose of advancing knowledge. But it has nothing to do with liberal education.

For liberal education we need a new type of teacher, and hence a new type of graduate school. It should be liberal, too. That is, it should be composed of teachers and students who have had a liberal education and who are eager to help others to acquire one. The members of the faculty should not be selected in terms of their competence in specialized fields, but in terms of their capacity to see knowledge as a whole, to engage in candid and intrepid thinking about fundamental problems, and to guide the student in his efforts to do such thinking for himself. It should be a community devoted to integration, to unification, to synthesis, to bringing order and intelligibility out of the chaos of the modern world.

The colleges and universities today are characterized by the loss of community within them. Since everybody is a specialist, nobody can communicate with anybody else. The conversation among the students is about athletics and among the faculty about the weather. Both students and faculty lose the sense of communal support in their intellectual enterprise, a sense which is of tremendous advantage in a college with a prescribed curriculum. But what is worse, it is impossible to rely on institutions which have no community within them to lay the foundation for a community in this country or a community in the world. The antics of alumni at reunions suggest that no community can be established among the products of the higher learning except by artificial exhilaration, and such community as results can hardly be described as moral, intellectual, or spiritual.

Some of the most venerable of our institutions of learning have now endorsed the movement to restore community to higher education. One of them has actually gone so far as to require the reading of eight of the great books of the Western world. Another suggests that a few of them might be read in the summer. We are getting on. The movement is now respectable, and it is to be hoped that it will gain momentum. But we may hope also that this movement will not fall a prey to the popular tendency to substitute names for things. For many years we have attached the name education to anything that went on in an educational institution, and the name research to anything that reflected the curiosity, however idle, of those who had found their way into academic life. Now we seem likely to attach the name liberal to anything that is not science and technology.

It is true that we do not need to emphasize the importance of science and technology. Now that they have won a war for us, the tendency of American students and American philanthropists to flock into these fields will be accentuated. It is true that our greatest problems are not how to improve the material conditions of existence and how to exploit the forces of nature. Our greatest problems are how to exist at all in the world which science and technology have made, and how to direct the power they have placed in our hands. Upon these problems science and technology shed little light. In the atomic age they cannot even defend us from the atomic bomb.

Nevertheless, natural science is a necessary part of a liberal education, for the citizen must understand the natural environment in which he lives. Though scientific research can contribute little to the moral, intellectual, and spiritual revolution upon which the future of civilization depends, the scientific method and the scientific spirit have a considerable part to play in it. Moreover, to say, we have had too much natural science; let us have more social science and humanities, is, in the present condition of the higher learning, to substitute names for things.

Does the student in the humanities and the social sciences learn the arts of communication? Does he learn to read and write? Does he master the disciplines which for centuries have been regarded as indispensable to the attack on any intellectual task? Does he come to understand the ideas and ideals which have animated mankind? Does he learn how to tell the good from the bad, the true from the false, the beautiful from the ugly? Does he discover what the ends of life are and what are the purposes of organized society?

Does he understand the tradition in which he lives? Does he learn how to be human, see the connection between man and man, and fit himself to become a member of a community which shall embrace all men? We know that ideas, understanding, criticism, and ethical and political theory have almost vanished from the humanities and the social sciences, to have their places taken by miscellaneous information, tours of the stockyards, and data collecting. We know that the fundamental problems of our time are philosophical. Yet philosophy has disappeared from the

social sciences. Instead of underlying all studies in the humanities, philosophy is confined to one department, which is steadily
losing influence as language, literature, art, and history vainly try
to become scientific.

What the world needs, then, is a liberal education worthy
of the name. This would be an education educating a man's
humanity, rather than indulging his individuality. It would be
an education appropriate to man, offering him the habitual vision
of greatness, and dealing primarily, in a world of rapid change,
with values independent of time or place. I believe that such
an education is supplied by a curriculum consisting of the great
works of the mind and the liberal arts. As the *Manchester
Guardian* said editorially the other day, "The more we understand the forces of nature, and so increase human power, the
more important it is that we should understand human character and draw inspiration from the great civilizing writers and
thinkers of the past. For the changes that simplify man's relations to nature complicate man's relations to man. Today, when
we have achieved intoxicating triumphs over nature, the nations
of the world are more afraid of each other than at any time in
their history."

Still, I do not insist upon the great civilizing writers and
thinkers of the past. If anybody can suggest a curriculum that
is more likely to achieve the objects I have named than the one
I have proposed, I shall gladly embrace him and it.

The new kind of graduate school needed to produce the new
kind of teacher which this program requires would not be concerned with the training of departmental specialists in the traditional fields, but with the education of men who were eager
to qualify themselves to understand and to help others understand the nature, the works, and the destiny of man.

We must now engage in the liberal education of everybody,
of all adolescents and all adults. Of these two adult education
is the more important. In fact, one of the principal purposes of
the liberal education of adolescents should be to prepare them
to go on with liberal education throughout their lives.

This program requires drastic changes in our educational institutions. But these changes are not impossible. They are those

which should have been made years ago, for everything that I have suggested is something we should have been doing all along. Until these changes are made, we cannot claim that the task which history has imposed upon us is beyond human achievement. All we can say is that we do not care enough about it to attempt it. By a clear definition of our purpose and a relentless exclusion of the irrelevant, the frivolous, and the trivial we may hope to reach the goal. We may hope to help our fellowmen to survive and to lead the good life if they do. It is better to try and fail than to decline the challenge.

APPENDIX

BIOGRAPHICAL NOTES [1]

BARUCH, BERNARD MANNES (1870-   ). A.B., College of
the City of New York, 1889; LL.D., Williams, 1923, University
of South Carolina, 1925, and several other colleges and universities; member of New York Stock Exchange, many years; appointed by President Wilson, member of Advisory Committee
on National Defense, 1916; member various committees on war
production, World War I; chairman, War Industries Board,
1918; member, Supreme Economic Council; economic adviser
for American Peace Commission, 1919; member, President's
Conference for Labor and Capital, October, 1919; President's
Agricultural Conference, 1922; unofficial adviser, various war
committees, World War II; American delegate, Atomic Bomb
Commission, 1946; awarded many decorations for services in
World War I; member, Phi Beta Kappa; author, *Making of
Economic and Reparations Sections of Peace Treaty*, 1920, also
treatises on various economic subjects.

BLAKELY, ROBERT J. (1915-   ). Born in Nebraska; attended Onawa, Iowa, public schools, graduating in 1933; A.B.,
State University of Iowa, 1937; graduate study in history, Harvard, 1937-38; editorial writer, Des Moines (Iowa) *Register
and Tribune*, 1938-42; Office of War Information, a special
assistant to Gardner Cowles, Jr., director of Domestic Branch of
OWI, 1942-43; United States Marine Corps Reserves, 1943-45,
commissioned, 1944; forward observer for artillery with the
Third and Sixth Marine Divisions; wounded, Okinawa; discharged as first lieutenant; with *Register and Tribune*, 1946-   ;
author of articles in *Foreign Affairs, Travel, Far Eastern Review,
American Library Association Bulletin,* and Council on Foreign
Relations publications.

[1] The chief sources of these notes are *Who's Who in America, Current Biogra-
phy, Religious Leaders in America, International Who's Who, Who's Who in
American Education, Directory of American Scholars,* and the *Congressional
Directory.*

BOWLES, CHESTER (1901-   ). Born in Springfield, Massachusetts; B.Sc., Yale, 1923; copy department of the George Patten Company, 1925-29; founder advertising firm, Benton and Bowles, 1929, chairman, 1936-41; rationing administrator, Connecticut, 1941-42; state director of Office of Price Administration, May 1942; general manager and later administrator of Office of Price Administration, 1943-46; Administrator, Economic Stabilization, 1946.

BRIGANCE, WILLIAM NORWOOD (1896-   ). Born in Olive Branch, Mississippi; A.B., University of Nebraska, 1916, A.M., 1920; University of Chicago, 1921, University of Wisconsin, 1922; Ph.D., University of Iowa, 1930; secondary school teacher, 1916-17, 1920-22; professor of speech, Wabash College, 1922-36; professor and head of Department of English, University of Hawaii, 1936-38; again professor of speech, Wabash, since 1938; teacher summer sessions, University of Nebraska, 1923-25, University of Southern California, 1932, University of Wisconsin, 1940, Louisiana State University, 1942; enlisted in regular army, 1917, later 2nd lieutenant, 32nd Division, with A.E.F., 13 months; member, American Association of University Professors; president, Speech Association of America, 1946; Lamda Chi Alpha, Tau Kappa Alpha, Phi Beta Kappa, American Legion; author, *The Spoken Word*, 1927; *Speech* (with W. G. Hedde), 1935; *Speech Composition*, 1937; *Your Every Day Speech*, 1937; *Speech-Making* (with R. K. Immel), 1938; *A Drill Manual for Improving Speech* (with F. M. Henderson), 1939; *American Speech* (with W. G. Hedde), 1942; *Speech for Military Service* (with R. K. Immel), 1943; editor (for National Association of Teachers of Speech) *A History and Criticism of American Public Address*, 1943; editor, *Quarterly Journal of Speech*, 1942-44.

BROWN, LEWIS H. (1894-   ). Born in Creston, Iowa; A.B., State University of Iowa, 1915; with Montgomery Ward and Company, 1919-27; president of Johns-Manville Company since 1929; trustee of Mutual Life Insurance Company; captain infantry, U.S. Army, 1917-19, A.E.F., France, 1918-19; received

Vermilye medal, 1939, from Franklin Institute of Pennsylvania for "outstanding contribution in the field of industrial management."

BYRNES, JAMES F. (1880-   ). Born in Charleston, South Carolina; admitted to bar, 1903; editor, *Journal and Review,* Aiken, South Carolina, 1903-07; court reporter, 1900-08; solicitor, 2nd Circuit, South Carolina, 1908-10; member 62nd to 68th Congresses, 1911-25; practiced law, Spartanburg, South Carolina, 1925-31; United States Senator, 1931-41; Associate Justice, U.S. Supreme Court, 1941-42; appointed head of the Office of War Mobilization, 1943; Secretary of State, 1944-   .

CHURCHILL, WINSTON LEONARD SPENCER (1874-   ). Educated at Harrow and Sandhurst; entered the army, 1895; served with Spanish forces in Cuba, 1895; service in India, 1897-98; with Nile army, 1898; correspondent with *Morning Post,* South Africa, 1899-1900; escaped prisoner, and in various battles of the Boer War, 1900; Member of Parliament, 1900-22; First Lord of Admiralty, 1911-15; an officer in the British Army in France, 1916; Minister of Munitions, 1917; various ministerial offices, 1918-22; Chancellor of the Exchequer, 1924-29; First Lord of the Admiralty, 1939-40; Prime Minister, First Lord of the Treasury, and Minister of Defense, 1940-45; author of a long list of books, including *Marlborough* (4 vols.), 1933; *Blood, Sweat, and Tears,* 1941; *Unrelenting Struggle,* 1942; *The End of the Beginning,* 1943; *Onward to Victory,* 1944.

COMPTON, ARTHUR HOLLY (1892-   ). Born in Wooster, Ohio; B.S., College of Wooster, 1913, Sc.D., 1927; M.A., Princeton, 1914, Ph.D., 1916; Cambridge University (England), 1920; honorary degrees from Ohio State University, Yale, Princeton, Brown and other universities; professor of physics, Washington University, 1920-23; professor of physics, University of Chicago, 1923-45; president of American Physical Society, 1934; Chancellor, Washington University, St. Louis, 1945-   ; president or officer of other learned societies; research in X-rays; Nobel prize for physics, 1927; a director, atomic bomb project,

Office of Scientific Research and Development, 1941 and after; author of *X-rays and Electrons*, 1926, and other publications on scientific subjects.

CONANT, JAMES BRYANT (1893-   ). Born in Dorchester, Massachusetts; A.B., Harvard, 1913, Ph.D., 1916; LL.D., University of Chicago, 1933, New York University, 1934, Bristol University (England), 1941; Sc.D., Cambridge University (England), 1941; D.C.L., Oxford University (England), 1936; honorary degrees from many other universities at home and abroad; instructor, assistant professor, professor of chemistry, Harvard, 1916-17, 1919-33; President of Harvard since 1933; chairman, National Research Defense Committee, 1941-43; lieutenant, Sanitary Corps, U.S. Army, 1917; major, Chemical Warfare Service, 1918; member of the atomic bomb project under Office of Scientific Research and Development, 1941 and after; member of Sigma XI, Phi Beta Kappa, and many learned societies; author of *The Chemistry of Organic Compounds*, 1933, and other books and articles.

DENNY, GEORGE V., JR. (1899-   ). Born in Washington, North Carolina; B.S., University of North Carolina, 1922; LL.D., Temple University, 1940; instructor in dramatic production, University of North Carolina, 1924-26; actor, 1926-27; manager of W. B. Feakins, Inc., 1927-28; director, Institute of Arts and Sciences, Columbia University, 1928-30; associate director, League of Political Education, 1931-37; founder and director, America's Town Meeting of the Air; treasurer, Economic Club of New York; member of executive board, American Association for Adult Education; President, Town Hall, Inc.; served, Students' Army Training Corps, 1918.

GITTELSOHN, ROLAND B. (1910-   ). Born in Cleveland, Ohio; Western Reserve, A.B., 1931; graduated as rabbi, Hebrew Union College, Cincinnati, Ohio, 1936; rabbi since June 1936, Central Synagogue of Nassau County, Rockville Centre, Long Island, New York; Executive Board, Long Island Zionist Region; committee on religious education, Central Conference of American Rabbis; commission on Jewish Education of Central Conference of American Rabbis and Union of American Hebrew Congregations; chaplain, United States Navy Reserve, June 1943, January 1946; received Navy Commendation Ribbon as Jewish chaplain of Fifth Marine Division for campaign of Iwo Jima; delivered dedicatory sermon, Fifth Marine Division cemetery, Iwo Jima; member, Phi Beta Kappa, Delta Sigma Rho; author of *Modern Jewish Problems* and numerous magazine articles.

HARDING, HAROLD FRIEND (1903-). Born in Niagara Falls, New York; A.B., Hamilton, 1925; A.M., Cornell University, 1929, Ph.D., 1937; studied in London, 1933; instructor in public speaking, Iowa State College, 1925-27; Cornell, 1928-31; assistant professor, George Washington University, 1931-38, head of the Department of Speech since 1946; major, lieutenant colonel, and colonel, Coast Artillery, United States Army, 1941-46; chief of staff, headquarters, Replacement Training Command in the Pacific Ocean Areas; awarded Bronze Star Medal, Legion of Merit, Rockefeller Foundation Postwar Fellowship in the Humanities; on various committees, National Association of Teachers of Speech; member and national treasurer, Delta Sigma Rho; author, *English Rhetorical Theory in the Eighteenth Century.*

HUTCHINS, ROBERT MAYNARD (1899-). Born in Brooklyn, New York; A.B., Yale, 1921, honorary A.M., 1922, LL.B., 1925; LL.D., West Virginia University, Lafayette College, and other institutions; Dean, Yale Law School, 1928-29; president, University of Chicago, 1929-44; chancellor, University of Chicago since 1944; in ambulance service, U.S. Army, 1917-19; Italian Army, 1918-19; decorated Croce di Guerra (Italian), 1918; member of numerous honorary and learned societies, including Phi Beta Kappa, Order of the Coif; author of *The Higher Learning in America,* 1936, and numerous other books and magazine articles.

JACKSON, ROBERT HOUGHWOUT (1902-). Born in Spring Creek, Pennsylvania; educated at Albany, New York, Law School, Union University; admitted to New York Bar,

1913, and began practice at Jamestown; appointed general council, Bureau of Internal Revenue, 1934; Assistant Attorney General of United States, 1936-38; Attorney General, 1939-41; Associate Justice of the United States Supreme Court since 1941;
Chief Counsel, International Tribunal to try Axis war criminals,
1945-46.

KUROKI, BEN (1919-   ). Born in Hershey, Nebraska;
attended public schools, Hershey; a Nisei, he enlisted, one day
after Pearl Harbor, in Army Air Forces; attended gunnery
school; flew thirty missions in Europe, including those over the
Ploesti oil fields in Rumania; later as gunner on B-29 in Pacific
theater, flew twenty-eight combat missions against Japanese
home islands, first Japanese-American to win Distinguished Flying Cross in fighting against Japan; won two Distinguished Flying Crosses and many other awards as a qualified turret gunner.

LEWIS, JOHN LLEWELLYN (1880-   ). Born in Lucas,
Iowa; educated in public schools; official United Mine Workers
of America, 1909-11; officer, American Federation of Labor,
1911-17; president of United Mine Workers of America since
1920; president of Congress of Industrial Organizations, 1935-
40; resigned with his United Mine Workers from the C.I.O.
in 1945; rejoined American Federation of Labor, 1946.

MACARTHUR, DOUGLAS (1880-   ). Born in Arkansas;
graduate, U. S. Military Academy, 1903; graduate, Engineer
School of Application, 1908; D.Sc., Pennsylvania Military Academy, 1928; many other honorary degrees; successively promoted
as member of the U. S. Army; Brigadier General, 1918; Major
General, 1925; General, 1930; served in Philippines, 1903-04,
Japan, 1905-06; army service schools, 1910-12; in Vera Cruz
Expedition, 1914; general staff, 1913-17; commander of 42nd
Division (Rainbow), 1918; Meuse-Argonne and other offensives;
twice wounded in action; army of occupation in Germany, 1918-
19; chief of staff, U. S. Army, 1930-35; commander, U. S. armed
forces in Far East since 1941; appointed supreme commander
land, air, and sea forces, Southwest Pacific, 1942; decorated

D.S.C., D.S.M., and awarded many other military honors; in charge of occupation of Japan, 1945-

MARSHALL, GEORGE CATLETT (1880-   ). Born at Uniontown, Pennsylvania; student Virginia Military Institute, 1897-1901; honorary graduate, United States Infantry-Cavalry School, 1907; graduate, Army Staff College, 1908; honorary degrees at Washington and Jefferson, Pennsylvania Military College, William and Mary, Trinity, and elsewhere; mounted through the grades to Major General, 1939; served in the Philippines, 1902-03, 1913-16; with A.E.F., 1917-19; on General Staff, and in Meuse-Argonne operations; in China, 1924-27; chief of staff with rank of General, 1939-1945; awarded the D.S.M. and many other military awards from United States, and various other countries; on military mission to China, 1945-46; "One of the principal brains and powers behind the vast military effort of the Allies in World War II"; author of *Selected Speeches and Statements of George C. Marshall,* 1946.

MURROW, EDWARD R. (1909-   ). Born in Greensboro, North Carolina; graduate of Washington State College, 1930; student at Stanford University and University of Washington; President of National Student Federation, 1930-32; assistant director of Institute of International Education, 1932-35; with Columbia Broadcasting System since 1935; chief of European service, 1937-46; vice president, Columbia Broadcasting Company since 1946.

NEWTON, JOSEPH FORT (1878-   ). Born at Decatur, Texas; student Southern Baptist Seminary, Louisville, Ky.; Litt.D., Coe, 1912; D.D., Tufts, 1918; LL.D., Temple, 1929; ordained Baptist church; pastor, Paris, Texas, 1897-98; St. Louis, 1898-1900; founder and pastor, People's Church, Dixon, Ill., 1901-08; pastor, Liberal Christian Church, Cedar Rapids, Iowa, 1908-16; at City Temple, London, England, 1916-19; Church of the Divine Paternity, New York, 1919-25; Memorial Church of St. Paul, Overbrook, Pennsylvania, 1925-30; St. James Church, Philadelphia, 1930-35; special preacher Philadelphia Churches, since 1935; associate editor, *Christian Century*, Chicago; author of many volumes, including *The Sword of the Spirit*, 1918; *The Theology of Civilization*, 1919; *Preaching in London*, 1923; *Preaching in New York*, 1924; *The New Preaching*, 1929; *The Angel in the Soul*, 1931; *His Cross and Ours*, 1940; also many pamphlets on patriotic and Masonic topics, and numerous addresses and sermons.

REUTHER, WALTER PHILIP (1907-   ). Born in Wheeling, West Virginia; apprentice tool and diemaker, Wheeling; employee, Briggs Manufacturing Company, Ford Motor Company (a foreman), Detroit; attended Wayne University for three years; traveller, via bicycle through Germany, Russia, China, Japan, student of auto plants and machine shops, 1933-35; organized auto workers in Detroit, 1935; member of the executive board, International Union of Automobile Workers, 1936-46; vice president of the United Automobile Workers, 1942-46; elected president in March 1946.

ROMNEY, GEORGE (1907-   ). Attended the Latter Day Saints' University, the University of Utah, and George Washington University; Latter Day Saints Missionary, Scotland and England, 1927-28; tariff specialist, under Senator David Walsh, of Massachusetts, 1928-29; assisted in drafting the Smoot-Hawley Tariff Act; with Aluminum Company of America, 1930, including assignment as Washington, D. C., representative of that company, 1930-39; Detroit manager, Automobile Manufacturers Association, 1939-42; general manager, Automobile Manufacturers Association, since 1942; managing director of the Automotive Council for War Production, 1941-45; active member of various trade organizations, both local and national.

SPELLMAN, FRANCIS JOSEPH (1889-   ). Born in Whitman, Massachusetts; A.B., Fordham, 1911; S.T.D., American College in Rome, 1916; LL.D., Notre Dame, Fordham, 1935; assistant All Saints Parish, Roxbury, Massachusetts, 1916-18; director of Catholic literature, Archdiocese of Boston, 1918-22, vice chancellor, 1922-23; editorial writer *Boston Pilot* (religious weekly), 1924; attaché Office of Secretary of State and translator of Papal broadcasts and encyclicals, Vatican, Rome, 1925-32; auxiliary bishop of Boston, 1932-39; archibishop of New York, 1939-44; inducted as cardinal, 1945; translator of *The Word of God, In the Footsteps of the Master.*

TAFT, ROBERT ALPHONSO (1889-   ). Born in Cincinnati, Ohio; attended public schools of Cincinnati and the Taft School; was graduated from Yale University, A.B., 1910; Harvard University, LL.B., 1913; attorney at law; Assistant Counsel for the United States Food Administration, 1917-18; Counsel for the American Relief Administration, 1919; member of the Ohio House of Representatives, 1921-1926, speaker, 1926; Ohio State Senate, 1931-32; United States Senate since 1939.

TRUMAN, HARRY S. (1884-   ). Born in Lamar, Missouri; student Kansas City School of Law, 1923-25; captain, Field Artillery, First World War; judge, Jackson County Court, 1922-24; presiding judge, 1926-34; United States Senator from Missouri, 1935-41, reelected for the term 1941-47; elected Vice President on the Democratic ticket, November 1944; sworn in as President of the United States on the death of President Roosevelt, April 1945.

UREY, HAROLD CLAYTON (1893-   ). Born, Walkerton, Indiana; B.S., University of Montana, 1917; Ph.D., University of California, 1923; at University of Copenhagen, 1923-24; D.Sc., Montana, Princeton, and other universities; chemist, Barret Chemical Company, Philadelphia, 1917-19; instructor in chemistry, University of Montana, 1919-21; associate in chemistry, Johns Hopkins, 1924-29; associate professor, chemistry, Columbia, 1929-34; professor, 1934-41; professor of chemistry, University of Chicago, since 1944; prominent in development of atomic bomb, World War II; member of many learned societies; author (with A. E. Ruark) of *Atoms, Molecules and Quanta,* 1930; editor, *Journal of Chemical Physics,* 1933-40; contributor to scientific journals; specialized in structure of atoms and molecules; discoverer of hydrogen atom of atomic weight two.

VANDENBERG, ARTHUR HENDRICK (1884-   ). Born in
Grand Rapids, Michigan; studied law at the University of Michigan, 1901-02, honorary A.M., 1925; LL.D., Hope College, 1926;
editor of *Grand Rapids Herald,* 1906-28; United States Senator,
1928-47; Chairman of Republican Senate Legislative Committee,
1933-34; received 76 votes for Republican presidential nomina-
tion, Philadelphia, 1940; American delegate, United Nations
Organization Conference, San Francisco, 1945; United States
Delegate of United Nations since 1945; member of Authors'
Club, London, England; author of *Alexander Hamilton, the
Greatest American,* 1921; *If Hamilton Were Here Today,* 1923;
The Trail of a Tradition, 1925.

CUMULATED AUTHOR INDEX

An author index to the volumes of *Representative American Speeches* for the years 1937-38 to 1945-46. The date following the title of each speech indicates the volume in which it appears.

Ackerman, C. W. Role of the press as a factor in public opinion and economic changes. 1937-38: 198-209

Barkley, A. W. Against Roosevelt's tax veto. 1943-44: 188-99; Foreign policies of Roosevelt. 1938-39: 53-9

Barr, Stringfellow. How can our schools meet the war emergency? 1941-42: 230-4

Barton, Bruce. Faith of Lincoln. 1939-40: 161-72

Baruch, Bernard. International control of atomic energy. 1945-46: 120-31

Baukhage, H. R. Tribute to Roosevelt. 1944-45: 167-9

Bell, B. I. Not taps but reveille. 1944-45: 307-13

Beneš, Eduard. What are we fighting for? 1942-43: 56-66

Berle, A. A. Jr. The warfare of free souls. 1941-42: 56-63

Biddle, Francis. Democracy and racial minorities. 1943-44: 172-87

Blackwelder, O. F. The contribution of the Christian faith. 1940-41: 255-62

Blakely, Robert J. Greatest lack. 1945-46: 241-61

Borah, W. E. Against the repeal of embargo. 1939-40: 38-52; Antilynching bill. 1937-38: 17-38; Possible results of a European war. 1938-39: 29-35

Bosley, Harold. If anywhere, then everywhere. 1943-44: 337-46

Bowles, Chester. Price control and inflation. 1945-46: 144-53

Brigance, W. N. Backwash of war. 1945-46: 75-84

Brown, L. H. Freedom or planned economy—there is no middle road. 1945-46: 133-43; Private agencies and public goals in the postwar world. 1942-43: 202-15

Burton, H. H. America's road to lasting peace. 1943-44: 106-15

Butler, N. M. The American plan to prevent war. 1941-42: 259-64; The responsibility of youth. 1944-45: 241-4; Which way is progress? 1937-38: 138-45; Why war? 1938-39: 13-17

Byrnes, J. F. Common Interests of the United Nations. 1945-46: 39-44; The war against inflation. 1942-43: 189-201

Cameron, W. J. Christmas, 1940. 1940-41: 232-4; Rock and flood. 1940-41: 235-7

Carleton, W. G. What of free enterprise? 1943-44; 209-29

Carter, Boake. Germany takes Austria. 1937-38; 97-100

Chapman, Virgil. On the war resolution again Japan. 1941-42; 40-3

Chester, C. M. Management's new responsibilities in our changing social economy. 1939-40: 293-305

Chiang Mei-ling (Madame Chiang Kai-shek). Fighting for the common cause. 1942-43: 81-4; Japan is first United States foe. 1942-43: 85-91

Churchill, Winston. Address to Congress. 1941-42: 19-29; Address to Congress. 1942-43: 30-46; British-American cooperation. 1943-44: 27-36; Germany surrenders. 1944-45: 40-2; Humanity's loss. 1944-45: 170-3; Sinews of peace. 1945-46: 20-32

Clark, B. C. Rearmament. 1938-39: 71-6

Coffee, J. M. What does freedom of speech mean to us today? 1941-42: 96-9

Coffin, H. S. God's mysterious education. 1941-42: 235-45

Compton, A. H. Science and religion. 1939-40: 421-6; Social implications of atomic energy. 1945-46: 109-19

Conant, J. B. Civil courage. 1945-46: 223-8; Unique ideal of American life. 1939-40: 337-45; Valedictory service address. 1942-43: 257-65

Conklin, E. G. Education for democracy. 1939-40: 346-63

Connally, T. T. America and postwar international cooperation. 1943-44: 96-105

Coughlin, C. E. Spirit of the reorganization bill. 1937-38: 111-21

Crocker, Lionel. Leadership and the spoken word. 1941-42: 100-9

Cushman, R. E. How to use civil liberty in wartime. 1941-42: 91-5

Cutten, G. B. Arise, let us go hence. 1938-39: 210-20

Danaher, J. A. Should the English-speaking democracies unite now? A debate. 1940-41: 209-24
Davis, Elmer. Finland surrenders. 1939-40: 63-7; If we're good enough, we can take it. 1941-42: 111-18
Day, E. E. What really threatens American democracy? 1938-39: 79-86
Denny, G. V. Jr. Should industry grant labor's demands for a thirty per cent wage increase? A debate. 1945-46: 165-79
Deutsch, M. E. The preservation of the university. 1942-43: 248-56
Dewey, T. E. Acceptance speech. 1943-44: 259-66; Calendar of unpunished crimes. 1939-40: 257-65; Governmental integrity. 1944-45: 143-51; Hines policy-numbers case. 1938-39: 181-3; Inside story of a racket. 1937-38: 163-75
Donovan, W. J. Shall we do whatever is necessary to insure a British victory? A debate. 1940-41: 33-48
Douglas, W. O. The function of democracy. 1940-41: 225-31
Durant, Will. Crisis in American civilization. 1939-40: 208-29
Duranty, Walter. Soviet Russia at war: Round table discussion. 1940-41: 168-83
Dykstra, C. A. Individual and the democratic adventure. 1939-40: 141-54

Eastman, J. B. How can we solve the railroad problem? 1938-39: 138-41
Eden, Anthony. America and Great Britain in the postwar world. 1942-43: 131-41; A job to be done. 1944-45: 76-81
Eisenhower, D. D. Quality of America's fighting men. 1944-45: 114-22

Farley, J. A. Politics as a profession for business men. 1939-40: 266-74
Fleming, D. F. An irrepressible issue. 1943-44: 138-42; What is it that we fight? 1942-43: 67-71; "Who says it can't be done?" 1941-42: 265-9
Fosdick, H. E. Being civilized to death. 1937-38: 210-19; Ethical problems of neutrality. 1939-40: 427-37; Jesus' ethical message confronts the world. 1938-39: 223-33
Frank, Glenn. Essential differences between the Republican and Democratic parties: A debate. 1939-40: 233-56

Fulbright, J. W. America and Internationalism. 1943-44: 83-95

Gannon, R. I. Wisdom before information. 1941-42: 191-200
Gilkey, C. W. Bridges into a better world. 1938-39: 234-44
Gittelsohn, R. B. That men may be free. 1945-46: 16-19
Gottschalk, Louis. Soviet Russia at war: Round table discussion. 1940-41: 168-83
Green, William. Labor, freedom and democracy. 1940-41: 243-54
Grew, J. C. The menace of Japan. 1942-43: 72-80

Hancher, V. M. Postwar planning—for what? 1943-44: 319-28
Hand, Learned. We seek liberty. 1943-44: 254-7
Harding, H. F. Can the liberal arts tradition survive? 1943-44: 306-18; New directions for higher learning. 1945-46: 229-40
Harper, S. N. Soviet Russia at war: Round table discussion. 1940-41: 168-83
Hayes, C. J. H. American war aims. 1942-43: 47-55
Henderson, Leon. Equality of sacrifice. 1941-42: 161-8
Hildebrand, J. H. Are we educating for national strength? 1940-41: 271-91
Hillman, Sidney. Agriculture, industry and labor. 1938-39: 142-57
Hocking, W. E. The crisis of our time: Discussion. 1944-45: 194-7
Holmes, J. H. One supreme issue of the hour. 1939-40: 391-407
Hoover, Herbert. National defense. 1939-40: 126-37; Protection of democracy. 1937-38: 80-96; The question of peace. 1940-41: 196-208
Howell, Wilbur. The democratic issue. 1941-42: 64-73
Hughes, C. E. Judiciary. 1937-38: 176-83; 150th anniversary of the first Congress. 1938-39: 161-5
Hull, Cordell. Foreign policy of the United States. 1943-44: 67-82; Opening of the Pan American Conference. 1938-39: 40-52
Hunt, Frazier. Those incredible Russians. 1942-43: 185-7
Hutchins, R. M. The crisis of our time: Discussion. 1944-45: 199-201; Issues in education. 1945-46: 262-72; Organization and subject matter of general education. 1938-39: 199-209; Philosophy of life. 1937-38: 184-9; Shall we do whatever is necessary to insure a British victory? A debate. 1940-41: 33-48; The university in war and peace. 1942-43: 235-47

Irwin, W. A. American way. 1939-40: 183-90

Jackson, R. H. Essential differences between the Republican and Democratic parties: A debate. 1939-40: 233-56; International military tribunal. 1945-46: 60-73.
Johnston, E. A. Intolerance. 1944-45: 175-85; A warning to labor *and* to management. 1943-44: 200-8
Jones, E. DeW. Faith of our fathers. 1942-43: 287-98

Kaltenborn, H. V. Czechoslovakia capitulates. 1938-39: 18-21; Germany invades Holland and Belgium. 1939-40: 68-75; Hitler's fifty-second birthday. 1940-41: 149-56
King, E. J. American postwar sea power and control of Pacific bases. 1944-45: 83-92.
Krause, Norman. We will not lay down arms. 1943-44: 123-37
Krueger, Maynard. Propaganda. 1939-40: 191-207
Kuroki, Ben. War isn't over at home. 1945-46: 208-13

LaFollette, R. M. Jr. American foreign policy. 1937-38: 69-79
Lasswell, H. D. Propaganda, good and bad: Discussion. 1941-42: 75-90
Lee, J. B. Drafting of wealth in time of war. 1938-39: 60-4; Technological unemployment and relief. 1938-39: 108-18
Lewis, J. L. In support of Willkie. 1940-41: 113-24; United Mine Workers' demands. 1945-46: 180-95
Lindbergh, C. A. Our air defense. 1940-41: 75-81
Lippmann, Walter. Education without culture. 1940-41: 292-309; In the service of freedom. 1943-44: 248-53; Rise of personal government in the United States. 1937-38: 122-37
Lochner, L. P. Inside Germany. 1942-43: 168-84
Lodge, H. C. Jr. A fruitful approach to a prolonged peace. 1942-43: 116-30
Luce, C. B. America and the postwar air world. 1943-44: 143-57
Lundeen, Ernest. America's policy toward insular possessions of other countries: Symposium. 1939-40: 75-90

MacArthur, Douglas. Surrender of Japan. 1945-46: 13-15
McKeon, R. P. Propaganda, good and bad: Discussion. 1941-42: 75-90
MacLeish, Archibald. Propaganda, good and bad: Discussion. 1941-42: 75-90; This cause is our cause. 1943-44: 243-7; Tribute to Wendell Willkie. 1944-45: 186-9
McNutt, P. V. Labor and the war. 1941-42: 169-77

Marshall, G. C. National military strength. 1945-46: 85-94
Mays, B. E. The inescapable Christ. 1944-45: 298-306
Miller, C. R. Propaganda. 1939-40: 191-207
Millikan, R. A. Science and the world tomorrow. 1938-39: 187-93
Moulton, H. G. Wartime price control. 1940-41: 82-92
Mundt, K. D. Peace—if we want it. 1944-45: 93-113
Murphy, Frank. Civil liberties. 1938-39: 173-80
Murrow, E. R. Farewell to England. 1945-46: 33-8; Orchestrated hell. 1943-44: 37-45; Spring comes to England. 1940-41: 157-62

Neibuhr, Reinhold. The crisis of our time: Discussion. 1944-45: 191-4
Nelson, D. M. MacArthur day address. 1941-42: 151-60
Newton, J. F. What to do with life today. 1945-46: 214-22
Nye, G. P. Jr. For an adequate defense. 1938-39: 65-70; Neutrality. 1939-40: 53-60; What does the European situation mean to us? 1937-38: 54-60

Patterson, R. C. The sixth column. 1941-42: 135-41
Pepper, Claude. All-out aid to Britain. 1940-41: 49-57
Peterson, H. C. Propaganda. 1939-40: 191-207
Phelps, W. L. Acceptance of American Education award. 1939-40: 364-74
Prentis, H. W. Jr. Competitive enterprise versus planned economy. 1944-45: 217-28; Preserving the roots of liberty. 1941-42: 201-17

Redfield, Robert. The crisis of our time: Discussion. 1944-45: 197-9
Reuther, Walter. Should industry grant labor's demands for a thirty per cent wage increase? A debate. 1945-46: 165-79
Reynolds, Quentin. The campaign and men in uniform. 1944-45: 123-33
Reynolds, Robert. America's policy toward insular possession of other countries: Symposium. 1939-40: 86-116
Robinson, E. E. Can democracy survive the war? 1942-43: 221-33
Rockefeller, J. D. The Christian church—what of its future? 1944-45: 291-7
Romney, G. P. Should industry grant labor's demands for a thirty per cent wage increase? A debate. 1945-46: 165-79
Roosevelt, E. A. Civil liberties—the individual and the community. 1939-40: 173-82

Roosevelt, F. D. America accepts the
challenge. 1941-42: 30-9; Canadian
position of the United States. 1938-
39: 25-8; Eight common principles
for a better world. 1941-42: 247-
50; Fall of Rome. 1943-44: 46-
51; Four human freedoms, 1940-41:
185-6; Fourth inaugural address.
1944-45: 153-5; Italy enters the
war 1939-40: 76-83; Keeping political faith. 1944-45: 134-42;
Message to Congress. 1939-40: 26-
37; Message to Congress. 1942-43:
15-29; Message to Congress. 1943-
44: 15-26; National defense. 1939-
40: 117-25; New Deal must continue. 1938-39: 97-107; Preservation of American independence.
1940-41: 19-32; Republican leadership and national defense. 1940-41:
125-36; Second inaugural address.
1937-38: 11-16; A state of emergency exists. 1940-41: 57-74; This
nation will remain neutral. 1939-
40: 21-5; Truths that inspired
Washington. 1942-43: 217-20;
United States policy toward war.
1938-39: 36-9; Victory dinner address. 1937-38: 101-10; War address. 1941-42: 15-18; Yalta Conference. 1944-45: 19-36
Russell, W. F. To bind up the
wounds in the schools of all nations. 1943-44: 287-305
Ryan, J. A. Religion, the indispensable basis of democracy. 1939-40:
408-20

Sayre, F. B. Corregidor. 1941-42:
179-85
Schuman, F. L. Design for a people's
peace. 1942-43: 142-57
Schwellenbach, L. B. America's policy toward insular possessions of
other countries. Symposium. 1939-
40: 86-116
Seversky, A. P. de. Will airpower
win this war? 1941-42: 186-9
Shapley, Harlow. A design for
fighting. 1944-45: 245-71
Sheen, F. J. Judgment of nations.
1942-43: 299-304; Liberty and the
republic. 1938-39: 245-52
Sheil, B. J. Tribute to Roosevelt.
1944-45: 165-7
Smith, T. V. Forward America: A
debate. 1938-39: 119-37
Snyder, F. B. Another "shot heard
round the world." 1941-42: 142-9
Sockman, R. W. This nation under
God. 1942-43: 267-75
Spellman, F. J. The one road to
peace. 1940-41: 187-95; Response
at a reception. 1945-46: 203-7
Stassen, H. E. American world policy
for peace and progress. 1944-45:
56-67
Stettinius, E. R. Jr. The United Nations Security Conference. 1944-45:
68-75

Stoddard, A. J. Education and the
people's peace. 1944-45: 272-89
Stoddard, G. D. Frontiers for youth.
1941-42: 218-29
Studebaker, J. W. Democracy shall
not be plowed under. 1939-40:
375-87; Morale building in our
schools and colleges. 1941-42: 119-
34
Sumners, H. W. Internal solidarity.
1943-44: 165-71
Swing, R. G. The meaning of the
home front. 1943-44: 159-64; The
wheel of judgment. 1940-41: 163-7

Taft, R. A. Forward America: A debate. 1938-39: 119-37; Price control veto. 1945-46: 154-63
Taylor, Deems. Universality of music. 1940-41: 238-42
Thomas, E. D. America's policy
toward the insular possessions of
other countries: Symposium. 1939-
40: 86-116
Thomas, Norman. Acceptance speech.
1943-44: 277-85; America's duty in
time of crisis. 1939-40: 275-89;
No democracy without civil liberty.
1937-38: 45-51
Thompson, Dorothy. Let's face the
facts. 1940-41: 137-48; Should the
English-speaking democracies unite
now? A debate. 1940-41: 209-24;
Stopping propaganda. 1938-39: 87-
93; What does the European situation mean to us? 1937-38: 60-7
Tittle, E. F. The price of peace.
1943-44: 329-36
Truman, H. S. Address to Congress.
1944-45: 156-63; Railroad strike
emergency. 1945-46: 196-201; V-E
day proclamation. 1944-45: 37-9
Tugwell, R. G. For a third term.
1938-39: 166-72

Urey, H. C. Atom bomb and war.
1945-46: 95-108

Valentine, Alan. Mobilizing the
mind. 1940-41: 263-70
Vandenberg, A. H. American foreign policy. 1944-45: 43-55; Memorial Day address. 1937-38: 39-
44; United Nations assembly: a report. 1945-46: 45-59
Vandercook, J. W. The soul of
France. 1942-43: 159-62

Wallace, H. A. America's part in
world reconstruction. 1942-43: 93-
104; Charter for postwar prosperity.
1944-45: 203-16; Community of interest between labor, capital and
agriculture. 1937-38: 142-62; Practical religion in the world of
tomorrow. 1942-43: 276-86; The
price of free world victory. 1941-
42: 45-55

Waymack, W. W. Challenge of America. 1939-40: 155-60

Weaver, A. T. The challenge of the crisis. 1944-45: 229-40

Welles, Sumner. America's foreign policy. 1943-44: 53-66; Postwar world leadership. 1941-42: 270-8

Wheeler, B. K. Against the resolution for collaboration for postwar peace. 1943-44: 115-22; United Mine Workers' Convention. 1939-40: 316-26

Willkie, W. L. Acceptance speech. 1940-41: 93-112; Economic freedom for the world. 1942-43: 105-15; The function of a political party. 1943-44: 267-76; Isolationism and the League of Nations. 1941-42: 251-8; Lidice. 1942-43: 163-7; Why are you unemployed? 1939-40: 306-15

Woll, Matthew. Labor's contribution to American democracy. 1939-40: 327-34

Wriston, H. W. Free enterprise. 1943-44: 230-41

Young, O. D. Science of better living. 1937-38: 190-7